THE
INDIAN CIVIL SERVICE

THE
INDIAN CIVIL SERVICE

1601-1930

L.S.S. O'Malley

GYAN

Published by

Gyan Publishing House
5, Ansari Road
Daryaganj, New Delhi-110002
Phone: 011-47034999, 9811692060
E-mail: books@gyanbooks.com

Distribution Network
gyanbooks.com
India, USA, Canada, UK, Australia

ISBN: 978-93-7097-335-0 (PB)

First Published, 1931

2nd Impression 2025

Printed at: Gyan Press, Delhi.

THE INDIAN CIVIL SERVICE
ARTHUR L.S.S. O'MALLEY

THE INDIAN CIVIL SERVICE:

1601–1930

THE INDIAN CIVIL SERVICE
1601-1930

BY

L. S. S. O'MALLEY, C.I.E.
INDIAN CIVIL SERVICE, RETIRED

WITH A FOREWORD BY
THE RT. HON. THE MARQUESS OF ZETLAND
G.C.S.I., G.C.I.E.

LONDON
JOHN MURRAY, ALBEMARLE STREET, W.

CONTENTS

PREFACE

IN *The Thackerays in India* Sir William Hunter mentioned with regret that no history of "the noble Service which formed the governing body in India" had been published. "Our early wars," he wrote, "still move before us in the living pages of Orme. The Bengal army, the Madras army, the Company's artillery and navy has each its separate historian; the soldier politicals have an honourable literature of their own. The Indian Civil Service has found no annalist." Over thirty years have passed since these words were written, but no complete record of the achievements of the Service has been produced. Its position has been changed materially during recent years, but the story of its development and of its work is still well worth telling. I have therefore attempted to give some account of them, not without being conscious how far the deed falls short of the will.

I desire to express my sense of deep gratitude to three retired members of the Indian Civil Service—Sir John Cumming, K.C.I.E., C.S.I., Sir Verney Lovett, K.C.S.I., and Mr. C. E. A. W. Oldham, C.S.I.—for the help which they have kindly given in the preparation of this book by reading through most of the manuscript and by supplying materials as well as much valuable criticism and advice.

L. S. S. O'M.

PREFACE

FOREWORD

NO one who is conversant with the facts, will be likely to cavil at a description of British India as a miracle of organization. To the "factors" and "writers" of the East India Company, brought into contact with a jumble of races separated by language, by religion, by social custom and by the standards of their civilization into innumerable entities great and small, existing fortuitously within the confines of a sub-continent itself vast in area and infinitely diverse in its physical characteristics, the evolution of an India such as we know to-day can have been neither calculated nor, indeed, even dimly imagined. How, and by whom, has the miracle been accomplished? How, and by whom, has the quite remarkable measure of political and administrative uniformity which characterizes British India to-day, been imposed upon a continent presenting in all other respects so great a medley of diversities, contrasts and contradictions? To that question an answer is provided in the following pages.

Everyone who knows anything of India is aware that in the fashioning of British India a paramount part has been played by a body of men known as the "Indian Civil Service." The story of such a body must clearly be suffused with the spirit of romance. Glimpses of it have been vouchsafed to the public from time to time by members of the Service who have told of their experiences in published Memoirs ; yet no consecutive account of the origin, the growth and the infinite variety of the work of the service has hitherto been written. It is such an account that Mr. O'Malley gives us ; and it is time that such a task was undertaken, for under stress of modern political movements the character of the Indian Civil Service is undergoing rapid change, and in its altered environment can scarcely hope to retain all those special characteristics which have made it unique among the administrative organizations of the world.

Let it be added that to no more competent hands could the task have been entrusted. For upwards of a quarter of a century Mr. O'Malley served as a member of the Indian Civil Service in Bengal. He served with success as an executive officer in the districts, in days of no little difficulty and anxiety when the Presidency was seething with political discontent ; later he served with distinction in the secretariat at the Head Quarters of Government during times of stress, when Constitutions were in the melting-pot and strange, unprecedented forms of Government were on the anvil, to emerge as patently transitional expedients —novel experiments in quasi-democratic systems carried out incongruously enough on the uncongenial soil of the immemorial East. At times duties devolved upon him—as, for example, when he was charged with the superintendence of the revision of the official gazeteers—entailing historical research and a display of literary ability. In these circumstances it was not surprising that when an author was sought by the Cambridge University Press for a volume on Bengal, Bihar and Orissa and Sikhim for the Provincial Geographies of

India series, choice should have fallen on Mr. O'Malley. All who are familiar with that volume will look forward with feelings of pleasurable anticipation to his story of the I.C.S.

When writing a foreword to a book there is always a temptation to select the more striking passages of the book itself for comment. I will confine myself to a single extract which illustrates the scope which existed in the early days of British administration, especially in the so-called Non-Regulation provinces, for individual enterprise and initiative. In the Regulation provinces suttee had been prohibited by a Regulation passed in 1829. In Sind the Regulation was not operative and the evil was left to be dealt with according to individual predilection. When it was represented by the Brahmans that it was a practice sanctioned by religion and one which should be respected, Sir Charles Napier replied—

"Be it so. This burning of widows is your custom. Prepare the funeral pile. But my nation has also a custom. When men burn women alive, we hang them and confiscate all their property. My carpenters shall, therefore, erect gibbets on which to hang all concerned when the widow is consumed. Let us all act according to national customs."

Some, as they read the earlier chapters of Mr. O'Malley's book, will sigh for these good old days; they will realize, as they read the concluding pages of his story, why it is that the good old days have gone never to return. It is with the future that we are now concerned, and we shall be the better prepared to face the future for a careful study of all that is to be learned from a perusal of Mr. O'Malley's informative and extraordinarily interesting story.

ZETLAND.

March, 1931.

CHAPTER I

A MERCHANT SERVICE: 1601–1772

THE term civil service, which is now applied to the general body of persons employed on non-combatant work connected with the administration of a State, was first used to designate those servants of the East India Company who were engaged in mercantile work. Employés of the Company were called its servants, and those who conducted its trade overseas were known as civil servants so as to distinguish them from those whose duties were of a naval or military nature. As the character of the Company changed and its trading operations were first supplemented by territorial dominion and eventually replaced by the responsibilities of Government, its civil servants were transformed from traders into administrators. The term civil service consequently acquired a new meaning, connoting not the status of non-combatants but the work of civil administration in which its members were engaged. The Indian Civil Service is, however, not altogether a civil service in the English sense of that term. It is only one, but the highest of the public services in India, a *corps d'élite* responsible for the higher branches of the administration and filling judicial as well as executive offices. It is not merely an executive agency of Government but helps to formulate and direct policy, for some of its senior members are Governors of provinces and are members both of executive and legislative councils. It is a small body consisting of only 1,014 men on 1 January, 1930; its effective strength at any one time, after deducting the number of men on leave, may be taken as from 800 to 900. This is not a large number when the variety of its duties is taken into account as well as the number of provincial Governments, each with its own Secretariat, and the salient fact that British India has an area of over a million square miles and a population of nearly 250 millions.

In this chapter an attempt is made to sketch the history of the civil service of the East India Company in the days when it was first a body of merchants with no ambitions or responsibilities other than those of trade, and next when those merchants became possessed of political power without, however, losing their commercial character. In the first stage they were intent on making a fortune or a competence according to their opportunities. In the second the way to making a fortune was open and easy, and the unscrupulous manner in which they took advantage of their position makes this a sordid chapter in the history of the Company's civil service.

The men who were sent out to India to carry on the Company's trade in the early years of its existence were called Factors,[1] a word meaning simply commercial agents, and the trading stations in which they lived were known as factories; they

[1] John Wheeler, Secretary to the Merchants Adventurers, wrote in 1601 in *A Treatise of Commerce*: "The Company of Merchants Adventurers hath no bank, nor common stock, nor common factor to buy or sell for the whole company, but every man tradeth apart, and particularly with his own stock, and with his own factor or servant." loc. cit. Sir C. P. Lucas, *The Beginnings of British Overseas Enterprise* (1917), p. 19.

were the headquarters of Factors and not places of manufacture. In 1675 the Company established a regular gradation of posts. At the bottom were apprentices, who were required to serve for seven years, receiving £5 a year for the first five and £10 a year for the last two years. When they had served out their term, they could obtain preferment to the next grade, that of Writers, subject to their giving security. The Writers were required to serve a "covenanted" term of five years, and, if found deserving in point of ability and faithfulness, could become Factors. The Factors again could rise to be Merchants, and the latter could become Senior Merchants. The Factors responsible for large factories were called Agents,[1] and those in charge of the chief factories to which the others were subordinate were dignified by the title of President and were assisted by a Council of Senior Merchants. The grading of the staff appears to have been copied from the Dutch. The Writer (Schrijver), Junior Merchant, Merchant and Senior Merchant were regular gradations in the official hierarchy of the Dutch East India Company, which also had a system of Presidents and Councils.[2]

[1] At the present time there is a similar system in West Africa, where, as stated in *The Times* (British West African number) of 30 October, 1928: "The big firms have chains of numerous trading stations, known as factories . . . and in them the sale of goods and the purchase of produce is carried on. . . . The bigger places act as parent factories to their neighbouring smaller ones, and the latter are grouped under their parent factory into an administrative unit under a European manager, who is called an 'agent.'"

[2] See Sir George Birdwood, *Report on the Old Records of the India Office* (1891), p. 55 note, and Introduction (p. 16) by Professor Geyl to *Journal of the East India Voyages of Bontekoe of Hoorn* (1929).

Apprentices were only sent out till 1694, when there was a batch of seven boys from Christ's Hospital, for whom as a special concession the Directors paid the cost of the voyage to India, "whereas all other servants do pay their passage outwards." After that year the lowest grade was that of Writers, a name, traced back by Sir William Foster[1] to 1645, which simply described the nature of the work done by them. Peter Mundy, for instance, wrote that on his first arrival at Surat in 1628 he was "imployed to write in the office as comonly all new Commers are, exceptinge men of place."[2]

In addition to carrying on the routine duties of trade, the Company's servants gained some experience of municipal government and judicial administration in the three settlements, Madras, Calcutta and Bombay, where the Company acquired territorial rights. Law courts and Corporations were established, and in Madras the love of English institutions led to the introduction of civic insignia, such as silver-gilt maces; the Mayor and Aldermen were required to ride in the same order as the Lord Mayor and Aldermen of London and to wear robes of scarlet serge, which must have been an uncomfortable attire in a climate which has been described as nine months hot and three months hotter. In Calcutta one of the Company's servants was entrusted with the management of land in the three villages held by it, and with jurisdiction over their Indian inhabitants. The first appointment was made in 1700, when Ralph

[1] Sir W. Foster, *John Company* (1926), p. 211.

[2] *Travels of Peter Mundy*, ed. Sir R. Temple (Hakluyt Society, 1914), Vol. II, p. 21.

Sheldon was given the designation of Jemidar, i.e., zamindar or landholder, his duties being "to collect the rents and to keep the three Black Towns in order." He had his own Court for the trial of civil as well as criminal cases in which Indians only were concerned, and like the modern Collector he dealt with land and revenue cases.[1] In Madras there was a similar officer called the Land Customer, who collected rent from the villages and land round the Fort and taxes on various articles, customs dues, market dues and rents on houses.[2]

Members of the mercantile staff were also called upon occasionally to undertake other duties in case of necessity. In 1675 orders were sent out to Surat that the civil servants were to apply themselves to acquiring a knowledge of military discipline so that if there was any sudden attack, or if they were found better qualified for military duties than for mercantile work, they might receive commissions and have the pay of military officers. Clive, as is well known, started his career as a Writer, and was consequently called by Lord Brougham the merchant's clerk who raised himself to celebrity. They might also be called upon to perform the duties of clergymen in default of men duly ordained, as we learn from the *New Account of the East Indies*, by Captain Alexander Hamilton, who was in India from 1688 to 1723. In Calcutta, he wrote,

"Ministers of the Gospel being subject to mortality, very often young merchants are obliged to officiate and

---

[1] C. R. Wilson, *Early Annals of the English in Bengal* (1895), Vol. I, p. 190.

[2] *Imperial Gazetteer of India*, Vol. XVI, p. 378.

have a salary of £50 per annum, added to what the Company allows them, for their pains in reading prayers and sermons on Sundays." [1]

The mortality, judged by modern standards, was often appalling. Between November, 1630, and May, 1633, out of 21 persons in the Surat factory, 14 died; the survivors were so enfeebled by sickness that scarcely one was able to write or set hand to paper.[2] Of Bombay Captain Alexander Hamilton wrote:

"It was a long time before the Island had people enough to fill a chapel, for as fast as recruits came from Britain, they died in Bombay, which got the island a bad name. Of seven or eight hundred English that inhabited before the war there were not above sixty left by the sword and plague, and Bombay that was one of the pleasantest places in India was brought to be one of the most dismal deserts."

It is not surprising that under such conditions it should be a common saying that the average life of a man in Bombay was two monsoons. Calcutta had no better record. Hamilton wrote of it:

"One year I was there, and there were reckoned in August about 1,200 English, some military, some servants to the Company, some private merchants residing in the town, and some seamen belonging to shipping lying at the town, and before the beginning of January

---

[1] It is not uncommon even now for a Judge or Collector of a district to read morning or evening prayers in a district headquarters where there is no clergyman; cases have been known of their also reading sermons.

[2] *The Travels of Peter Mundy* (Hakluyt Society, 1914), Vol. II, p. 275.

there were four hundred and sixty burials registered in the Clerk's Book of Mortality." [1]

Such a heavy loss of life was due to the ravages of disease, bad sanitary conditions, ignorance or neglect of the principles of hygiene and diet essential in India, and unfortunately also gross intemperance. Apart from actual loss of life, the mercantile staff of the Company had at various times throughout the seventeenth century to suffer the hardships incidental to imprisonment and loss of property when they had given offence to the Mughal Government. Thus, in 1624 the merchants at Surat and elsewhere were put in irons and imprisoned for some months. Again, in 1688 the factory at Dacca was seized and the merchants thrown into prison; there they were joined by others from out-stations, "all in a most miserable and tattered condition, laden with fetters of about 8 lbs.; and all were thrown into prison, fettered and chained together at night two and two."

This harsh treatment was a reprisal for hostilities undertaken by the Company. Previously it had acted on the dictum that war and trade are incompatible. Its ambitions went no further than freedom to buy and sell without payment of customs duties. "All war," the Directors declared in 1681, "is so contrary to our interest that we cannot too often inculcate to you our aversion thereunto." Five years later they abandoned their pacific attitude in consequence of the stoppages of trade caused by disregard of their charters and unauthorized exactions. They thought the policy

[1] *A New Account of the East Indies* (1727), Vol. I, pp. 185, 237.

of the mailed fist would be more effectual, but were so ignorant of the power and resources of the Mughal Empire as to imagine that it could be brought to terms by the dispatch of ten ships with 1,000 soldiers on board, reinforced only by two vessels with 160 soldiers. The little war which they light-heartedly levied ended in an ignominious failure and a contrite submission.

After this brief bellicose interlude, the former pacific policy was resumed. The Company's servants were reminded that they were the representatives of a body of merchants, and instructed to live and act accordingly. They had to conform to the usages of the local Governments. In case of difference their weapons were the language of diplomacy, backed by the customary presents and *douceurs*. On a few occasions stronger action was taken, as in 1701, when Aurangzeb issued orders for the arrest of all Europeans on the ground that they were guilty of piracy and the seizure of ships conveying pilgrims to Mecca. Thereupon the President at Calcutta, Beard, roundly declared that he could no longer be "always giving to every little rascal," strengthened his garrison—even so it numbered only 120 men—and laid an embargo on the sailing of all Mughal ships until the orders were withdrawn. Otherwise the attitude of the English was conciliatory, care was taken not to offend Indian susceptibilities, and they won a reputation for just dealing. Ovington, a Chaplain who went to Surat in 1689, has left it on record that the factory chapel contained no figures of living beings, so as to give no occasion for offence to the Moslems, and that the English were held in such veneration and esteem by the Indian population that those who were injured or distressed applied for relief to the President rather than to their own Governor.

The Company paid little heed to the text that the labourer is worthy of his hire, and gave salaries so small as to be nominal. Even as late as 1744 at such an important place as Dacca the annual salaries were only £40 for the Chief, £30 for a Junior Merchant, £15 each for the Factors and £5 for a Writer. Service in a distant country, so precarious and so poorly remunerated, was only made tolerable by the trade which the mercantile staff conducted on their own account, shipping Indian goods from port to port in India or exporting them overseas. The Company fought against the practice from an early period of its existence, on the ground that those engaged in it sacrificed the Company's interests to their own. Stringent bonds were taken from the Factors, and actions were brought against them on their return from India. The Company even obtained a proclamation from King Charles I in 1628 prohibiting private trade except so far as it might be licensed by the Company itself—an extraordinary admission of its incompetence to control its own servants; but so little importance did the men in India attach to this that one of them in 1631 contended that the prohibition of private trade was understood to be merely a matter of form for the Company's satisfaction.[1] In the end, the Company was obliged to recognize the right of private trade, and the exiguous salaries which it paid may be regarded as a kind of retainer, its servants being actually dependent for their living

[1] Sir W. Foster, *The English Factories in India, 1630–1633*, p. 157.

on the profits which they made from their own trade.

One feature of the trade which should be mentioned was the employment of, and dependence on, Indian brokers called Banyans, a system which persisted with pernicious results when the traders became administrators. The Banyans were under little control owing to the Company's servants' ignorance of Indian languages. According to *Fryer's Travels in India* (1696), the Banyans' commission was supplemented by "what they squeeze secretly out of the price of things bought: which cannot be well understood for want of knowledge in their language; which ignorance is safer than to hazard being poysoned for prying too nearly into their actions." The Company's servants were in their hands to such an extent that at one time it was commonly said at Surat that they were President and Council and governed the Company's affairs at their pleasure.[1]

The position which the Company and its officers occupied until the middle of the eighteenth century cannot be better summarized than it was in a farewell letter which Henry Verelst, Governor of Bengal, wrote to the Council at Calcutta in 1769.

"In the infancy of our settlement, with all our care and prudence, we could ill defend ourselves from the forged accusations or open attacks of the Government; we looked no further than the provision of the Company's investment[2]; we fought advantages to our trade

---

[1] Sir W. Foster, *The English Factories in India, 1630–1633*, p. 17.

[2] The investment was the purchase of merchandise for export to England, this being the method adopted for remitting any surplus of revenue.

with the ingenuity, I may add selfishness, of merchants. All our laws were local and municipal, reaching no further than our exigencies and conveniences; all our servants and dependents were trained in the same notions; the credit of a good bargain was the utmost scope of their ambition."

The English were, in fact, a colony of merchants, governed and influenced by commercial principles, at the mercy of a Government which was ever ready to take advantage of their weakness. Within a decade they acquired an ascendancy which, as Verelst was the first to point out, was in the number of those events which are distinguished by a series of fortunate and unforeseen circumstances and are not the outcome of any definite plan or policy. Even after the battle of Plassey there was no idea of supplanting the Nawab's government in Bengal. There were no territorial acquisitions till 1760, when Mir Kasim Ali Khan ceded to the Company three districts, Burdwan, Midnapore and Chittagong, in order that their revenues might defray the cost of the defence of Bengal by the Company's army.

Clive left for England early in 1760, and the Company's servants, free from the control of his strong hand, proceeded to exploit the weakness of the Nawab's government. As Sir Alfred Lyall said, "finding themselves entirely without restraint or responsibility, uncontrolled either by public opinion or legal liabilities (for there was no law in the land), they naturally behaved as in such circumstances, with such temptations, men would behave in any age or country." [1]

[1] *Rise of the British Dominion in India* (1893), p. 120.

Their first step was to make money by trading without payment of the internal customs duties. Any officer who tried to levy duty on their boats passing up and down the great rivers of Bengal was defied and, if necessary, overpowered. Needless to say, Indian merchants were handicapped by having to pay duties until they adapted themselves to the new order of things and paid the English for the privilege of trading in their name with the same freedom from duties. It was a case of wholesale and rampant smuggling, which the revenue officers were powerless to prevent or check. What made this free trade worse was that the country folk were tyrannized over by the traders' agents and underlings, suffered from their exactions, and had to sell their goods to them at less than the market price. The authority of the Nawab's government so completely collapsed that there was a general scramble for the fortunes that could so easily be made. According to Clive, "the evil was contagious and spread among the civil and military [1] down to the Writer, the ensign, and the free merchant," i.e., the independent trader having no connexion with the Company.

"All," wrote Verelst, "who were disposed to plunder, assumed the authority of our name, usurped the seats of justice, and carried on what they called trade by violence and oppression. The Nabob's officers fled before them, or joining the invaders divided the spoil. . . . Mahomedan, Portuguese and Armenian alike, nay, every illiterate mariner who could escape from a ship,

---

[1] There were many military "Nabobs." General Richard Smith is believed to have been the original of Sir Matthew Mite in Samuel Foote's play *The Nabob*.

erected our flag and acted as lord of the district around him."[1]

In May, 1765, Clive arrived to resume office as Governor at the head of a Select Committee of four members besides himself, with the oft-quoted resolution of "cleansing the Augean stable." His first step was to deal with the chief offenders, the men of senior standing who filled the higher posts. There were honourable exceptions, such as Verelst, Sykes and Cartier, men of inflexible integrity, proof against all temptation; but the majority were men with whom self-interest was the only standard of conduct. Their latest offence was disobedience to the Directors' orders about presents, which the Company's servants had hitherto been at liberty to accept. The giving of presents to persons able to exercise power or confer favours was an immemorial custom, and also an immemorial curse, in India. A man who had his present refused took it to mean that it was not of sufficient value and would reappear with a larger present. The conception of a just judge was that of a man who took presents from both parties, and then decided according to the merits of the case and gave back the present of the unsuccessful party. It is not surprising that merchants, familiar with the system of commissions, took advantage of what seemed to them a very agreeable custom.

The flagrant abuses which the custom gave rise to led the Directors to issue orders that covenants should be executed binding military as well as civil officers to pay into the Company's treasury all presents received from Indians exceeding Rs.

[1] *View of the Government of Bengal* (1772), p. 106.

4,000 in value, unless their receipt was sanctioned by the Directors, and not to accept any present above Rs. 1,000 in value without sanction from the President and Council. Thirteen days after these orders reached them the Council had concluded an agreement by which Najm-ud-daula paid 20 lakhs of rupees for his succession to the throne. Clive peremptorily ordered, and indeed forced, the Members of Council to sign the new covenants upon pain of instant dismissal, and the junior men followed suit. Spencer and a few senior men were dismissed; one man committed suicide, and others were forced to resign or did so on their own initiative. Clive proceeded to bring in some fresh and purer blood. No measure could, in his opinion, be more salutary or better calculated to teach the men in Bengal a lesson than to supersede them by men brought from Madras, where, he said, the conduct of the gentlemen upon the establishment "is in general so unexceptionable that to present Bengal with such examples of regularity, discretion and moderation would, I think, be a means of restoring it to good order and government."[1] Later, as is well known, the Madras men seized their opportunities for making money easily and were as sordid and unscrupulous as their fellows in Bengal. The staff in Bombay was at this time too small to be able to spare any men. The lot of the Writers there was not a very happy one. In his *Oriental Memoirs* James Forbes wrote that after his day's work he found that a dish of tea and a walk "gave a keener appetite for supper than

[1] Letter of Clive to the Directors dated 30 September, 1765, Appendix No. 73, to the Parliamentary Committee's Report of 1773.

our scanty pittance of thirty rupees per month could furnish," and that a salary of £65 a year, which he drew in 1766, was insufficient for the moderate necessities of life.

More drastic measures followed for the prevention of abuses in the interior of Bengal. Orders were issued for the recall of all the Company's servants in Bengal from the "aurungs," or trading stations in the interior, where they could not be properly supervised. Only the men employed in the factories at Patna, Dacca, Cossimbazar and Chittagong, and the assistants to the Supravisors at Burdwan and Midnapore, were to remain "up the country." European "free merchants" were to be deported. They were numerous at this time and carried on a large and lucrative trade: indeed, the Select Committee spoke of "the shoals of free merchants annually imported, who being encumbered with no public business nor confined to residence in Bengal, can carry on a free trade with every port in India to much greater advantage than your servants." The Directors laid down that the proper place of these men was in the sea service, as captains or supercargoes in the coasting trade, or settled as merchants in Calcutta. Any who went up-country despite these orders were to be shipped back to England. Their policy was summed up in the words, "We are determined to have as few Europeans as possible in the country." [1]

Clive was alive to the fact that it was impossible to prohibit private trade altogether so long as the Company persisted in paying meagre salaries, and pointed out a fact which the Directors blindly over-

[1] H. Verelst, *View of the Government in Bengal* (1772), p. 120, and Appendix, p. 184.

looked, viz., that owing to the extent of the Company's own trade it was impossible for anyone who really did his duty by it to acquire anything considerable by private trade.[1] He found a solution of the difficulty by making a monopoly of the inland trade in salt, betel and tobacco, the profit from which was to be divided among the Company's servants, military and ecclesiastical, as well as mercantile, according to their rank. The Company itself was to receive an *ad valorem* duty of 35 per cent. This scheme was designed to ensure to Members of Council and Colonels £7,000 and to Majors and Factors £2,000 a year. Officers of lower rank were left out in the cold, and had only the pittances allowed by the Company. The Directors refused to sanction the scheme, though they had no alternative to suggest, but under various pretexts it was continued till September, 1768. The privilege of private trade was withdrawn so long as the monopoly lasted, and this, combined with the absence of any provision for adequate pay, made the position of the younger members of the staff impossible. In 1767 the Select Committee had to point out that the majority were reduced to a bare monthly allowance, which would force them into debt; and they urged that a competent subsistence should be given to save them, and especially the Writers, from penury and want. The Writers naturally turned to their Banyans for help, received loans from them, and became their tools.

Clive's chief administrative measure was what is called the assumption of the *Diwani*, which meant simply that the Company assumed the control of revenue administration and received the revenue.

[1] See R. Muir, *The Making of British India* (1917), p. 89.

All the rest of the civil administration was left to the Nawab and his Ministers. Of actual control of the revenue administration there was very little. There were only two British officers to exercise it under the Select Committee, viz., the Resident at Murshidabad (the Nawab's capital) and the Chief at Patna. Otherwise the whole administrative staff was Indian, or Persian, for the Select Committee recorded the fact that the instruments of government were generally Persian adventurers, strangers to the customs, and indifferent to the welfare, of the people of the country. The Company's servants had nothing to do with the civil government except in the ceded districts of Burdwan, Midnapore and Chittagong, where their administration was attaining a creditable standard and ensuring peace and prosperity. There, according to a report sent by Richard Becher in 1769, the system of letting out the land for a reasonable term of years "and English gentlemen to superintend the collections and the administration of justice has occasioned the province to flourish, when the countries adjacent to it under the government of the Ministers are in a very declining state." [1]

The system of dual government consequent on the assumption of the *Diwani* soon broke down. The Company's servants were repeatedly and peremptorily forbidden to assert any public authority over the officers of the Nawab's government and enjoined to retain their primitive characters of merchants with the most scrupulous delicacy.[2] The Indian and Persian collectors of revenue, left

[1] See R. Muir, *The Making of British India* (1917), p. 94.

[2] *View of the Government of Bengal* (1772), Appendix, p. 122.

without proper supervision and control, colluded with those who had to pay it; their dependents and underlings oppressed and plundered the people. It was, moreover, impracticable to replace them by the Company's civil servants, who had neither the necessary numbers—many had been killed in the Massacre of Patna—nor the requisite training and experience. "The power of supervising the provinces," Clive said, "though lodged in us should not, in my opinion, be exercised. Three times the number of civil servants would be insufficient for the purpose."[1] Verelst took the same view, saying that it would have been impossible for the Company to have taken the *Diwani* into the hands of its own staff, because its strength was barely sufficient for even the current commercial business.

In 1769 the Select Committee were almost reduced to despair over the system of revenue administration. They came to the conclusion that the only possible remedy was to associate some selected English officers more directly with it by placing one in charge of each district under the name of Supervisor (or in its archaic form, as then used, Supravisor), his duty, as the title implied, being to supervise the proceedings of the Indian officials. High hopes were entertained of the outcome of this experiment. The Supervisors would be able to detect and correct any abuses of official power, and a succession of able and vigorous administrators would be secured. The instructions given to the Supervisors were inspired by high ideals: indeed, they would be a suitable model at any time for those engaged in Government service in India.

[1] Letter of 30 September, 1765, to the Directors.

"Among the chief effects which are hoped for from your residence in that province, and which ought to employ and never wander from your attention are to convince the Ryot [1] that you will stand between him and the hand of oppression; that you will be his refuge and the redresser of his wrongs . . . that after supplying the legal due of Government, he may be secure in the enjoyment of the remainder; and finally to teach him a veneration and affection for the humane maxims of our Government.

"The exploring and eradicating numberless oppressions which are as grievous to the poor as they are injurious to the Government; the displaying of those national principles of honour, faith, rectitude and humanity which should ever characterize the name of an Englishman; the impressing the lowest individual with these ideas, and raising the heart of the Ryot from oppression to despondency and joy, are the valuable benefits which must result to our nation from a prudent and wise behaviour.

"Versed as you are in the language, depend on none where you yourself can possibly hear and determine. Let access to you be easy, and be careful of the conduct of your dependents. Aim at no undue influence yourself, and check it in all others. Great share of integrity, disinterestedness, assiduity and watchfulness is necessary not only for your own guidance but as an example to all others; for your activity and advice will be in vain unless confirmed by example. Carefully avoid all interested views by commerce or otherwise in the province whilst on this service . . . for though ever so fair and honest, it will awaken the attention of the designing. . . . You have before a large field to establish a national and private character." [2]

These admirable instructions were almost a dead

[1] The tenant or cultivator.

[2] H. Verelst, *View of the Government of Bengal* (1772), Appendix, pp. 228 and 238.

letter. The Supervisors, whose title was changed subsequently to that of Collectors in order to denote their duty, viz., collecting revenue, were handicapped by ignorance of the language and customs of the country, which made them rely on subordinates. In the absence of any orders from the Directors about pay, they had to be allowed the right of private trade. The old abuses continued, and again we see the cloven hoof of the Banyans, who according to Warren Hastings were devils. "The Banyan," he said, "is in fact the lord of every Supervisorship. All the business of the district passes through the hands of the Banyan to his master. No complaints can come before the latter without the permission of his *maître de palais*." Amid all the hyperbole of his speech impeaching Warren Hastings, Burke scarcely exaggerated in saying that without the Banyans, Europeans were nothing, that "while we are boasting of the British power, we are, in more than half the service, nothing but the inferior tools and miserable instruments of the tyranny which the lower part of the natives exercise."

The root cause of the abuses prevalent at this time was the obstinate and foolish refusal of the Directors to pay their employés decent salaries. They were not alone in this penny-wise policy. The French did the same in Canada and the Dutch in South Africa, with the same result, viz., that their underpaid officers indulged in private trade. On this subject Sir Charles Lucas writes:

> "It seems transparently obvious that if employers are to be honestly served, they must pay good wages; yet the history of colonial administration abundantly shows that no lesson has been so imperfectly learnt and so con-

stantly forgotten. Have few officers, work them hard, pay them well, hold them responsible, and trust them—this is the only way to secure capable and honest administrators. In the latter part of the seventeenth and throughout the eighteenth century no government acted on these lines, and companies could hardly be expected to do so. Their business was not to train just and wise rulers, but to buy the services of their staff as cheaply as possible. They paid salaries on which men could hardly live, and the subject races had to make good the deficiency."[1]

The Company's servants were, in any case, men of their age, and the age was in many ways ruthless and corrupt. It was not so long since the British Parliament itself had been notorious for corruption, and few had any true conception of the duties of trusteeship where subject races were concerned. They were, moreover, not so black as they were painted in England. There credulity and ignorance laid to their charge crimes of which they were innocent. Even the great famine of 1770, which was due to the failure of the rains, was attributed to men who had humanely endeavoured to alleviate its ravages or who were not even in India at the time. Both Sir Francis Sykes, who had left Bengal 18 months before it commenced,[2] and Richard Becher, the Resident at Murshidabad, whose heart was wrung by the horrors of the famine and who made every effort to prevent starvation, were calumniated as the authors of this terrible visitation. Becher was apparently traduced because a large stock of grain had to be

[1] *Historical Geography of the British Colonies (South Africa: Part I)* (1913), pp. 74–5.

[2] Lord Teignmouth, *Memoirs of the Life of Lord Teignmouth* (1843), Vol. I, pp. 46–7.

purchased to feed the army; as a matter of fact, the British and their dependents were absolutely prohibited from making purchases of grain for private profit.[1] This libel was perpetuated in Disraeli's *Sybil*, where a portrait is given of Warren as a Nabob who made a fortune by a corner in rice during a famine in India. On the other hand, Thackeray in *The Newcomes* derided the tradition of the Nabob as

> "the jaundiced monster of romances and comedies who purchases the estates of broken-down English gentlemen, with rupees tortured out of bleeding rajahs, who smokes a hookah in public and in private carries about a guilty conscience, diamonds of untold value, and a diseased liver."

[1] *Memoir of Lt.-Col. Richard Scott*, "Naval and Military Magazine," March, 1827, pp. 154–5.

CHAPTER II

CREATION OF A CIVIL SERVICE: 1772–93

THE creation of a Civil Service in the modern sense of the term may be said to have been the work of both Warren Hastings and Lord Cornwallis. The former laid the foundations on which the latter built up a superstructure. To Warren Hastings belongs the credit of reorganizing the revenue administration, remodelling the judicial system, and freeing trade from its abuses. He had scarcely assumed office as Governor of Bengal in 1772 when he received a letter from the Directors announcing their decision to undertake the management of the revenue system by the agency of the Company's servants. Warren Hastings was directed to dismiss the Naib Diwan and the Indian officers under him—in other words, to make a clean sweep of the existing agency except for the Collectors, whom he had "always considered as tyrants" and would have liked to have got rid of.

"But," he observed, "there were among them so many sons, cousins, or *élèves* of Directors, and intimates of the Members of Council, that it was better to let them remain than provoke an army of opponents against every act of administration by depriving them of their emoluments. They continue, but their power is retrenched; and the way is paved for their gradual removal."

As a step in this direction, Indian officers, called *Diwans*, were associated with the Collectors, and various restrictions were imposed on them, e.g., Banyans and their servants were not allowed to farm any portion of the revenue, the Collectors and their servants were prohibited from giving loans to middlemen, and an interdict was laid on the receipt of presents from zamindars. The control of the revenue administration was transferred to the President and Council at Calcutta, which replaced Murshidabad as the capital, a change significant of the position now assumed by the Company. In 1774 the Collectors were recalled from the districts, while their functions in revenue and civil administration were transferred to Indian officers called *Amils*; the superior control of revenue administration was vested in six Provincial Councils composed of Company's servants. These arrangements continued till 1781, when the Collectorships were reinstituted under a Committee of Revenue, the members of which were bound by oath to receive no perquisites and were remunerated by a commission of 1 per cent on the net collections.

As regards trade, Warren Hastings considered it a fixed and incontrovertible principle that commerce can only flourish when it is equal and free.[1] Accordingly, the customs duties were made the same for all, unauthorized exactions were stopped, abuses were firmly repressed; and the control of customs was transferred from the Collectors to Commissioners paid by a commission on their collections. The work of reform was

[1] W. Seton-Karr, *Selections from the Calcutta Gazette of 1784–1788* (1864), p. 190.

facilitated by the Regulating Act of 1773, which prohibited Collectors and persons engaged in either the collection of the revenues or the administration of justice from participating in trade, and forbade persons holding military or civil offices to accept presents from any of "the natives of Asia," the only exceptions being lawyers, medical men, and Chaplains, who might receive fees in the way of their profession. Another provision, which appears strange in the light of modern conditions, was that no British subject was to take more than 12 per cent as interest on loans; at Madras usury was common and flagrant. The prohibition of private trade, it will be noted, was limited in its extent. It did not apply to men not engaged in revenue or judicial work, i.e., to those who carried on the Company's trade; but in their case Warren Hastings effected a reform by a Regulation issued in 1774 which prohibited advances and required cash payments: the abolition of the system of advances left weavers and others free to work for whomever they liked.

Perhaps the greatest reform of Warren Hastings was in connexion with the judicial system. In the Muhammadan courts justice was prostituted; almost every decision was a corrupt bargain with the highest bidder. The people were so far from supposing justice to be due from a judge that one quarter of the property in dispute was retained by him as a reward for his trouble.[1] In the interior, moreover, these courts had been replaced by unauthorized tribunals presided over by the zamindars or local landholders, so that, in Warren

[1] H. Verelst, *View of the Government of Bengal* (1772), p. 136, and Appendix, p. 229.

Hastings's words, the regular course of justice was everywhere suspended. He first established civil and criminal courts for every district with appellate courts at Calcutta. The judges of the district courts were Indians, but they were presided over by the Collectors. Criminal jurisdiction was still an appanage of the Nawab, but it was brought under the inspection and control of the Company's servants, who were required to see that the judges' decisions were fair and impartial. The administration of civil justice was also transformed in 1781, when Hastings separated revenue from civil jurisdiction and set up courts under English judges, whose jurisdiction extended over rent as well as civil cases; previously cases about rents had been heard by revenue officers. These judges were also given some executive powers, being invested with the power of arresting but not of trying dacoits and other criminals. Warren Hastings made no attempt to proceed *per saltum* by abolishing Indian judges or by substituting English for Hindu and Muhammadan law. It was his declared policy "to found the authority of the British Government in Bengal on its ancient laws," "to point the way to rule this people with ease and moderation according to their own ideas, manners, and prejudices." So far did he carry his respect for ancient customs that the barbarous penalties of the Muhammadan law were allowed to continue; for instance, a dacoit might be impaled or have a hand and a foot cut off, a thief might have 30 stripes every day for six months, etc.[1] Savage punishments, however, were not

[1] See Sir Henry Cotton, *Indian and Home Memoirs* (1911), p. 162.

unknown in England. They were common under military law, as may be gathered from two cases, both of which occurred in India in 1771. In one an English private, found guilty of mutinous conduct, was sentenced to 3,000 lashes, of which 2,000 were inflicted, the remainder being remitted by the General ; in the other three men, caught stealing while troops were on the march, had their ears cut off and were kept by the roadside with drums beating and a man proclaiming the nature of their offence till all the troops had marched past.[1]

Warren Hastings initiated the system of codification, which has been the secret of the success of judicial administration of India, by having a code of Hindu law compiled. Despite his own want of legal training he drew up a code of regulations for the courts, which embodied real reforms. The system by which law officers were paid by means of fines and court fees was abolished ; and he renounced for the Company the right, authorized by Muhammadan law and hitherto exercised by the Mughal Government, to a commission on the amount of all debts and on the value of all property recovered by decrees of the courts. Subsequently an admirable code of procedure was drawn up by Sir Elijah Impey after his appointment as Chief Judge of the Sudder Diwani Adalat, i.e., the supreme court, which did not merely decide appeals in civil cases, but also revised the proceedings of the lower courts and supervised their procedure.

Another cardinal principle of Warren Hastings's administration was that the people must have easy access to the representatives of Government.

[1] W. C. Macpherson, *Soldiering in India, 1764–1787* (1928), pp. 56, 81.

Instructions were issued that each officer of the Company must set apart a fixed portion of his time, daily or as often as his other duties permitted, to hearing and deciding all complaints brought before him. It was also laid down that there should be a box for petitions at the door of each cutcherry, or court house, of which he alone was to have the key: all petitions found in the box were to be read out to him on each court day. It was by attention to such details that Warren Hastings sought to bring justice to the people without its having to pass through the corrupt channel of subordinates.

Much of Warren Hastings's work was necessarily experimental. He himself did not claim the honour of being a reformer but merely that he made a number of "chops and changes"; but he succeeded in evolving order from the chaotic conditions which confronted him when he assumed office, and he laid the foundations of a civil service in the modern sense (so far as India is concerned) of an administrative *corps d'élite*. In the earlier part of his government he seems to have been so disgusted with the abuses prevalent under the system of English Collectors that he preferred to employ an Indian staff in the districts under the control of selected servants of the Company. These abuses, be it added, he attributed to a defective constitution and not to depravity of principle in the Company's servants.[1] It was not till 1780–1 that the revenue and judicial administration in the districts was entrusted to English officers. From that time onwards there may be said to have been the nucleus of a Civil Service

[1] Letter to Laurence Sullivan dated 21 March, 1776.

with the systematization and specialization of functions which are essential to such a service, e.g., the separation of customs from the revenue department and of revenue from judicial functions.

In appraising the work of the civil servants at this time allowance must be made for the facts that they were originally merchants and had to learn the work of civil administration, and that the country was in such a disturbed condition that the establishment of order was one of their first duties. In some districts, especially in North Bengal, lawlessness was a chronic danger. Dacoits or robbers, called " banditti " in the early records, roamed over the country in large bands often 1,000 and more strong. Some were hereditary dacoits described by Warren Hastings as a race of outlaws who lived from father to son in a state of warfare against society, plundering and burning villages and murdering the villagers. Their numbers were swollen by soldiers whose profession was gone when the large armies of the Nawabs were disbanded, by the retainers of noblemen whose establishments were reduced, and after the famine of 1770 by bands of peasants forced into crime by actual want : in 1772 we are even told of the country in North Bengal being overrun by hordes of robbers numbering 50,000. Ordinary work was thus frequently interrupted by the measures which had to be taken for maintaining the public peace. Making allowance for all the disadvantages under which they worked, the judgement passed by Kaye on these early days of administration seems just, viz. :

" The Company's servants had everything to learn as administrators, and those great lessons were not to be learnt in a day. But considering the strangeness of the duties which then devolved upon them, the magnitude of the labour imposed, and the extreme difficulty of acquiring a competent knowledge of the language, the institutions, the usages, and the character of the people, in all their multiform social aspects, a people whom before they had only known in the one relation of trader, the wonder is not that they advanced so little towards good government, but that they advanced so much." [1]

By 1785, when Warren Hastings laid down his office, there was a distinct improvement of *morale*, though corruption had by no means been eradicated and there were still black sheep in the service. Responsibility had already inspired a new sense of duty. When he assumed office in 1772, Warren Hastings had been fierce in denunciation, e.g., of "the boys of the service" who were "rulers, heavy rulers of the country." His views thirteen years later were very different. In a valedictory minute he testified to "a disdain of sordid emolument with a spirit of assiduity and the consequent expertness in business exceeding, I dare venture to affirm, the habits of any community under the British empire." And, alluding to the general stigma laid on all who served in India, he looked forward to the time when his testimony might help to disperse the clouds of prejudice which obscured the real worth of the service.[2] Valedictory testimonials are apt to be flattering, but there can be doubt as to the change which was taking place. Paternal despotism had begun to replace selfish

[1] J. W. Kaye, *The Administration of the East India Company* (1853), p. 87.

[2] W. Seton-Karr, *Selections from the Calcutta Gazette of 1784–1788* (1864), p. 133.

exploitation. Many of the men in the service were a blessing instead of, as formerly, a curse to the people. Hastings's statement is confirmed by some statistics quoted by his agent, Major Scott, in the House of Commons debate on Pitt's India Bill. He declared that the time when large fortunes were made in Bengal was past, and pointed out that out of 508 civil servants appointed from 1762 to 1784, only thirty-seven had returned to England, 150 were dead—a lamentably high proportion—321 were still in Bengal, and, inferentially, had not been able to return with fortunes. Out of the thirty-seven who had retired only two were members of Parliament, none had immense fortunes, many had less than £20,000 and some not a shilling.[1] Pitt himself said in the House of Commons that after the first five years persons employed in the Company's service might be supposed to save out of their salaries £2,000 a year without being suspected of peculation ; but Scott, whose information was more accurate, declared that nineteen out of twenty would be exceedingly happy at a prospect of being worth £10,000 in ten years.[2]

A few actual cases throw more light on the position of the Company's servants at this time than such generalizations. Henry Thomas Colebrooke, writing to his father in 1785 after six years

[1] According to Mackrabie's diary, George Vansittart was supposed to have taken £150,000 home with him in 1776, and Barwell, who retired in 1781, was credited with a fortune of £40,000. These, however, had been in Bengal in the earlier days of unlimited opportunities.

[2] J. M. Holzman, *The Nabobs in England* (New York, 1926), pp. 27, 28, 30.

of service, told him that India was no longer a gold mine; everyone was disgusted, and all who could do so were leaving it as fast as possible. He himself had drawn a total pay of Rs. 661 (*sicca*) in the preceding year.[1] We have also fortunately a reliable record by John Shore, who was afterwards Lord Teignmouth, which shows that the early years of service were lean years. Shore may be regarded as a man of the new and better school of officials, and his career as illustrating the changed conditions of service. He started his service in 1769 with the meagre salary of Rs. 96, which was equivalent to £12 a year, and could pay little more than half the rent of a miserable, close, and unwholesome dwelling. He complained bitterly that the Writers had had a customs-free trade before the arrival of "Lord Clive of infamous memory" and even since then, but they were now debarred from all such profit, because the orders of the Directors had deprived them of their right to trade, which was conferred, though under severe restrictions, by their covenants. Within a year of landing, when only twenty years of age, Shore was discharging the duties of a Judge: in a year he decided 600 cases with only two appeals from his judgements. During the first five years of his service his salary never exceeded £500 a year, and in the first ten he saved nothing. It was not till he had spent twelve years in the country that he was in a fair way to earning a competency by honest means; and after twenty years, the latter of which were in high office, he returned with a fortune of £25,000 honourably acquired. Not all were so fortunate: Shore could give a long list of persons

[1] D. Dewar, *Bygone Days in India* (1922), p. 181.

ruined beyond all hope of recovery because of former youthful extravagance.[1]

On the other hand, if a man had a shrewd commercial mind and was not hampered by scruples, it was easy to make money, as may be seen from the candid and rather naïve record of a transaction of the Hon. Robert Lindsay, son of the Earl of Balcarres. In the early years of his service he was stationed at Dacca, where consignments of salt, a monopoly of the Company, were sold at public auction. Lindsay noticed that lots fell, as they were put up, to dependents of the Members of Council; in fact, there was a ring. Lindsay, who had had a commercial education at Cadiz, saw a fair opportunity of bettering himself without injury to the public. He entered into a partnership with an Indian merchant, who advanced him money to buy up salt, and at the next sale he bought to the extent of £20,000. "The speculation turned out so well as fully to enable me to pay off all the debt I had contracted during my long residence in Calcutta, and to place a few thousand rupees in my pocket." The sequel was not to be wondered at. "This, I have reason to think, soon after facilitated my removal from Dacca."[2] When he was posted to Sylhet in 1773 he wrote: "My pay as Resident did not exceed £500 per annum, so that fortune could only be acquired by my own industry." He acquired it by trade in lime and by ship-building. The revenues were collected in cowries, of which 700 millions were remitted annually to Dacca, and this canny young man hit

[1] Lord Teignmouth, *Memoir of Lord Teignmouth* (1843), Vol. I, pp. 25–7, 38, 39, 77, 140, 224.

[2] *Dacca District Gazetteer* (1912), p. 40.

on the bright idea of keeping the cowries for current expenditure in Sylhet and of remitting their value in limestone, for which he held the contract.[1] *Ornatur propriis industria donis* would have been a suitable motto for this shrewd merchant-administrator.

Many of the Company's servants were still intent on sordid money-making. In 1787, within a year of assuming office as Governor-General, Lord Cornwallis found abundant evidence of frauds, peculation and corruption. A glaring case was that of the Resident at Benares, who, in addition to his salary of Rs. 1,000 a month, obtained from irregular emoluments little less than Rs. 400,000 a year, exclusive of a monopoly of the trade of the surrounding country.

> "I have," Cornwallis wrote in this same year, "every reason to believe that at present almost all the Collectors are under the name of some relative or friend deeply engaged in commerce, and by their influence as Collectors and Judges of Adaulet they become the most dangerous enemies of the Company's interest and the greatest oppressors of the manufacturers." [2]

Cornwallis was fond of making sweeping charges of corruption, such as his dictum "Every native of Hindostan, I really believe is corrupt," and his description of Sir John Macpherson's government as "a system of the dirtiest jobbings"; but we know from other sources that his charge against the Civil Service had some foundation of fact. Many took advantage of the frequent opportunities

[1] Sir W. W. Hunter, *The Thackerays in India* (1897), pp. 86, 92, 93.
[2] C. Ross, *Correspondence of Marquis Cornwallis* (1859), Vol. I, pp. 238, 250, 282.

for enriching themselves which were presented by the recurring settlements of revenue. John Shore said that as President of the Committee of Revenue he could easily have made £100,000 on a single mission and that some of the Company's servants realized vast sums from the landlords for understating the amount of their rentals.[1] There were also gross breaches of the orders about private trade, as may be judged from the frankly selfish account of François Grand, whose wife was divorced by him for her liaison with Sir Philip Francis and afterwards married Talleyrand. Grand, who was Collector of Tirhut from 1782 to 1787 and as such was debarred from engaging in private trade, wrote bemoaning the hardship of his dismissal by Cornwallis.

"I introduced the manufacturing of indigo after the European manner, encouraged the establishment of indigo works and plantations, erected three at my own expense and thus possessed a fortune of £15,000 sterling. My manufactories, my houses, land, furniture, tents, equipages, horses, boats, stood upon a valuation of £10,000 more. By one stroke of his Lordship's pen, every hope and fair-built prospect was completely blasted. Thus the blow was struck, and from that day I fell, perhaps, never to rise again. View the portrait and feel."

The remedy which Cornwallis steadily urged was simple. The Company wanted men of experience, ability and character to serve in a country where health was precarious, and it must pay them properly. Salaries should be given sufficient to enable them to live in a decent and comfortable

[1] Lord Teignmouth, *Memoir of Lord Teignmouth* (1843), Vol. I, p. 75.

D

manner and to make such savings as would give them a prospect of being able in a moderate number of years to return and spend the latter part of their days in easy circumstances at home.[1] The Directors were guilty of false economy by not giving adequate salaries to men who held offices of great responsibility, in which they could soon make their fortunes by irregular means. The salaries of Collectors had, it is true, been raised to Rs. 1,200 a month (equivalent to £1,300 a year), but a Collectorship could only be attained after twelve years' service; and it was impossible on such a salary for an honest man to save enough to live on after retirement. Eventually, the Directors agreed that men employed in the collection of the revenues should be paid partly by a salary and partly by a commission of about 1 per cent. on the amount of the collections.[2] The latter commission formed a great part of the Collector's emoluments, for the Directors, then as always, hated the idea of high salaries appearing in the balance sheets; it varied from district to district according to the revenues collected, and could not exceed

[1] The scale which the Directors thought sufficient for life in England was low. In 1786 when a number of civil servants had had their posts abolished owing to retrenchment, all that they would sanction was: for a Senior Merchant who had a private fortune of under £10,000, an annuity of £400 a year; for a Junior Merchant with under £7,500 of his own, £300 a year; and for a Factor or Writer with under £6,000, an annuity of £200. In each case the Company would provide only the amount necessary with the interest of the men's own money to bring the annuity to this total. W. Seton-Karr, *Selections from the Calcutta Gazette of 1784–1788* (1864), pp. 123–4.

[2] C. Ross, *Correspondence of Marquis Cornwallis* (1859), Vol. I, pp. 278, 286, 290.

Rs. 27,500 a year. In one of the largest districts the Collector drew a salary of Rs. 1,500 a month and an average commission of a little over Rs. 2,000 a month. This Cornwallis considered not excessive considering the very high responsibility laid upon him, the temptations to which he was exposed, the prohibition of other emoluments, the incessant labours of his office, and the zeal which must be exerted to promote the prosperity of the revenues and—an important addendum—of the country at large. Liberty of private trade, however, continued to be a recognized right of the Commercial Residents and Agents, who were employed solely in the trading business of the Company and received a commission on articles purchased for the Company.[1]

After 1786 a single officer combined the offices of Collector, Judge and Magistrate, the duties of the last until 1791 being merely to apprehend and not to try dacoits, robbers and other offenders. The union of these offices, and the consequent abandonment of the principle of separating executive from judicial functions, was decided upon by the Directors both because it tended to simplicity and economy, and also because they felt that they ought to be guided by "the manners and usages of the people rather than by any abstract theories drawn from other countries or applicable to a different state of things"—an important principle which was neglected when the Permanent Settlement was concluded. The actual pay was attached to the office of Collector, to which the offices of Judge and Magistrate were

[1] Lord Teignmouth, *Memoir of Lord Teignmouth* (1843), Vol. I, p. 161.

regarded as appanages. In a few years it was found that the duties of the Judge and Magistrate were neglected when they interfered with those of the Collector. The system by which revenue cases, or cases affecting rights in the soil, were tried in the civil and not the revenue courts had been given up, and they were now exclusively cognizable by the Collector. The latter looked upon the collection of revenue as his chief duty, and naturally so, for failure in collections might entail dismissal. To remedy this defect, judicial powers were withdrawn from the Collector in 1793 and transferred to the civil courts. There were thus two chief administrative officers in each district, the Collector, whose duties were confined to the collection of the public dues, and the Judge-Magistrate, who united in his person the powers of Civil Judge and Magistrate and also controlled the police. Of the two the Judge-Magistrate had the higher rank and station, Cornwallis having proclaimed that Judgeships were to be considered the first appointments in importance in the service.

The most important administrative reform introduced by Cornwallis was in connexion with the administration of criminal justice, which was till 1790 under the Nawab. The Magistrates had in 1787 been authorized to hear petty cases, but otherwise the criminal courts were held exclusively by Muhammadan officers though subject to inspection and control by the Company's officers. The system was open to three objections. The cruel punishments of mutilation inflicted under the Muhammadan law were shocking to humanity; the courts were vitiated by a spirit of corruption;

murders, robberies and other violent crimes were lamentably frequent and little checked. Another objectionable practice was that of sentencing accused persons to imprisonment, without defining its period, until reparation was made for the injury done or security for good conduct was obtained: in one district jail it was found in 1792 that 100 out of 300 prisoners were confined in this way for an unlimited period. Cornwallis saw no prospect of reform so long as Indian officers constituted the judiciary. It was his declared conviction "that all regulations for the reform of that department would be useless and nugatory whilst the execution of them depends upon any native whatever." Accordingly, he announced at the end of 1790 that he had resolved to take over the administration of criminal justice, and the criminal courts were transferred to the Magistrates. It was at first laid down that decisions should be regulated by the Muhammadan law, except that murder was not to be compromised by the dead man's relatives; but in 1791 mutilation was abolished as a punishment.

The work of codification was also continued, the regulations of Sir Elijah Impey being revised and enlarged in 1793 by Sir George Barlow. Objections have been raised to this code on the ground that it was so complicated and overlaid with formalities as to obstruct the even course of justice. Sir Thomas Munro also held that appeals should have been kept within narrower limits and not have gone beyond the District Judge; but the right of appeal to a higher court had already been granted by Warren Hastings. In spite of its defects the new judicial system was such a success that in 1802 Sir Henry Strachey stated that the poor looked to the laws and not to the patronage of the powerful for protection [1]; in other words, the reign of law had begun.

The great merit of Lord Cornwallis's government was that it gave some stability to the administration. Nowhere was the need for stability greater than in the revenue system, where, as the result of want of knowledge of the intricate system of land tenures, as well as of experience on the part of the staff, there had been constant changes and experiments ever since the Company took over the *Diwani*, new measures being hastily adopted and fresh experiments tried and as hastily abandoned. Whatever its demerits, the Permanent Settlement had the advantage of introducing some finality in a department which had been in such a state of flux that it was some time before the people, habituated to frequent changes, could believe that the settlement could or would be lasting.

Before Cornwallis's administration ended, a Civil Service in the modern sense of the word had been organized. Its charter of rights was contained in the Charter Act of 1793, which provided that all vacancies occurring in any of the civil offices in India, below that of Member of Council, should be filled up from among the Civil Servants of the Company belonging to the Presidency in which they occurred and not otherwise. There were restrictions as to the length of residence in India required for posts carrying a certain salary, viz., three years if the salary was over £500 a year, but

[1] J. W. Kaye, *The Administration of the East India Company* (1853), p. 343.

otherwise the general principle was established that posts in the civil administration were to be reserved for the Civil Service. This barred the door on outsiders and prevented them obtaining an entrance by means of patronage in England; jobbing of this kind had been stoutly opposed by Cornwallis, who threatened to resign if it was continued. The same motive led to a provision that promotion was to go by seniority. The duties of different departments were defined; fixed salaries proportionate to responsibility were attached to specific appointments; perquisites and allowances were done away with. Redundant establishments were reduced and sinecures abolished. A civil auditor was appointed for the regular examination and check of all civil expenditure; and this Cornwallis declared to be the only new office he had created.[1] It was also laid down in 1793 that all officers of Government were amenable to the Courts for acts done in their official capacities, while Government itself agreed to submit its rights to be tried by them in cases in which it was a party with its subjects in matters of property.[2] There was thus a double check, financial and judicial, on irregularity.

There was an undoubted improvement both in honesty and efficiency. Sir John Shore in 1789 declared that it would be difficult to point to any salary for which some equivalent duty was not exacted; for one sinecure place in Bengal there were ten in England. There were, he believed,

[1] C. Ross, *Correspondence of Marquis Cornwallis* (1859), Vol. I, p. 541.

[2] A. B. Keith, *Speeches and Documents on Indian Policy* (1922), Vol. I, p. 177.

more honesty, principle and humanity, comparatively speaking, in India than in England, and no country in the world where the officers of Government devoted more time and attention to public business. Official duties were inconceivably laborious to those who performed them with zeal and assiduity.[1]

"That there is and ever will be peculation in India is only saying it is not a desert; for where men are, some knaves will be found; but there is as much virtue, principle, and active zeal here as in any part of the world. The Company until lately considered mankind in a new light. They placed their servants at a feast where they were starving and told them to help all but themselves."

Five years later he wrote that there were as few little peculations and sinister emoluments as anywhere in the world, and in 1798 he assured his successor in the office of Governor-General that he would find as great a measure of integrity, zeal and assiduity in the officers of the Government of India as in any part of the world.[2]

[1] The office hours were from 7 a.m. to 4 p.m., but probably then, as now, much work had to be done out of office hours. Rules about revenue returns were strict to a degree of harshness. One Collector was warned in 1783 that he would be liable to immediate dismissal if he failed to submit his monthly accounts punctually. Three years later this drastic order was modified. It was then laid down that a Collector whose accounts were not received by the due date would be liable to a fine of half a month's pay for the first offence and of a whole month's pay for any subsequent unpunctuality.

[2] Lord Teignmouth, *Memoir of Lord Teignmouth* (1843), Vol. I, pp. 140, 165, 171, 180, 285, 329, 463.

It is to this period rather than to the administration of Warren Hastings that Kaye's remark should be applied

> "that there was gradually springing up a race of trained administrators around whom the old commercial traditions did not cling, who had not graduated in chicanery, or grown grey in fraud and corruption, and who brought to their work not only a sounder intelligence but purer moral perceptions and a higher sense of what they owed to the people of the soil."[1]

This conclusion may be confirmed by some actual cases taken from different branches of the Service. The first is that of Jonathan Duncan, a Civil Servant of the new order, for he joined the service in 1772. He was appointed in 1788 Resident at Benares, where he induced the Rajkumars of Jaunpur to give up female infanticide, and was for sixteen years Governor of Bombay. The monument erected in his memory at Bombay, where he died in 1811, bears the inscription: "He was a good man and a just." This epitaph was well deserved. A man of large tolerance and wide sympathy, he knew and was revered by the people: it was said, indeed, that he had been Brahmanized by long residence in India. Bishop Heber, questioning the people at Benares in 1824, found that though they usually spoke of Wellesley and Warren Hastings as the greatest rulers they had known, they spoke with most affection of Jonathan Duncan; *Duncan Sahib ka chhota bhai*, i.e., "Mr. Duncan's younger brother" was still "the usual term of praise applied to any public man who appeared to be actuated by an unusual spirit of kindness

[1] *The Administration of the East India Company* (1853), p. 88.

and liberality toward their nation."[1] The second case is that of a man called to less exalted stations and simply doing the work of a District Officer, viz., Tilman Henckell, Collector of Jessore in Bengal from 1781 to 1789, of whom it has been written:

"The idea of his administration was that it was the duty of Government to procure the peace and comfort of the mass of the inhabitants, though it might involve some harm in respect of the Company's commercial interests. . . . Mr. Henckell was never unmindful of his employers' mercantile interests, but he set this before him—to guard the then almost helpless natives from the oppressions to which they were subjected by the commercial officers of the Company as well as by their own zamindars."[2]

So well did he act up to this ideal that a contemporary record (1788) stated that his benevolence to the poor manufacturers of salt aroused such reverential gratitude that they made an image of him and worshipped it among themselves.[3]

Instances of improved *morale* might also be cited from the commercial branch, which in the previous passage has been referred to as a source of oppression. Many of the Commercial Residents and Agents now began to stand out as upright men and public benefactors, besides doing much to develop local manufactures and industries. Charles Grant, afterwards one of the "Clapham Sect," who was appointed Commercial Resident at Malda in 1781, started, as he was entitled to do, an indigo estate

[1] Bishop Heber's *Journal* (1828), Vol. I, p. 438.

[2] Sir James Westland, *Report on the District of Jesore* (1874).

[3] W. Seton-Karr, *Selections from Calcutta Gazette* (1864), p. 253.

of his own, besides managing the Company's silk filatures. He grew rich so fast that, to satisfy his own scruples, he asked Lord Cornwallis to have his private accounts examined with his public accounts. They were returned with the remark that the Governor-General wished that all servants of the Company were equally scrupulous. His successor at Malda, George Udny, was described in the history of Bengal called *Riyazu-s-Salatin* (1788), which was dedicated to him, as the Hatim of the world of bounty, the Naushirwan of the world of justice,[1] the generous man of the age, whose lips scattered pearls, while the tray of his bounty was filled with gold for the poor and needy.

Another commercial worthy was John Cheap, who came to India in 1782 and was for forty-one years Commercial Resident in Birbhum, where he died in 1828. He was known as " Cheap the Magnificent " and has been immortalized in the *Annals of Rural Bengal* by Sir William Hunter, who wrote : " In his person Government appeared in its most benign aspect. . . . Happy was the infant on whom his shadow fell." He was an unofficial judge to whom the people brought their disputes for arbitration, and a friend before whom they laid their troubles. He fostered new manufactures, e.g., by introducing indigo cultivation and an improved process of sugar manufacture, and to him the people were indebted for the only good roads they possessed. A Frenchman named Frushard, who as Commercial Agent for the Company in the same district (1782–1807) spent

[1] Hatim was a prince of Arabia famous for lavish hospitality, Naushirwan a king of Persia whose justice was proverbial.

Rs. 150,000 a year for the Company alone, was another small unofficial providence. He decided the cases which the villagers brought to him without any sanction but their own consent, arrested the dacoits who preyed on them, cleared their villages of the tigers which infested them, and made his silk filature the centre of a circle of cultivation and prosperity.[1]

[1] See E. G. Drake-Brockman, *Notes on the Early Administration of the District of Birbhum* (Calcutta, 1898).

CHAPTER III

UNDER THE COMPANY: 1793–1858

IN 1786, when Cornwallis's government began, the British possessions consisted only of the Bengal Presidency, i.e., Bengal, Bihar and Benares; of the Madras Presidency, which included a few scattered districts (Madras, a small adjacent tract and the Northern Circars); and of the Bombay Presidency, which comprised merely the island of Bombay and Salsette with a small area on the mainland. The Bombay Presidency was of such little account from the administrative point of view that Cornwallis, while acknowledging its value as a naval and military base, thought that a small factory there and another at Surat, with a staff recruited from Bengal or Madras, would answer all purposes. It was to him perfectly incomprehensible that Bombay should have a Council, Senior and Junior Merchants, Factors and Writers merely to load one ship in the year and to collect a very small revenue.[1] The only acquisition made by Cornwallis was that of the territory ceded by Tippu in 1792, but annexations were made so fast as the result of the wars waged by Wellesley that by the beginning of the nineteenth century the Company had become the master of an empire, and its servants, though bearing the old commercial designations, were, as he pointed out to the

[1] C. Ross, *Correspondence of Marquis Cornwallis* (1859), Vol. I, p. 389.

Directors, no longer to be considered as the agents of a commercial concern but, in fact, the ministers and officers of a powerful sovereign, required to discharge the functions of magistrates, judges, ambassadors and governors of provinces, and carrying out duties which were those of statesmen in other parts of the world.

With the extension of its duties the Civil Service came to be divided into different branches, viz., judicial, political, revenue, and mercantile. Political was the name which was, and is still, applied to what is generally known as diplomatic work. The distinction between judicial and revenue was weakened by the transfer of magisterial work from the Judges to the Collectors in 1831, when the modern system of district administration under a District and Sessions Judge and a Magistrate-Collector came into being. The commercial department disappeared in 1833, when the Company, being prohibited from trade by the Charter Act of that year, ceased to be a trading corporation, and its officers were confined to administrative work. The old titles of Merchants, Factors and Writers were, however, retained in official registers till 1842,[1] though the mercantile duties which they connoted had disappeared.

The Service continued to maintain the standard of integrity and efficiency which had resulted from the exercise of responsibility and the receipt of reasonable rates of pay. As observed by Lord Minto, Governor-General from 1807 to 1813, the old fashion of corruption had gone out since the Company had given up the policy of parsimony as regards its officers' pay. In his judgement, a more

[1] See article on Factor in *Hobson-Jobson* (1903), p. 345.

pure and highly honourable administration did not exist than that of the East India Company in India. The Abbé Dubois wrote in *Hindu Manners, Customs and Ceremonies* in 1822, after thirty years in South India:

> "The justice and prudence which the present rulers display in endeavouring to make these people less unhappy than they have been hitherto; the anxiety which they manifest in increasing their material comfort; above all, the inviolable respect which they constantly show for the customs and religious beliefs of the country; and, lastly, the protection which they afford to the weak as well as to the strong . . . all these have contributed more to the consolidation of their power than even their victories and conquests. . . . For uprightness of character, education and ability it would be hard to find a body of public servants better capable of filling with zeal and distinction the offices, more or less important, that are entrusted to them."

In 1833, again, Macaulay could declare in the House of Commons that civil and military functionaries resembled in nothing but capacity and valour the adventurer who seventy years earlier had returned to England laden with wealth and infamy. He viewed with reverence and delight the honourable poverty which was the evidence of a rectitude firmly maintained amidst strong temptations; he rejoiced to see his countrymen, after ruling millions of subjects, after administering the revenues of great provinces, after judging the causes of wealthy zamindars, after residing at the Courts of tributary kings, return to their native land with no more than a decent competence.

Although the Charter Act of 1793 had reserved for the Civil Service all offices below that of Member of Council, it was found in practice to be impossible to maintain such a monopoly. The practice of employing military men in civil offices had already been introduced by Lord Cornwallis; and these Military Civilians (as they are commonly called) were an important part of the executive as well as the diplomatic staff. For instance, in 1792 the settlement of the ceded districts of Madras was entrusted not to civil servants, but to soldiers. From that year till 1807 Sir Thomas Munro, one of the first and greatest of a line of soldier-statesmen, was engaged in what is called revenue work, such as adjusting the payments due to the State by peasant-proprietors, which was the basis of the *ryotwari* settlement adopted for the Madras Presidency and associated with his name. It was natural that the army should be drawn upon to help in the administration of India. With the expansion of English power vast tracts were annexed one after the other. The Civil Service could not spare men enough for both their government and pacification, e.g., the suppression of bands of marauders, for which officers of the army were the best fitted. It is difficult at this length of time to realize how unsettled newly annexed territories were, but some idea may be gathered from a description of the border districts of the Punjab, where, Sir Harry Lumsden wrote in 1846:

> "Every man ploughed with his sword by his side and matchlock handy, with a piece of dried cowdung burning near, ready to light the match, while the cattle of the village were escorted out to graze by an armed party from each village."[1]

---

[1] Sir P. S. Lumsden and G. R. Elsmie, *Lumsden of the Guides* (1899), p. 39.

Sometimes the administration was entirely in the hands of Military Civilians, as for instance in Arakan, where they were most successful in introducing settled government after its annexation in 1826. It was here that Sir Arthur Phayre first made his reputation between 1834 and 1848, after he had acquired valuable experience in civil work in Assam.

The employment of military men in civil administration was naturally a grievance to the regular Civilians. Their feeling on the subject was voiced by Henry Torrens in *A Ballad* (1833), in which he satirically contrasted the Writer required to pass examinations in Indian languages, and then appointed as "seventh sub-assistant" to a Collector, with the young Ensign who was thought to have an intuitive knowledge of languages and was called from the regimental mess to rule over districts. The "orthodox Bentinckian creed," as Torrens called it, was recited in doggerel verse, which refers to Lord William Bentinck's appointment of Indians, as well as of military men, to civil offices:

"All but B.C.S.[1] Collectors for their offices sufficient are!
All Moonsiffs[2] are immaculate, all Judges inefficient are!
No military favourite (whatever his condition) errs!
And Colonels of Artillery are heaven-born Commissioners!"

At no time was the employment of Military Civilians pushed further than during the brief government of Lord Ellenborough, who liked soldiers as much as he disliked Civilians. Those of the latter who wore moustaches he derisively dubbed "Cutcherry (i.e., court-house) Hussars," and he added injury to ridicule by substituting army

[1] Bengal Civil Service.

[2] Indian judicial officers dealing with civil suits in the first instance.

officers for them wherever he was within his legal rights in so doing. He had no scruple about appointing to posts of high responsibility military men without administrative training and experience, and by the time he left India few Civilians had been left either in the political service or in the Non-Regulation provinces. The exclusion of the Civil Service was also carried to an extreme by Sir Charles Napier in his administration of Sind (1843–7). He soon got rid of the few Civil Servants who had been sent there when it was annexed, and he put army officers in charge of the whole revenue and judicial administration, with unfortunate results, for those whom he selected were not competent to deal with difficult questions of revenue and with a complicated system of land tenures. They were, moreover, preoccupied by military duties, suppressing robber bands, obtaining supplies for the troops, etc. Elsewhere, however, splendid work was done by Military Civilians, who were chosen for their special qualifications. Indeed, some of the greatest names in the history of British India are those of soldiers who were engaged in civil administration, such as Sir Henry Lawrence, Sir Herbert Edwardes, Sir Arthur Phayre, Sir Mark Cubbon, Sir Robert Sandeman, Outram, Nicholson, Sleeman, Abbott, Lake, Rennell Taylor, Sir Henry Ramsay, and others too numerous to mention. Nor is the line of great soldier-administrators extinct; in modern times, for example, may be mentioned Colonel Deane, the first Chief Commissioner of the North-West Frontier Province, his successor, Sir George Roos-Keppel, and Sir Henry McMahon, who was Chief Commissioner of Baluchistan and Foreign Secretary to the Government of India.

The provinces in which military officers were employed were known as Non-Regulation, while Civilians were exclusively employed in the Regulation provinces. The latter were the older provinces governed by the laws made under the Charter Acts, which were called Regulations until 1834, when the more modern designation of Acts was adopted. The Non-Regulation provinces were less advanced areas, in which the introduction of the ordinary law with its formalities and more elaborate procedure was considered inadvisable and which were accordingly excluded from the operation of the Regulations and Acts in force elsewhere in British India. The Governor-General in Council had, instead, power to make laws for them by executive orders, for which a parallel is the issue of Orders in Council made by the Crown for Crown Colonies. The officers of Government serving in them were at the same time required to "ordinarily conform to the principles and spirit of the Regulations" and to act according to justice, equity, and good conscience in cases not covered by laws or rules.

The working of this system may be illustrated by a concrete instance. In Regulation provinces the practice of suttee was prohibited by the Regulation passed by Lord William Bentinck's Government in 1829. In Sind, where this Regulation was not in force, suttee, a rare practice there, was put down by an executive order. When the Brahmans pleaded that it was a sacred custom of Hindus which should be respected, Sir Charles Napier replied:

> "Be it so. This burning of widows is your custom. Prepare the funeral pile. But my nation has also a custom. When men burn women alive, we hang them and confiscate all their property. My carpenters shall

therefore erect gibbets on which to hang all concerned when the widow is consumed. Let us all act according to national customs." [1]

The Brahmans saw the force of this *argumentum ad hominem* and the practice was given up.

Of the general system followed in Non-Regulation areas inhabited by primitive races no better example can perhaps be given than the administration of Kumaon after its cession by the Nepalese. Under Nepalese rule the people had been subjected to gross oppression. To escape the exactions of their masters they fled into the jungles, leaving their villages waste. Under British rule they became a prosperous and contented peasantry, so conscious of the change that it became proverbial to speak of any act of oppression as the end of the Company's rule and the restoration of that of the Gurkhas. The man who was primarily responsible for this transformation was George William Traill, who was Commissioner of Kumaon from 1816 to 1835 and was known as the " King of Kumaon," an unofficial title of honour afterwards borne by Sir Henry Ramsay, a soldier-Civilian who was Commissioner of Kumaon from 1856 to 1884. Traill's administration was one of personal government of a patriarchal type, which was described as follows by Brian Houghton Hodgson, who was his Assistant in 1819–20:

" I was much struck by the simple yet efficient method of administering the province, a new acquisition tenanted by very primitive and poor tribes. The Commissioner (Traill), who spoke and wrote the local language, dis-

---

[1] Sir William Napier, *History of General Sir Charles Napier's Administration of Scinde* (1851), p. 35.

pensed with all formalities, settled cases in court like the father of a family and encouraged every one who had a complaint to put it in writing and drop it in a slit in the court door, of which he kept the key. Answered *viva voce*, in court or not. He was of active habits and went everywhere throughout the province, hearing and seeing all for himself. His cheerful, simple manners and liking for the people made him justly popular." [1]

The Non-Regulation system with its simple methods of administration and avoidance of complicated forms and procedure was peculiarly suited to aboriginal races. The danger of applying the elaborate Regulation system to primitive peoples, and the injustice which it might inflict on them, were forcibly brought home to the Government of India by the Santal Rebellion of 1855. The Santals had migrated in large numbers to the district (now in Bihar and Orissa) known as the Santal Parganas, where they cleared the forest and brought the land under cultivation. Their traditional belief was that the soil belonged to the man who reclaimed it from jungle, and they found themselves exploited and oppressed by alien landlords. Simple and improvident, they fell into the hands of moneylenders, whose exactions were enforced by legal process. The courts were distant, the Santals were equally ignorant and afraid of their procedure. Their only records of monetary transactions were strings in which knots represented the number of rupees which they had taken as loans and spaces between them the years which had elapsed. They rose *en masse* armed with axes, bows and arrows, with the idea of exterminating moneylenders and expelling land-

[1] loc. cit. Sir William Hunter, *Life of Brian Houghton Hodgson* (1896), p. 57.

lords from their country; and in pursuance of these objects, swept over the country and committed ghastly atrocities. A large military force had to take the field, and it was only after a campaign of six months that the rising was crushed. It served one good purpose, for it showed that the Santals had been driven into rebellion by the rigour of the Regulation system and the absence of contact with their rulers. The district was brought under the Non-Regulation system, the principal features of which were that the Santals had direct access to British officers, and that all judicial proceedings were of the simplest form, the parties and their witnesses appearing before the magistrates without the intervention of either pleaders or official underlings.

Nowhere did the Non-Regulation system achieve such admirable results as in the Punjab. Its success there was due to several causes. The administrative staff was small—under sixty in all—but they were picked men, half military officers, half the best Civilians to be found in the North-West Provinces, then regarded as the model administration; they were chosen by Dalhousie himself, a shrewd judge of character. They were men inspired by a spirit of service to the people, prompt in decision and action, and not impaired by age; Sir Richard Temple, the Secretary to the Punjab Government, had only a few years' service. In this small *corps d'élite* soldier and civilian colleagues worked harmoniously. Those soldiers to whom civil was less congenial than military work reverted to their regiments: it was not every soldier who found civil administration to his taste. One such was Sir Harry Lumsden, who in 1849, when the new system of government was introduced in the Punjab, complained that military men were not on equal terms with young Civilians who had legal procedure at their fingers' ends. He chafed at the idea of having "a young gentleman of the black cloth" promoted over his head or of having a Civilian held up to him as an example. Even Sir Herbert Edwardes, who had the reputation of being the cleverest man in India with his pen, was told on one occasion that a man who had been only two years in the Civil Service would not have made such mistakes as he had.[1]

The system of administration followed in the Punjab was the joint work of the two Lawrences—Henry, the soldier, and John, the Civilian. The foundations were laid by Henry Lawrence, who in a letter to one of his officers laid down its guiding principles.

> "In a new country, especially a wild one, promptness, accessibility, brevity and kindliness are the best engines of government. Have as few forms as possible and as are consistent with a brief record of proceedings. Be considerate and kind, not expecting too much from ignorant people. Make no change, unless certain of decided improvement in the substitute—light assessment, considering the claims and privileges, even when somewhat extravagant, of the privileged classes, especially when they affect Government and not ryots."[2]

---

[1] Sir P. S. Lumsden and G. R. Elsmie, *Lumsden of the Guides* (1899), p. 75.

[2] With this may be compared the remark made by one of the Punjab Civilians, Needham Cust, in *Memoirs of Past Years*: "We were taught in the Punjab to have an iron hand in a velvet glove; a firm rule, soft words, and conciliation."

The system, based on these general principles, was built up and made complete by John Lawrence, who declared that he desired earnestly to show what a man bred and educated as a Civilian could do in a new country. There were three cardinal points in his system. First, the concentration of authority and responsibility in the District Officer, who was not only Magistrate and Collector but also Judge: Lawrence considered that the union in one person of the administration of civil justice and of revenue was essential for the preservation of the indigenous system of land tenures, which would break up if subjected to civil courts without knowledge or experience of them. Secondly, the districts must not be so large as to make this undivided responsibility impossible and they must be small enough for the District Officer to get a complete knowledge of them and the people. Thirdly, the administration was grounded on a set of simple laws and rules, which respected Indian institutions.[1]

Personality was not obscured or overlaid by routine but had full play. All were ready to take the initiative and accept responsibility. There was, therefore, much personal government, but it was by no means a substitute for government by law. One of John Lawrence's maxims was "Do a thing regularly and legally if you can do it as well and vigorously in that way as irregularly and illegally." The officers under him were required to follow a code (drafted by Sir Robert Montgomery and Sir Richard Temple) which explained the main provisions of the several systems of Indian law on such matters as inheritance, marriage, adoption, the

[1] Sir Charles Aitchison, *John Lawrence* (Rulers of India series), 1897, pp. 60–1.

disposition of property by will or otherwise, and also set forth the chief principles to be observed in other branches of law, such as contracts, sale, debt and commercial usage. There were full provisions for the admission of evidence; there were also complete arrangements for reference to arbitration and for ascertaining local custom. Formalities and technicalities were reduced to a minimum, for every other consideration was made subordinate to the necessity for making justice cheap and quick, sure and simple. Justice, according to a contemporary account, was dealt out in a fashion combining the salutary promptness of the Oriental with the scrupulous investigation of the European court.[1] So far was the judicial administration from being rough and ready that the Government of the Punjab has been held to have deserved the name of a government by law better than that of either the North-West Provinces (now the United Provinces) or Bengal. A proof of this is that when the codes were introduced less change had to be made in the judicial system, civil as well as criminal, in the Non-Regulation than in the Regulation provinces.[2] Where the system proved of especial value was in its preservation of the democratic constitution of the Sikh villages, i.e., the management of their communal affairs by representative bodies, the structure of government being based on real local self-government. The people managed their own affairs, taxation was light, and there was general contentment. The fruits of this policy were seen in the Mutiny, when the Punjab stood staunch;

[1] *Calcutta Review*, March, 1854.

[2] Sir John Strachey, *India: Its Administration and Progress* (1911), pp. 101–2.

and it is no exaggeration to say that the saving of India was in a large measure due to the Non-Regulation system in the Punjab. It may be added that the respect shown to ancient customs sometimes led to quaint proceedings. Thus, it was the duty of Sir George Campbell to enforce the customary obligation of Jat widows to marry their deceased husbands' brothers. Disputes were frequent but this young Solomon soon settled them; he would sometimes perform the marriage ceremony offhand by throwing a sheet over the woman, as was the custom for second marriages.[1]

In the Regulation provinces, where the superior staff was drawn exclusively from the Civil Service, the basic principle of administration, after the experimental period which had produced such an exotic as the Permanent Settlement, was also the maintenance, as far as possible, of Indian systems of law and social organization. In Bengal (including Bihar) the Permanent Settlement divorced District Officers to a certain extent from direct contact with the people in the important sphere of revenue (but not of other) work and proved a dissolvent of indigenous institutions like the village community. This measure was extended in 1795 to Benares and an adjoining area (constituting one-tenth of the present United Provinces) and in 1802 to some districts in Madras (about a quarter of that Presidency); but it went no further, for its defects were realized. In view of the diversity of conditions in different parts of the country there was no attempt to impose uniformity. The forms of administration therefore varied greatly. In Madras

[1] Sir G. Campbell, *Memoirs of my Indian Career* (1893), p. 83.

Sir Thomas Munro established the principle of the indigenous revenue system, called *ryotwari*, which secured his rights to the peasant-proprietor. In Bombay, where the organization of administration, begun in 1803, was completed during the Governorship of Mountstuart Elphinstone (1819–27), the change from native rule is said to have been in men rather than in measures. Elphinstone, who was appointed Governor after twenty-four years' service, made it his aim to cherish whatever was good in the existing system. In the territories of the Deccan conquered from the Peshwa the guiding principles of the revenue administration were to maintain the existing system except for the farming out of land, to make light assessments of revenue based on actual cultivation, to impose no new taxes and do away with none unless obviously unjust; "and, above all, to make no innovations." The districts were organized on the Bengal model, which itself was based on the Mughal system; and in 1827 Elphinstone issued a systematic code of Regulations, of which a novel and important feature was that it dispensed with the Muhammadan criminal law followed elsewhere.

In the North-West Provinces, where the village system was in danger of being destroyed by the encroachment of powerful interests, its vitality was preserved by a settlement based on a regular survey and investigation of tenures and rights, as well as of the customs of each village. There had been a flood of litigation and the judicial courts had been unequal to the task of determining and protecting the rights of the cultivators. The settlement, which dealt with 70,000 square miles and affected the interests of over 20 million people, was based on principles established by Holt Mackenzie and embodied in Regulation VII of 1822. It was completed in ten years (1832–42) by Robert Bird, who was described by Sir James Abbott as " the greatest benefactor the people of India have ever known." The policy pursued in this province was admirably explained by Mr. James Thomason, Lieutenant-Governor from 1843 to 1853, in his Directions for Collectors of Land Revenue issued in 1846.

> " We have not swept over the country like a torrent, destroying all that is found, and leaving nothing but what itself deposited. Our course has rather been that of a gently swelling inundation, which leaves the former surface undisturbed, and spreads over it a richer mould from which the vegetation may derive a new verdure, and the landscape possess a beauty which was unknown before. Such has been our course in the civil administration."

There was a dual system of judicial administration. In each Presidency the Supreme Court, which was composed of Judges belonging to the English, Scotch or Irish Bars, who were appointed by the Queen, had complete jurisdiction over the Presidency town (Calcutta, Bombay or Madras, as the case might be) and exclusive criminal jurisdiction in all but some minor cases over all Europeans in whatever part of the Presidency they might be. The Sudder, i.e., Chief, Courts, criminal and civil, consisted entirely of members of the Civil Service, who had risen through the successive stages of the Service, and were courts of appeal for all courts in the country, other, of course, than the Supreme Courts. The Supreme Courts administered English law. The law, both civil and criminal, administered by the Company's courts was remarkable for its variety. In civil matters they administered Hindu law to Hindus and Muhammadan law to Muhammadans; commercial cases were decided according to commercial customary law; cases not covered by any existing law were decided according to equity and good conscience, so that there was a fair amount of discretionary latitude. Procedure was defined by numerous regulations, in addition to which there was a mass of case-made law. The simpler procedure of Non-Regulation provinces was unknown, and there was no attempt to bring parties together to settle disputes by compromise and conciliation without recourse to lawyers and litigation.

The criminal law in the Presidencies of Bengal and Madras was still nominally Muhammadan law, but this had been largely superseded by Regulations and Acts made by different legislatures and containing widely different provisions. It had, in fact, according to a report submitted in 1838 by the Indian Law Commission (under Macaulay), become distorted to such an extent as to deprive it of all title to the religious veneration of Moslems, but retained enough of its original peculiarities to perplex and encumber the administration of justice. In Bombay Regulations and Acts took the place of Muhammadan law entirely after 1827; but the Indian Law Commission found that its penal code had no superiority over the penal law of the other Presidencies except that of being codified, while the principles according to which crimes should be classified and punishments apportioned had been less regarded than in the legislation of Bengal and Madras.

Owing partly to the inchoate state of the law and

partly to the prevalence of perjury the judicial administration was held in low repute. In 1853 Lord Campbell, referring to the experience he had had in hearing appeals as a member of the Judicial Committee of the Privy Council, said in the House of Lords that " as far as regarded the administration of justice in the inferior courts, no language could be too extravagant in describing its enormities"; and John Bright declared in the House of Commons that there appeared to be throughout the whole of India, on the part of the European population, an absolute terror of coming under the Company's courts for any object whatever.

Indian legal experts, both Hindu and Muhammadan, who had the title of Law Officers, were long associated with the courts as the exponents of Muhammadan and Hindu law. In civil cases the Judges, under a Regulation passed in 1780, had to refer to Maulavis and Pandits for advice on points of Muhammadan and Hindu law respectively in cases respecting succession, inheritance, marriage, caste, religious usages and religious institutions. Muhammadan Law Officers also long sat with the Judges at sessions trials and delivered *fatwas*, i.e., rulings as to the nature of the crime and the punishment due under Muhammadan law. A Judge was bound to consult the Law Officers, and if he differed from them, had to refer the matter to the Sudder Court. As Muhammadan law was gradually superseded, the functions of the Law Officers were contracted and Judges did not consult them unless they were in a difficulty. They are said to have been accommodating and to have had a convenient general ruling for any case not specifically covered by Muhammadan law, viz., that the accused was liable to discretionary punishment; this gave the Judges considerable latitude. In 1832 it was provided by Regulation that a Judge might dispense with *fatwas* if he obtained the opinions of a *panchayat* (a kind of extra-judicial jury whose duty was merely to inquire and report) or of assessors, who sat with him during a trial. Assessors were generally summoned, and their opinions taken, in preference to the Law Officers, whose services were used less and less. As they died out, no one was appointed in their place, and they were at length formally abolished in 1864.[1]

At the time of the transfer of government from the Company to the Crown, the framework of the organization of the Civil Service was in many respects the same as at present. The Executive Council of the Government of India consisted of five members, viz., the Commander-in-Chief, the Legislative Member, and three ordinary members who had to be members of the Company's services: of the latter two were generally Civilians and one a military officer. Madras and Bombay had each two members of Council belonging to the Civil Service of the Presidency; no other province had a Council till 1912. The Secretariats of the Regulation provinces differed in strength, but all were numerically small. Bombay had a Chief Secretary and three other Secretaries, Madras had a Chief Secretary and two other Secretaries, Bengal and the North-West Provinces had each only one Secretary, who dealt with all departments.

[1] See article on Law-officer in *Hobson-Johnson* (1903), pp. 510–12; also Sir G. Campbell, *Modern India* (1853), p. 477, and *Memoirs of my Indian Career* (1893), Vol. I, p. 162.

The Secretaries were selected exclusively from the Civil Service and each had a junior Civilian as his Deputy Secretary. Boards of Revenue in control of the revenue administration had been constituted for Bengal (3 members), for the North-West Provinces (1 member) and for Madras (4 members); Bombay had no Board but two Revenue Commissioners working directly under the Government. In Bengal, Bombay and the North-West Provinces there were Commissioners holding charge of divisions, or group of districts, and supervising the work of the District Officers; then, as now, there were no Commissioners in Madras. These officers were introduced in 1829 and originally did judicial as well as revenue work, going on circuit as Sessions Judges in place of the provincial Courts of Appeal. The latter had become resting-places for members of the Service who were considered unfit for higher responsibility and were accordingly abolished. Subsequently the judicial work of the Commissioners was transferred to the Judges.

Judicial administration was controlled by the Sudder Courts at Calcutta, Bombay, Madras and Agra, which had appellate powers and general authority over the lower courts. Judges also did the work of Magistrates till 1831 and were consistently overworked, if we can believe the account given in *Notes on Indian Affairs* published in 1837 by the Hon. F. J. Shore, himself a Judge-Magistrate. Work had to be done both before and after office hours (9 a.m. to 5 p.m.), and some even had police reports read to them during breakfast. A Judge-Magistrate who really attempted to do his duty had, he declared, to work without intermission from one year's end to another.

"I have known men go through this drudgery for five, six, aye, ten years together, sacrificing their time, their health, the comforts of domestic life and the society of their friends in a vain attempt to give satisfaction to those under their authority.[1]

It will be noted that his aim was to satisfy not any High Court or Government, but the people under him.

The magisterial functions of the Judges were transferred to the Collectors in 1831, thus making the District Judge the chief judicial and the District Magistrate and Collector the chief executive officer in each district of the Regulation provinces. This arrangement was soon given up in Bengal, where the offices of District Magistrate and Collector were separated in 1837, as it was found that magisterial work suffered from the heavy duties devolving on the Collector in connexion with the resumption of revenue-free tenures; this was a temporary difficulty which was treated as if it was permanent. The separation of the two offices was condemned by Dalhousie in 1854 as injurious both to the administration and the interests of the people. The District Magistrates were junior officers overworked and inadequately paid, and their experience was insufficient to qualify them for their responsibilities. The Collectors, on the other hand, who were senior men, were well paid and had not enough work. The arrangement consequently gave colour to mischievous and exaggerated phrases such as

[1] See D. Dewar, *Bygone Days in India* (1922), p. 185. Mr. Dewar points out that Shore was somewhat eccentric. He took to wearing Indian dress, as a result of which a Government Order was issued prohibiting the wearing of such dress by the Company's European servants.

Collectors "shaking the pagoda tree," "boy judges," etc. It was finally given up in 1859, when Bengal came into line with other provinces by having its districts under a District Officer filling the offices of District Magistrate and Collector. The arrangement by which local executive authority is concentrated in one man has worked well and is well suited to the needs and predilections of the people. They appreciate undivided responsibility and are accustomed to look to one man as the representative of Government. The idea of "two kings in Brentford" is foreign to them, whereas they understand and appreciate there being one man who can hear their complaints, who can give orders to the local staff, and who can see that they are carried out: *hākim*, the word for a Magistrate in Northern India, means literally one who gives orders. It is his power to give orders that makes the District Officer what he is, for it is his function not to do everything himself but to direct and control the work of his staff and to co-ordinate the different departments of the local administration.

In Madras and Bombay the Judge and the Magistrate-Collector were of equal standing; in the North-West Provinces the Judges held the higher rank. In Bengal (up to 1859) the Magistrate was inferior in status to the Collector; the latter, who was not comparable in importance with the Magistrate-Collector elsewhere, both because his duties were limited to revenue matters and because the land revenue was fixed by the Permanent Settlement, was lower in rank and drew less pay than the Judge. Below the District Magistrate came the Joint Magistrate and Deputy Collector, a grade created by Lord William Bentinck, and at the bottom of the scale was the Assistant Magistrate. The usual course of promotion in Bengal was for the Assistant Magistrate to become a Joint Magistrate and Deputy Collector, and then in succession a District Magistrate, a Collector, and a Judge, after which he might become a Commissioner, his duties in each office being entirely different. In all provinces the executive service seems to have been preferred to the judicial service and to have been manned by officers of a better stamp.

Leave on full pay might be granted for one month in a calendar year—the prototype of privilege leave—and furlough for three years after ten years of service. If the furlough was spent in Europe, the officer received an allowance of £500 a year and ceased to have a lien on his appointment. If, however, he spent his leave in Ceylon, Australia, South Africa and certain other places, he was allowed to draw one-third of his pay, he retained a lien on his appointment, and his leave counted for service. This anomaly was introduced during the administration of Lord Ellenborough.

The rule that promotion should go by seniority, which was laid down by the Charter Act of 1793, was not abolished until 1861. It had the merit of preventing favouritism and unfairness, but it had the equally manifest defect that ability and keenness had little encouragement. Promotion, though it might be delayed, came at last to the least as well as to the most competent. Men were allowed to retire on pensions of £1,000 a year after twenty-five years' service, of which only three years might be spent on furlough: the amount is still the same, but its value much less owing to the change in the value of money, the increase in the cost of living, the imposition of the income-tax and its progressive rise. Civil Servants subscribed to their pensions, being required to pay 4 per cent of all pay and allowances. All members of the Service, whether married or unmarried, were obliged to subscribe to a family pension fund, from which widows received £300 a year, sons of deceased Civilians £100 a year till the age of 21, and daughters the same amount till marriage. The saying that a Civilian is worth £300 a year, dead or alive, dates back to this period.

The District Officer was the pivot of the administration, combining revenue, magisterial and general administrative duties. His work was much the same as that now devolving on the District Officer, but it was not of the same volume even though he had to do much that is now done by Departments and local bodies. He took a much more active part in the suppression of crime, including the pursuit and breaking up of gangs of robbers and dacoits. Their numbers and their audacity made the latter formidable. In 1856, for instance, the Deputy Commissioner of Gonda went in pursuit of a band of dacoits with a few mounted police, and pluckily, but rashly, entered a village to which they had been traced with only one of his men. Their leader shot him and, cutting off his head, hung it up in a tree. A company of Irregular Infantry which had been detailed for the pursuit of the band came up soon afterwards, only to find that it had decamped. A second company had to be detached to hunt it down, and at last it was run down in the Nepal Hills. A regular battle ensued, in which most of the dacoits were killed after they themselves had killed and wounded a number of the soldiers.[1]

The District Magistrate also did much that is now done by local bodies in connexion with the maintenance of roads, the promotion of education, medical relief and measures of public health. Local self-government by representative bodies had not been introduced outside the Presidency towns. Laws, it is true, had been passed in 1842 and 1850 by which towns which asked for a municipal constitution could have it, but there was no desire to take advantage of this permissive legislation. In Bengal an attempt to go beyond the voluntary principle was quashed by judicial process. A District Magistrate made one town a municipality under the orders of the local Government and was promptly sued by its inhabitants in the Supreme Court, which decreed damages against him on the ground that the majority of the inhabitants did not desire a municipal form of government. In Bareilly also the inhabitants rose in opposition to the unwelcome privilege of taxing themselves for a town police force and local improvements, and were only put down by the active use of military force.[2]

It was left to the District Magistrate to provide for sanitation, drainage and other civil requirements; and he had sometimes to force improvements on an unwilling people. This was the experience of Frederic Gubbins, when District Magistrate of Benares in 1852. His predecessors had tried to clear the town of accumulated filth by a system of drainage and to keep the roads free from encroachments; but they were baffled

[1] Col. John Bonham, *Oude in 1857* (1928), pp. 15–16.

[2] G. Campbell, *Modern India* (1853), pp. 200, 260.

not merely by the *vis inertiae*, but by the active opposition, of the people. When Gubbins renewed the attempt, the people attacked him and drove him out of the town. As he still persisted in his health campaign, the shopkeepers shut up their shops, and stopped the supply of grain on which the troops depended. Gubbins foiled this effort by importing grain and, hearing that a conspiracy was on foot, arrested the ringleaders. Next day he had all the shops opened and the opposition collapsed.

It is unnecessary to enlarge on the well-known fact that much more was done by executive action than is now possible under a more highly organized government and a comprehensive legislation. One example will suffice. Sir George Campbell tells us that in 1843, when he was a young Magistrate in the North-West Provinces and a large fair took place, there were stocks for the accommodation of 300 bad characters, and they were all filled. Known criminals and bad characters were previously detained at the police stations, all suspicious persons found at the fair were sent to the stocks, and there was a general clearance of the gipsies, dancing women, monkey-men, bears, etc., who were deported to the next district. He thought that a vigour somewhat beyond the law was exercised, but "altogether the arrangements turned out beautifully."[1] No one is likely to combat this view, or to deny that much of the fun of the fair must have been lost.

Although officers had more of a free hand than at present, it must not be imagined that there was

[1] Sir G. Campbell, *Memoirs of my Indian Career* (1893), Vol. I, p. 21.

simple autocracy. On the contrary, the officers of Government, from the lowest to the highest, were subject to a number of checks, legal, financial, and administrative. There was a body of substantive law, revenue, judicial and police, incorporated in Regulations up to 1833 and in Acts after that year, and official action was also regulated by codes of rules, which, however, were not as comprehensive and numerous as at the present time. Financial control was close and rigid. Expenditure could not be incurred by executive officers unless it had the previous sanction of superior authority. The local Governments were similarly subordinate to the Government of India to a surprising extent; Dalhousie found, to his annoyance, that as Governor of Bengal his hands were so tied by financial rules that for the creation of a petty post or a slight increase in the pay of one already in existence he was obliged to refer to and obtain sanction from the Government of India, of which he himself was the head. Executive proceedings were subject to appeal as much as judicial proceedings, and persons aggrieved by the order of an officer freely exercised the right of appeal to his superior officers or to Government itself. Each officer worked in subordination to higher officers, and Government was highly centralized.

"It is," wrote Sir George Campbell in *Modern India* (1853), "the great principle of all grades of the Indian administration that each official grade is always kept constantly cognizant of all that is done by that below, by means of an infinite variety of statements submitted periodically, showing in every possible form every kind of business and devised to include everything in every shape. The Governments receive abstracts of correspondence and annual statements and reports from the Boards, Boards monthly statements and reports from the executive officers of districts, and executive officers daily reports and figured statements from their native subordinates."

Even in the Punjab the same system obtained. Monthly reports of the work of the different courts were submitted to, and criticized by, the Government. At the close of the year they were collected, division compared with division and district with district, and a brief review was issued by Government pointing out defects and suggesting improvements. Every court, according to John Lawrence, worked under a constant sense of supervision and with the great objects to be aimed at (viz., cheap, quick, sure, simple, and substantial justice) perpetually in view.

The power of appeal in executive as well as in judicial matters, and the strict subordination of each office to a higher, naturally led to an extraordinary amount of writing. To quote again from *Modern India*, which is the best authority for the administrative methods of this period,

"In India all business is conducted in writing to an extent quite beyond anything known in this country, even in our most important courts of record. There is more official writing and recording in a case of petty theft in an Indian police court than in the gravest case in Westminster Hall. All petitions, statements, applications of every description, are filed in writing; all evidence is recorded in writing, and all orders and instructions of every kind are formally written and signed."

One other characteristic of the conditions of service at this time should also be referred to. In modern times the complaint is frequently made, and with good cause, that the administration suffers from the unduly frequent transfer of officers, for, as Lord Curzon once said, one cannot have good administration without continuity and intelligent administration without local knowledge.[1] The same was the case before 1857, when too the complaint was made that transfers were so common as to give little opportunity for the acquisition of local knowledge. Men were transferred from one district to another, and from one department to another, with little reference to local administrative experience. Some extreme instances of this vicious practice were quoted by John Bright in the House of Commons in 1859. One officer held twenty-one offices in as many years, another twenty-four in thirteen years, a third seventeen in thirteen years, and a fourth twenty-one in eighteen years.

Even before the Mutiny life in the Service was often hazardous, more especially by reason of the dangers of political work and the open violence of armed revolt. Thus in 1799, Wazir Ali, the desposed Nawab of Oudh, who had been allowed to retire to Benares, rose in revolt, murdered Mr. Cherry, the Governor-General's Agent, and then marched on the house of the Judge, Mr. Samuel Davis. Davis took refuge with his family on the flat roof of his house, and standing at a trap-door which gave access to it, defended them with a spear, his only weapon, against a horde of assailants until rescued by some British cavalry. This defence was given the name of "a domestic Thermopylæ" and its hero that of a second Leonidas.[2]

[1] Sir T. Raleigh, *Lord Curzon in India* (1906), p. 77.

[2] Colonel W. F. B. Laurie, *Sketches of Some Distinguished Anglo-Indians* (Second Series, 1888), pp. 1–3.

A rising which took place at Kittur in the Belgaum district of Bombay in 1824 resulted in the death of two Civilians and the imprisonment of two others. When the revolt broke out, St. John Thackeray, the Collector and Political Agent, who was an uncle of the novelist, was killed in an attempt to capture the Kittur fort. A British detachment was cut up, and two Assistants of Mr. Thackeray, Sir Walter Elliot and Mr. Stevenson, were made prisoners. Two months later Mr. Munro, Sub-Collector of Sholapur, a nephew of Sir Thomas Munro, was killed in the final attack on the fort. The two prisoners were released after its capture.

The tragic consequences of a communal riot are recalled by the inscription on a tomb at Cuddapah in Madras, which relates that in 1832 Charles Edward Macdonald, aged 24,

> "a Civilian of the fairest promise, while attempting in the fearless and conscientious discharge of his duty to appease by prompt and persuasive measures the fury of a fanatic rabble of Moormen [Muhammadans], was, though completely unarmed, attacked, deserted by all his peons and barbarously murdered."

His wife, it goes on to say, survived him only twenty-one days and died broken-hearted in the twentieth year of her age. William Fraser, Resident at Delhi, was shot dead there in 1835 by a hired assassin of the Nawab of Firozpur. Sir William Macnaghten fell in 1841 in the massacre at Kabul; his mutilated body was flung into a ditch, and the bones were recovered two years later and buried in Calcutta. There is no more generous tribute to his memory than that paid by the historian Marshman, who described him as being

"as noble and brave an officer as ever fell in the service of his country." "Throughout seven weeks of unparalleled difficulties, he exhibited a spirit of courage and constancy of which there is not another example in the annals of the Company. He was the only civilian at Cabul, and one of the truest-hearted soldiers in the garrison. He had served several years in the Madras army,[1] and there can be little doubt that if he could have assumed the command of the force, it would have escaped the doom that befell it."

Mr. Vans Agnew was barbarously killed by the Sikhs at Multan in 1848—an outrage which led to the second Sikh war and the annexation of the Punjab. A memorial to him and Lieutenant Anderson may be seen in the Cathedral at Calcutta with an inscription, composed by Macaulay, which runs: "Not near this stone, nor in any consecrated ground, but on the extreme frontier of the British Indian Empire, lie the remains of Patrick Alexander Vans Agnew and William Anderson." In 1855 Mr. H. V. Conolly, District Magistrate of Malabar, who was about to take his seat as Member of the Executive Council at Madras, was murdered in his house, in the presence of his wife, by a gang of Moplahs armed with great war knives, with which they inflicted twenty-seven wounds. He was a brother of the unfortunate Captain Arthur Conolly, who after long imprison-

[1] He served in the army in South India from 1809 to 1814, when he was appointed to the Civil Service. Another Civilian was a victim of the Kabul massacre of 1879, viz., William Jenkyns, a Punjab officer, who was attached as interpreter to the staff of Sir Louis Cavagnari.

ment in a loathsome dungeon was, with his fellow-prisoner, Lt.-Col. Stoddart, publicly beheaded by the Amir of Bokhara in 1842.

During the Mutiny thirty-three members of the Service were killed and nine others died from sickness or exposure—forty-two in all or about one-twentieth of the total (886 in 1857). Of those whose names were on this roll of honour one may be specially mentioned, Robert Tucker, the Judge of Fatehpur. The civil station there was beset by rebels and, resistance being regarded as hopeless, the other Europeans—only ten in all—decided to abandon it and managed to escape by night. Tucker refused to leave his post and fought single-handed, killing sixteen men before he was over-powered, after which he was subjected to a mock trial and executed: as a last indignity his head, hands and feet were cut off. Tribute to the courage of others is paid by a soldier-writer, who states:

> "It is impossible to wade through the Bengal registers which tell the tale of the fearful Mutiny of 1857 and not think of the devotion and gallantry of those Civil Servants who with such a chivalrous and high-souled heroism faced the murderous rebels in the defence of life and home and fell dying like the bravest and best soldiers." [1]

Two members of the Service were awarded the Victoria Cross. They were Ross Mangles and Fraser McDonell, both of whom joined as volunteers the expedition, commanded by Captain Dunbar, which unsuccessfully attempted to relieve the small body of civil officers and Sikhs which was besieged

[1] Colonel W. F. B. Laurie, *Sketches of Some Distinguished Anglo-Indians* (1887), p. 179.

at Arrah. The expedition fell into an ambush and had to retreat under heavy fire for about twelve miles. The ditches, houses, patches of jungle, and other places of cover along the road by which the survivors retreated were lined by rebel sepoys. Ross Mangles, who had had nothing to eat for over twenty-four hours, and no sleep for two nights, carried a wounded soldier for five miles along this bullet-swept road till he reached a stream, where he swam out, got a boat and placed him in it. No one would have known anything of this deed of valour had not the soldier after twelve months' search found out the name of his rescuer. McDonell, with thirty-five others, many of them wounded, got into a boat, of which the rebels had removed the oars and lashed the rudder. It was close to the bank on which the rebels were massed, when McDonell climbed up and cut the rudder free amidst a hail of bullets.[1]

Equally worthy of mention is Herwald Wake, the life and soul of the defence of "the little house" at Arrah, where a small band of Englishmen and fifty Sikhs held out against over 2,000 sepoys for a week—a defence which was described at the time as a miniature edition of Lucknow. Another extraordinary but fortuitous feat to the credit of a Civilian was the single-handed capture of three guns by Sir George Campbell. Suspecting that a band of rebels was trying to make off with guns through some crops after an action, Campbell galloped off to reconnoitre. His Arab ran away with him and carried him straight towards the enemy. Campbell, who was quite alone, unable

[1] Ball, *History of the Indian Mutiny*, Vol. II, p. 115; I. G. Sieviking, *A Turning Point in the Indian Mutiny* (1910), pp. 62–8.

to hold in his horse, saw nothing for it but to shout and wave his sword. This was enough. The enemy imagined that he was leading a body of troops in pursuit and fled, leaving three guns as Campbell's prize.

A convulsion like the Mutiny naturally gave rise to the belief that the system of government in India was to blame. We are not concerned here with criticisms of the constitution, but only with the attacks upon the Indian Civil Service. It was attacked largely because it was identified with the Government. John Bright, in a somewhat unbalanced tirade against it, declared that the Governor-General was a creature of the civil and military services and that India must not in future be governed "for that Civil Service whose praises are so constantly sounded in this House," but for the non-official mercantile classes from England who settled in India, and for the Indians themselves. He urged that a beginning should be made of uniting the Government with the governed by appointing Indians to places of power and trust, and pointed out that the Charter Act of 1833, declaring their eligibility for office, high as well as low, had not been given effect to. The Civil Service was still exclusively British and nothing had been done to admit Indians to it, though they were employed freely and fully in lower offices; but for this the Service could not be blamed. Patronage lay with the Directors; the Service itself had no power to settle its personnel or the methods of selection.

The attack on it generally took another line, viz., that it had adopted a selfish, dog-in-the-manger attitude towards British fellow-subjects, an attitude summarized and satirized in the catch-words "India for the Civil Service." It was made a charge against it that it had discouraged the settlement of British non-officials in India, and their association with the work of government. They had undoubtedly been excluded up to 1833. In its anxiety to keep its trade monopoly the Company had tried to keep "interlopers" out. Private Europeans before 1833 were allowed to settle in India only under licence, and there were some irritating restrictions, e.g., ladies who took maid-servants with them from England had to give security to send them back within two years; we find that the selection of a maid for Macaulay's sister in 1833 was a matter of anxious deliberation.[1] The reason for discrimination in this case was simply that English maid-servants behaved badly in India, were insolent to Indians and were likely to bring discredit on their country. The embargo on the free entrance of Europeans into India was removed, however, by the Act of 1833. After that there was nothing to prevent them settling in India and developing its resources, but they did so only to a limited extent.

The commonest of the objections to the Civil Service at this time was that it was exclusive and had a monopoly of the higher offices in India as against other British subjects. In *The Red Pamphlet* (1857) it was even urged that indigo planters should be made Magistrates instead of "unfledged boys ignorant of the people and imperfectly acquainted with the language of the country." An effective reply to this objection was made by Mill in *Repre-*

[1] G. O. Trevelyan, *Life and Letters of Lord Macaulay* (1908), Vol. I, p. 248.

sentative Government, where he said that as much bitterness was manifested against the system, and as much eagerness displayed to overthrow it, as if educating and training the officers of Government for their work were a thing utterly unreasonable and indefensible, an unjustifiable interference with the rights of ignorance and inexperience. It was not unjust that trained officials should be exclusively eligible for offices requiring special knowledge and experience.

"The 'monopoly' of the Civil Service, so much inveighed against, is like the monopoly of judicial offices by the bar; and its abolition would be like opening the bench in Westminster Hall to the first comer whose friends certify that he had now and then looked into Blackstone."

His conclusion was that the system had succeeded in training persons fit for the responsibilities of administration, and because it had done so, British rule in India had lasted and been one of constant, if not very rapid, improvement in prosperity and good administration.

CHAPTER IV

UNDER THE CROWN: 1858–1914

MENTION may be made in the first instance of the changes which have taken place in the nomenclature of the Service since the transfer of the government of India to the Crown. As we have already seen, the Charter Act of 1793 provided that vacancies occurring in any Presidency should be filled from among the Civil Servants in the Presidency, a provision which was reaffirmed in the Charter Act of 1833. There were three Presidencies in 1793, viz., Bengal, Bombay, and Madras, and their number was not added to. As different territories were brought under British rule they were attached to the Bengal Presidency, so that in course of time it came to include the whole of British India outside the Bombay and Madras Presidencies. A Bengal Civilian might therefore serve in Bengal, Bihar, Orissa, Assam, Arakan and Tenasserim, the North-West Provinces (which was constituted a Lieutenant-Governorship in 1836), or the Punjab. The members of the Service in the three Presidencies had separate pension funds, and the Service in each Presidency adopted its name as a designation, i.e., Bengal Civil Service, Bombay Civil Service, and Madras Civil Service. Collectively and officially, however, the Service was known as "the Covenanted Civil Service of India," to distinguish it from the lower service employed in civil administration, which was mainly Indian in personnel and was known as the Uncovenanted Civil Service. The reference was, of course, to the covenants executed, then as now, in England, by which members of the former service engaged to subscribe to pension funds, not to accept presents, etc. Members of the other Service, who were recruited in India, executed no covenants.

The restriction of service to the limits of different Presidencies naturally caused difficulties, and was finally abolished, at the suggestion of the Government of India, by Lord Salisbury, the then Secretary of State for India, who directed, in 1878, that it should be laid down as a general rule that every Covenanted Civil Servant "is bound to serve wherever the Government at any period of his career, requires him to go." Although service was no longer restricted to a particular Presidency, the names Bengal Civil Service, Bombay Civil Service, and Madras Civil Service still continued to be used for some time: in 1886, for example, members of the Service appointed to the Public Services Commission, generally known, after the name of its President, as the Aitchison Commission, were described as "Bengal Civil Service," etc. The order of 1878 by which the Service became what is now called an "all-India Service" does not appear to have received legislative sanction till 1912, when the Bengal Presidency was created with its present limits and section 4 of the Government of India Act, 1912, repealed the long obsolete provisions as to appointments in each Presidency being restricted to Civil Servants belonging to it.[1]

[1] See Sir C. P. Ilbert, *The Government of India* (1916), p. 133.

The Aitchison Commission recommended that the use of the term "Covenanted Civil Service of India" should be discontinued and that it should be replaced by the term "Imperial Civil Service of India" in distinction from the proposed Provincial Civil Service. This suggestion was not accepted by the Secretary of State for India, Lord Cross, who ordered that the Covenanted Service should be designated "the Civil Service of India," that each branch of the Provincial Civil Service should be designated by the name of the province to which it belonged, e.g., Punjab Civil Service, Madras Civil Service, etc., and that the use of the terms "covenanted" and "uncovenanted" should be entirely discontinued. The name "the Civil Service of India" did not obtain general recognition[1]; few members even of the Service itself know that this designation has been officially prescribed. The name Indian Civil Service is general, both in official and popular use: colloquially, the initials I.C.S. are in vogue. The name Indian Civil Service had indeed come into use before Lord Cross's orders. A member of the Service, Mr. Cotterell Tupp, published in 1876 a book entitled *The Indian Civil Service and the Competitive System*, and two years later, when he was officiating Accountant-General at Madras, an *Indian Civil Service List*. In the latter he explained that the accepted division of the Service into Bengal, Bombay and Madras, though still convenient for some purposes and necessary as long

[1] The order as to the local names of the branches of the Provincial Civil Service was also a dead letter; it is only in recent years that the name of the Province has been used by each branch.

as there were separate Funds,[1] was antiquated and generally useless as a Civilian might serve anywhere in British India. He therefore ignored the distinctions of Bengal, Bombay and Madras Services and treated all three as "one great Indian Civil Service having the same prospects, conditions, origin and constitution"; but curiously enough he described himself on the title-page as "Bengal Civil Service."

The transfer of the government of India to the Crown was a constitutional change which made practically no difference to the position and prospects of the Indian Civil Service. To a certain extent there was a sense of greater security owing to the discontinuance of the periodical commissions of inquiry into the administration which had preceded the renewals of the Company's charter. The imminence of these commissions had always created some uneasiness as to the possibility of changes affecting the Service. The rights which it had enjoyed since 1793 were, moreover, confirmed by the Indian Civil Service Act of 1861, which reserved to its members the principal civil offices, all of which were set forth in a schedule. Promotion by seniority, which had been prescribed by the Charter Act of 1793, was at the same time abolished. Power, it is true, was taken to permit of the appointment to the reserved posts of outsiders, i.e., of persons other than covenanted officers, but this authority was carefully safeguarded. Previous residence of at least seven years in India was properly prescribed as a necessary qualifi-

[1] The Bengal, Bombay and Madras Civil Funds were closed to new entrants in 1879, after which date all men admitted to the Service subscribed to a common fund.

cation; outsiders appointed to revenue or judicial posts were to be subject to the same tests and examinations as members of the Civil Service; all appointments had to be reported to the Secretary of State, and unless approved by him within twelve months, were void. This provision was intended to guard against the possibility of the Civil Service being numerically unequal to the posts reserved for it. Only two substantive appointments under the local governments were, in fact, made under this authority, and both were of Indians; the power was also exercised to appoint some military officers to posts in the Secretariat of the Government of India, and some Indians to temporary judicial posts.[1]

The system of selecting candidates on the results of a competitive examination had recently been introduced, and so far from discouraging candidates by introducing outsiders to their prejudice, efforts were made to attract them. The Civil Service Commissioners in 1859, indeed, took special pains to make public the numbers, value and importance of the Writerships offered for competition: the retention of the term "Writerships" was a curious link with the past. It was set forth that

> "the emoluments of a Writership, the steady advancement in the Service of those who devote themselves to it with zeal and perseverance, the infinite opportunities of public usefulness which it presents, the dignity, honour, and influence of the positions to which it may probably lead, and the liberal and judicious provisions for retirement at a moderate age, all render the Civil Service a career full of interest and pecuniary advantage."

---

[1] Report of the Public Service Commission, 1886–7, p. 24.

The Mutiny made far less difference to the work of administration than might have been expected. Great though the upheaval in the districts affected by it had been, normal conditions were restored, and civil authority re-established, in a remarkably short space of time. Even in January, 1858, at a time when military operations were still in active progress, Mr. Charles Raikes, passing through a district in the United Provinces of which he had formerly been in charge, found that the people turned out in crowds and thanked God that the English had come back.

"For the last six months," they said, "every man has been knocking his nearest neighbour on the head." "The arm of the Magistrate had been paralysed; the Magistrate himself had been murdered or driven away; and anarchy prevailed all over Upper India as a necessary consequence when authority disappeared. . . . At the first flush of the matter men were glad to throw off authority. They had no passion for paying land-revenue and keeping up police stations. But before many months of misrule had passed, the mass of the people were praying for the return of the Magistrate." [1]

The same story was told of other districts from which the civil officers had temporarily withdrawn. Strong landlords had attacked weaker landlords, one village had preyed on another, robbers had knocked down and fleeced solitary travellers; the people were disgusted with what was known as Hindustani Raj, and welcomed back the British officers.[2] Even in Oudh, which had been under British rule for only a year before the Mutiny, and

[1] C. Raikes, *The Englishman in India* (1867), pp. 304–5.

[2] See, for instance, Sir Mortimer Durand, *Life of Sir Alfred Lyall* (1913), pp. 61–9.

which was a centre of rebellion during it, the people received them as if they had been accustomed to British administration all their lives and nothing particular had happened. How little the people of Oudh actually were familiar with British methods may be grasped from the fact that shortly after the Mutiny a basket of heads was sent to the head of the criminal administration by a village headman, who explained that thieves had attacked the village but had been captured, of which their heads were the tangible, but ghastly, proof. That this could happen at a time when, for instance, education had so far advanced that a University was established at Calcutta is one of the anomalies of a country where there are so many different stages of civilization. Among aboriginal tribes, primitive beliefs and practices were and still are common. In one district of Chota Nagpur they took advantage of the cessation of British authority during the Mutiny to kill off all persons suspected of being witches or wizards. Some years later there was a case of human sacrifice in the same part of the country. The chief of an aboriginal tribe had been engaged in litigation and had won his case in the Indian courts. His opponent appealed to the Privy Council, and the chief, not having means to fee lawyers in England, "took measures according to his lights, caught an idiot beggar, carried him to the top of a hill, and there formally sacrificed him to propitiate the gods who rule the Privy Council."[1] In 1882 there was a revival of human sacrifice in the State of Kalahandi, where it had been abolished over thirty

[1] See Sir G. Campbell, *Memoirs of my Indian Career* (1893), Vol. II, pp. 29, 70, 200–1.

years previously. The Khonds there rose because they were being ousted from their land by Hindu cultivators imported by the Raja and sacrificed twenty of them with the old ceremonies, hacking pieces of flesh off the victims and burying them in the fields as an offering to the Earth Goddess in the belief that abundant crops would ensue. Even as recently as 1907 the Khonds of the Agency Tracts of Madras solemnly petitioned the District Magistrate of Ganjam to sanction human sacrifice as a special concession because their crops were suffering from drought.

It is not surprising that the Non-Regulation system described in the last chapter still continued. In the interior large tracts were inhabited by aboriginals at a low level of civilization. The history of the frontier in Assam was one of fierce raids by wild tribes, some of whom were savage head-hunters, and of punitive expeditions. Elsewhere there were newly acquired or unsettled areas; Pegu came under British rule in 1852, the Berars in 1853, the State of Nagpur in 1854, and Oudh in 1856. The area administered under this system was largely extended in consequence of the annexation of Upper Burma in 1885. Upper Burma is twice as large as Lower Burma, and officers had to be found for its administration at short notice. In addition to men who had already served in Lower Burma, some Civilians[1] were brought from

[1] Of these two may be mentioned—Mr. (afterwards Sir Frederic) Fryer from the Punjab and Mr. (afterwards Sir Digges) La Touche from the North-West Provinces. The former became Chief Commissioner and first Lieutenant-Governor of Burma, the latter Lieutenant-Governor of the United Provinces.

other provinces, but these could not spare enough trained officials for the newly conquered territory, and a staff had to be improvised. A Commission, as the higher staff was called, was created, on which were Civilians from other parts of India, who had official training but no knowledge of the Burmese language, military officers with no administrative training, and others who knew Burma but were ignorant of civil work. The difficulties of this composite Commission were aggravated by unsettled conditions. The campaign of conquest had occupied only three weeks, but it was followed by two years of guerrilla warfare; among those who fell in action was Robert Phayre, a nephew of Sir Arthur Phayre, who was a Burma Civilian with ten years' service. Large bands of dacoits terrorized the country, and their victims, stripped of all that they had, were forced to join their ranks. Dacoity became so universal that it may be said to have been almost national. Sir Frank Gates, who was in charge of a sub-division in the early part of 1886, states that for about six months there was nearly one dacoity a day and that it was hopeless to try to catch all the criminals.[1] But administrative organization went on at the same time that robber bands were hunted down.

"Within two years," Lord Dufferin wrote, "a territory larger than France, which had been for generations a prey to lawlessness and intestine strife, has been reduced to peace and order, and furnished with a strong and efficient government complete in all departments which minister to the security, the prosperity and the comfort of the people. In no previous epoch of our government

---

[1] *Asiatic Review*, April, 1928, p. 244.

in India has it been found possible to achieve such results in such a brief period of time."

Sir Bampfylde Fuller, indeed, in *Some Personal Reminiscences* refers to the pacification of Burma as "one of the greatest accomplishments that the Indian Civil Service can take to its credit"; but it would be more correct to say that it shares in the credit, for though the head of the administration was a Civilian (first, Sir Charles Bernard, and then Sir Charles Crosthwaite), the Commission consisted of military civilians and uncovenanted officers as well as of members of the Indian Civil Service.

The continued and extensive employment of officers of the Indian army in the Non-Regulation provinces was for some time a grievance of the Civil Service. Lord Dalhousie in 1856 had fixed the proportions of officers to be employed at one-half military and one-half civil, and in 1867 the proportion of Civilians was raised to two-thirds, that of military and uncovenanted officers being reduced to one-third. The Non-Regulation provinces, having been excluded from the purview of the Act of 1861, were a field for the exercise of patronage, which excited resentment. Civilians filled posts in the lower grades, while appointments to higher grades were made in India from outside the Civil Service, with a consequent stagnation of promotion. Complaints were made that a cavalry officer with no experience of civil work could be appointed to a Deputy Commissionership in a province in which ten out of eleven Deputy Commissioners in charge of districts were already military men; that even men who had not served in the army but had the backing of interest were jobbed in, the very abuse to guard against which the Civil Service was created. These complaints were not without foundation. The Duke of Argyll, as Secretary of State, in a dispatch sent out to India in 1870 expressed the displeasure of the Government at a system which appeared to be growing up of appointing Englishmen in India to posts which should, as a rule, only be filled by Civilians who had gained their places by open competition; and in 1875 it was expressly laid down that the claims of Civilians should be brought forward and considered by the Government of India when any office fell vacant in Non-Regulation provinces, or any chief office in special Government departments which were mainly administrative, for which Civilians were eligible, and to which no other officer had a superior claim by reason of seniority, local standing, or special qualifications.

As the country became more settled, and the methods of administration more regular and precise, military officers were gradually superseded by members of the Indian Civil Service, and mixed Commissions, as the administrative corps were called, fell into desuetude. The employment of military officers for civil work was given up in 1876 in Oudh, the Central Provinces and the Non-Regulation areas of Bengal and the North-West Provinces, in 1885 in Sind, in 1903 in the Punjab, and in 1907 in Assam.

It has continued up to the present in Burma and the North-West Frontier Province. The Government of the former province in 1906 strongly opposed a proposal of the Government of India that it should be abandoned. It took the view that no advantage would accrue from the sole employment of Civilians. Work was of a very varied nature and officers of diverse qualifications were required. Military officers were not wanting in intellectual qualifications and possessed qualities equally essential to the administration, such as resource, force of character, knowledge of and sympathy with the people. The limited recruitment of military officers for civil posts under the existing system had provided Burma with many officers of exceptional capacity and merit, and it might be expected to do so in the future. The Government of India accepted this view, and Burma continued to have a composite Commission with a happy combination of Civil Servants and Military Civilians.

The former distinction between Regulation and Non-Regulation provinces has now become obsolete, though traces of it are found in nomenclature, e.g., in the District Officer being designated Deputy Commissioner in old Non-Regulation areas. The corresponding distinction in modern administration is between the areas under the ordinary laws and the less advanced parts of British India known as "scheduled districts." In the latter districts also administration has tended more and more to follow the same lines as in the older districts, but the process of assimilation has not been pushed so far as to overlook the fact that axioms based on community of race, religion, or custom in one part cannot be applied to another. The land revenue systems in particular are still marked by great diversity, and in most scheduled districts there are survivals of a simpler and more primitive procedure. Sind, for instance, which is nominally a scheduled area, has actually been brought under the operation of the ordinary laws and procedure, but in some parts of it the Sind Frontier Regulations are still in force by which a District Magistrate can refer murders and other offences likely to provoke reprisals among Baluchis and Pathans to a *jirga*, or council of their elders, and himself punish those found guilty by such a tribunal.[1]

The tendency to uniformity in the widely differing areas making up British India is largely the result of codification, of which the most remarkable example is the Indian Penal Code. The Code was the result of many years of deliberation and examination. It was in the first instance drafted by the Indian Law Commission appointed under the Charter Act of 1833, of which Macaulay was President, the other members being two members of the Civil Service, Mr. (afterwards Sir John) Macleod, of Madras, and Mr. (afterwards Sir William) Anderson, of Bombay, and an English barrister, Mr. Cameron (afterwards Law Member of the Governor-General's Council). The Commission ceased to exist in 1853 and the Code did not become law till 1860. The Penal Code, supplemented by the Code of Criminal Procedure, introduced uniformity in the administration of criminal justice in British India and had the great advantage of making the penal law available in a handy form both to those who had to administer it and to those who had to obey it. Combining conciseness of form with perspicuity of matter, the Code was a boon to the members of the Indian Civil Service.

"If," Sir George Trevelyan remarks in *The Life and Letters of Lord Macaulay*, "it be asked whether or not the

---

[1] *Imperial Gazetteer of India*, Vol. XXII, pp. 421–2.

Penal Code fulfils the ends for which it was framed, the answer may safely be left to the gratitude of Indian Civilians, the younger of whom carry it about in their saddlebags, and the older in their heads."

This is scarcely an overstatement. Sir James Fitzjames Stephen, himself a great lawyer, expressed the belief that no English lawyer or judge had anything like so accurate and comprehensive a knowledge of the criminal law of England as the average Indian Civilian had of the Indian Penal Code.[1]

Codification was steadily carried on until British India had a set of codes which have been described by Sir Henry Maine, who is still the acknowledged head of English jurisprudence, as standing, in form, intelligibility, and comprehensiveness, against all competition, and as approaching the highest standard of excellence which this form of legislation has reached.[2] As the jurisprudence became more crystallized, the administration became legalized to an extent which cannot be better explained than in the remarks made by the Government of India in 1907.

"In every branch of the duties on which an Indian Civilian is employed a knowledge of law is necessary. Law is the basis of our whole system of administration. Not only as a Magistrate or as a Judge, but also as a revenue officer, the Civilian deals with a system of codified law; he must be acquainted with the procedure of civil justice, and must be prepared to meet the questions raised by skilled legal practitioners. As an executive officer, he must be able to apply enactments to facts, must be expert in the law of contracts, must be com-

---

[1] *History of the Criminal Law of England*, Vol. III, p. 322.

[2] T. H. Ward, *The Reign of Queen Victoria* (1888), Vol. I, p. 503.

petent to conduct executive investigations in accordance with legal methods, and not infrequently he requires sufficient legal skill to draft rules that will have the force of law. Not only his conclusions but the methods and procedure by which he arrives at them are open to criticism and must be legally valid. Most important of all, he must know the legal limitations of the extensive powers that are entrusted to him. From the very commencement of his career in India, the young Civilian is in part a lawyer and in part a judge." [1]

Codification was extended to practically every branch of the administration in the form of manuals which contain the law on the subject as well as rules and regulations, e.g., on land acquisition, police, jails, registration, stamps, excise, etc. The existence of codes and manuals is a necessity in a country where there is only a small superior staff organized under a system of carefully regulated supervision and appeal. They have been instrumental in systematizing the administration and to a certain extent in making it uniform for different areas. They have also helped to simplify work, for the procedure or line of action to be followed by an officer in certain circumstances is either prescribed or indicated. At the same time, line upon line, precept upon precept, they have limited independence. There is less scope for individual initiative, and the officer of Government has become more the interpreter of rules and regulations. But rule and procedure cannot provide for all contingencies. The art of administration cannot be codified, and work in India now, as always, calls for qualities of leadership and resource.

[1] loc. cit. Report of the Royal Commission on the Public Services in India (1917), pp. 166–7.

At no time are these qualities more essential than during a famine. It has been well said that a famine campaign can no more be conducted by famine codes than a battle can be fought on the instructions in a military manual. One of the finest, if not the finest, of the administrative achievements of this period is the way in which famines have been prevented or mitigated, a triumph all the greater because it followed a lamentable failure—the Orissa famine of 1866. This was a tragedy comparable with the Irish Famine of 1846–7, for it is estimated that a million persons perished from starvation or from diseases consequent on or aggravated by privation and want. The causes of failure were several. Orissa was at that time an isolated tract dependent on locally grown produce. The rice crops failed, and what drought had spared, floods destroyed. The Bengal Government thought that the ordinary law of supply and demand would operate to supply the deficiency; but its dependence on an economic principle was not fortified by local knowledge. The local officers did not realize that the stocks of food were not enough to feed the people. When the dearth of food was realized, every effort was made to import food, but it was too late. Disastrous floods swept across the country, the roads were unbridged and impassable, there were no railways, and ships could not pass the surf barrier on the coast.

Even after allowance has been made for the difficulties the justice of the statement made in the House of Commons by the Secretary of State for India, Sir Stafford Northcote, must be admitted :—

"This catastrophe must always remain a monument of our failure, a humiliation to the people of this country, to the Government of this country, and to those of our Indian officials of whom we had perhaps been a little too proud." But, he added, from this deplorable evil lessons of value might be learnt and good ultimately arise.

The lesson was learnt, and measures were taken to prevent the recurrence of such a calamity. So far from relying on the law of supply and demand, the State stepped in to provide a supply where it might not otherwise be forthcoming, as well as to create conditions under which that law might operate. Canals were constructed both to provide transport and to irrigate areas liable to suffer from the vagaries of the monsoon and consequent crop failures. Railways were constructed and extended which enabled food to be brought where it was wanted. There is always food enough in the country to feed the people in areas suffering from dearth if only it can be brought there; but until there was a network of railways transport presented insuperable difficulties. Pack-bullocks and the slow-moving bullock-cart were often the only means of transport, and in times of famine bullocks die of starvation. Cases have been known, when famine has occurred in areas remote from the railway, of great stores of rice rotting in the station yards for want of bullocks to remove them; when bullocks are available, they have to be fed from the loads they carry simply because there is no fodder to be got and not a blade of grass to be seen. Railways and canals have added to the resources of the country and strengthened the power of resistance to famine, and a definite famine policy has been formulated, e.g., famine codes have been compiled for the different provinces, famine programmes of works to be executed in times of scarcity are kept in readiness for execution, and financial provision for famines is made in advance in each province, a surplus being set aside for the purpose.

Two of the great irrigation schemes, viz., the Chenab and Jhelam schemes in the Punjab, deserve special mention because of the almost unique work done by Civil Servants in connexion with them. Millions of acres which were formerly waste and unpeopled except by wandering graziers and cattle-thieves were made capable of cultivation by the fertilizing streams of water which engineering skill brought to them. The engineers having done their work, the Civil Servant came in to people the waste and establish what are known as Canal Colonies. Each of the areas brought under irrigation was placed in charge of a Civil Servant bearing the title of Colonization Officer, whose task it was to arrange for the settlement of cultivators, artisans and others. The land was like a blank sheet for them to work on; farms had to be laid out and allotted, roads constructed, towns and villages planned and built. Colonization in the Chenab Colony was begun in 1892 by Mr. (now Sir Edward) Maclagan, who was afterwards Governor of the Punjab, and the chief work was done by Lieutenant (afterwards Sir Frank) Popham Young (1892–9) and after him by Mr. L. H. Leslie Jones, who was Colonization Officer from 1899 to 1904. By the latter year the colony was practically complete. An area equal to Kent, Middlesex and Surrey combined had been brought under cultivation and was inhabited by about a million persons, chiefly peasant farmers—from the outset the policy was to preserve the tradition of the Punjab as a country of peasant farmers. There was an extensive system of roads and railways centred on Lyallpur (named after Sir James Lyall, Lieutenant-Governor of the Punjab in 1896, when it was founded), and a great trade in wheat and oil-seeds had been established. The prosperity of the people may be gauged from the fact that it was said, with some hyperbole, that, as in the days of Solomon, silver was nothing accounted of. Their feelings were reflected in a Punjabi ballad of forty-three stanzas which was sung by a blind poet in 1899, when Sir Frank Popham Young left the colony. It is full of praises of him and the English, as may be judged from the translation of one typical verse, which runs:

> "The English are absolute saints; this is the truth, believe me, and no lie. In the twinkling of an eye they made the waste land disappear. Contractors and labourers acquired wealth, and wages were paid in thousands. Young Sahib has peopled the land."

In the Jhelam Colony, which was started at the end of 1901 with Mr. (now Sir) Malcolm Hailey as Colonization Officer, the progress of colonization was at first checked by an epidemic of plague. Sir Malcolm Hailey, while seeing to the disinfection of houses, was himself attacked by plague, but his life was spared, and the work went on until the land became an expanse of rich cultivation, supporting a large and thriving population—"a wonderful work, truly, to have been done in a few brief years sliced out of a young man's life."[1]

[1] S. Low, *A Vision of India* (1906), p. 190. An interesting account of the work of colonization is given in a chapter aptly entitled "The Blossoming of the Wilderness."

When he took over charge as Colonization Officer, Sir Malcolm Hailey had only six years' service and was under thirty years of age; he subsequently became Governor first of the Punjab and then of the United Provinces.

Famines in the old sense may now be said to be a thing of the past, i.e., those dreadful times, of which there are records as far back as history goes, when food enough to feed the people could not be had for money or the people had not enough money to buy food. Now food is available, the destitute are supported by means of work, food or money provided by Government, and the era of famine involving starvation has been replaced by an era of relief. This relief is given on a scale which taxes the resources in men and money of the local Governments. For the local officers a famine means a time of immense labour, long wearing anxiety, and constant exposure—the subordinate staff has to be improvised, instructed, stimulated and kept up to the mark by constant inspection. It may also involve tragic loss of life: by the roadside at Jubbulpore may be seen a cross with the inscription, "To the memory of the officers of the Central Provinces who sacrificed their lives to their duty in the struggle to save life during the great famine of 1896–1897"; the reverse side bears the names of five members of the Indian Civil Service, one Executive Engineer, one Police Officer, and two Lieutenants of the Indian Army. As Lord Curzon said in 1907, a great famine brings out the heroic qualities of officers, British and Indian, civil and military, and shows the capacity of human nature for self-sacrifice and its sense and power of duty.

"Let those," he said, "who wanted to see what the British Government was capable of doing in India go there, sad as the experience might be, not in prosperous times but in the throes of a great famine, and they would see what no Government in the world has ever attempted to undertake in the past, what no Government in the world, except our own, was capable of undertaking now, and what he firmly believed that no Government, European or Indian, by which we could conceivably be supplanted or succeeded, would dream of undertaking in the future."[1]

Among other developments of this period to which prominence should be given is the protection of the tenantry against oppression or exploitation by landlords and money-lenders. Their rights in the land, to which they are passionately attached, have been safeguarded by agrarian legislation and settlement proceedings, in which the Service has played a leading and honourable part. Since the beginning of the present century a sustained effort has been made to effect a further improvement in the economic condition of the peasantry, a class frugal in small but improvident in large ways, by the establishment of the co-operative credit system in the villages. This has been introduced not spontaneously by the people themselves, but by the initiative of Government, and the movement, which has already been of great value, has been largely directed by members of the Civil Service. The potential importance of it cannot be over-estimated.

Another triumph of administrative organization considering the want of education of so many of the people—even now only 10 per cent can read

[1] *Journal of the Royal Society of Arts*, 1907, p. 424 (*a*).

and write—is the census, with which the Service has from the outset been closely associated. It was first carried out in 1872 and as a synchronous enumeration in 1881. It was a work of peculiar difficulty, the population being mostly illiterate, the enumerators an unpaid agency, and many of the people suspicious of its objects. Some thought it was a prelude to new taxation; many aboriginals feared that they were being numbered in order to be taken away as slaves. The alarm of one aboriginal tribe was allayed by the ingenious explanation that the census was required to settle a bet between Queen Victoria and the Czar of Russia as to which of them had the greatest number of subjects. After this the tribe was cheerfully enumerated to a man. The census has now become part of the regular work of administration, undertaken every ten years and carried through, without an expert agency, by the District Officers and their staff working in co-operation with the people themselves. These facts speak for themselves and show what can be done in a country which is on a low level both educationally and economically, which has neither the revenues of a European state nor its capacity for taxation, and in which therefore it is not easy to maintain European standards.

Less spectacular was the work done by the Service in raising the *morale* of the Indian executive and judicial staff. In the days of the East India Company the latter had a bad reputation as regards both integrity and capacity. According to Sir William Hunter, when India came to the Crown, the native judicial service was underpaid, weak in numbers, deficient in qualifications, and generally believed to be corrupt[1]; and in 1857 Colonel Malleson voiced this belief by writing in *The Red Pamphlet* of "the terrors of subjection to a Hindoo or Mahomedan magistracy." The change which took place during the next fifty years has been well expressed by Sir Andrew Fraser, who had thirty-seven years' service (1871–1908) and was Chief Commissioner of the Central Provinces and Lieutenant-Governor of Bengal. In the early days of his service, he said, any officer of experience who was asked would say that, though a few Indian officers might be trusted in every way, the great majority were corrupt and untrustworthy; at its close the answer would probably be that three or four were certainly open to suspicion, but the vast majority might be implicitly trusted.[2]

The Indian Civil Service has been like leaven leavening the lump, and it can take pride in the standard of integrity and efficiency attained by both executive and judicial officers in association with British officers. It has meant a long fight against corruption and nepotism, and all the greater credit is due to the Indian officers themselves because they have risen above the atmosphere of acquiescence in such practices in which they were brought up. Their own countrymen have long regarded it as natural that a man in authority should accept presents or bribes: it is a survival from the time when justice could not be obtained without them. The head of the Public Health Department in one province once said that some of the Indian officers under him were just as upright and capable as their British colleagues, but

[1] *The India of the Queen* (1903), p. 27.
[2] *Among Indian Rajahs and Ryots* (1911), p. 42.

this belief of their countrymen crippled their work. When these Indian officers went into villages to carry out some much-needed but unpopular work of sanitation, they would be offered presents to induce them to go away and leave the villages in insanitary peace. The villagers would not dream of doing this in the case of British officers and could not believe that their own countrymen were working not for their own advantage, but for that of the people.

As with the Indian Civil Service itself, a reformation has been effected by reasonable salaries and the consciousness of responsibility, combined with the knowledge that good work will be appreciated. Members of the Service have been able to infuse their subordinates with their own energy and have taught them that a man's career depends not on interest or family connexion but on honest and thorough work. In the case of the higher officers there has been admirable material to work upon. As justly remarked by the Simon Commission:

> "To the evolution of the higher Indian subordinate the training, organization and example which British officials have given have largely contributed, but these would have been wasted had there not everywhere existed human material endowed with capacity and a strong sense of loyalty, often fortified by long traditions of public service."

The result is seen in the number of upright and capable Indian officers known to all who have served in India.

During the fifty-six years under consideration it was rarely necessary to employ military force to support civil authority in the maintenance of peace and order. Troops had to be called out in 1879 to suppress disturbances in part of the Bombay Presidency, which were known as the Deccan Dacoities. These were the outcome of agrarian discontent due to economic causes. The movement began with attacks on and robberies of the local money-lenders. It gained cohesion and assumed a more serious aspect when the peasants found a leader in an educated Brahman, who gave out that he was Sivaji the Second, proclaimed that it was a national revolt and offered a reward for the head of Sir Richard Temple, the Governor of Bombay. The tactics of Sivaji were copied, and the insurgents operated in the same tract of country. Organized bands descended from the mountainous country found in the Western Ghats, plundered the villages at their foot and retired laden with booty to their fastnesses. The trouble lasted three months and only ended when three regiments of Native Infantry and one of Native Cavalry took the field against the insurgents, who displayed resolute courage in their encounters with them. In 1893 again there was a fanatical movement among Hindus against the killing of cows. In the town of Bombay there was a riot lasting three days and resulting in eighty deaths, which had to be repressed by military force; and there were serious disturbances in the district of Azamgarh in the east of the United Provinces. As is not uncommon in times of unrest, the cry was raised that the British Raj (rule) was at an end, and agitators actually appointed their own local officers with the usual official titles, such as Collector and District Superintendent of Police. This lasted only a fortnight, however, and the movement collapsed as soon as a regiment was marched through the district to serve as an ocular demonstration of the continued existence of British rule. It was a general rule that disturbances could be and were checked by the show rather than the use of armed force. Thus, when in 1896 grain riots, i.e., riots due to merchants making a corner in grain during a time of scarcity, broke out in the city of Nagpur and the surrounding district, troops were called out, but had neither to use the bayonet nor fire a shot, and in one town, which was in the hands of a mob of 1,500 men, the streets were cleared of the rioters by Mr. (afterwards Sir Charles) Cleveland, then Commissioner of Excise in the Central Provinces, who rode out post-haste with fifteen mounted Gunners from a battery.

The work of the Service during these years steadily increased in volume and complexity. It entailed more and more office work, and it was affected by greater centralization as well as by the creation of special departments of Government and of local self-governing bodies. Increase of work was inevitable owing to the increase of population, the development of the country, and last, but not least, the growth of the legal profession both in numbers and power. The last development which is known in India, not as the rule of law, but as the rule of the lawyer (*Vakil ka raj*), may be traced back for over half a century. Sir Henry Maine noticed in 1868 the immense multiplication of legal practitioners and the increased influence of the Indian Bar.[1] About forty years later the Maharaja of Darbhanga, the greatest land-owner

[1] *Village Communities in the East and West* (1871), p. 211.

in Bihar, complained to the Lieutenant-Governor of Bengal: "You," i.e., the British, "have thrown all power into the hands of the pleaders. They rule the courts; they have all the power of the local bodies; and they have a practical monopoly of the Legislative Councils. We cannot oppose them."[1]

Nor is centralization a new thing; as shown in the last chapter, it had proceeded far under the Company, whose administration was based on a system of carefully regulated supervision and control of lower by higher officers. Voluminous writing was also a weakness of the Government in India even under the Company and drew from Sir William Hunter the sarcastic comment that he governed most who wrote most.[2] The tyranny of the pen was not confined to Secretariats; the multiplication of reports, returns and correspondence, and the consequent obsession of office work, made local officers realize that though the pen is a good servant, it is a bad master. A Bengal Civilian, who joined the Service in 1859, echoed this feeling in two poems on *The Successful Competitor.*[3] In 1863 he deplored the lot of the Collector "chained to the desk"; ten years later he wrote:

> "The crack Collector, man of equal might,
> Reports all day and corresponds all night."

Even more forcible were the comments made in 1875 by Sir Henry Montgomery, of Madras, who was a member of the Indian Civil Service from

[1] Sir Andrew Fraser, *Among Indian Rajahs and Ryots* (1911), p. 58.

[2] *The India of the Queen* (1903), p. 14.

[3] J. F. Bignold, *Leviora* (published in Calcutta, 1888).

1825 to 1857 and of the India Council from 1858 to 1876:

"It is to me lamentable to see the increased amount of correspondence on trifles which now exists. Acts of the Legislature are now thought necessary to allow of doing what in my day any Collector worth his salt would have done without asking any leave. . . . Now the system is to incur no responsibility and to write on every occasion for orders, and Collectors are esteemed in proportion to their power of drawing up long reports and having their accounts neatly prepared and regularly submitted. Of course it is right that this should be—but I fear the more important duties of a Collector are often neglected or hustled over to effect these objects." [1]

The tendency to centralization was accentuated rapidly after the transfer of India to the Crown. When it took place only the principal cities were connected by telegraph and there were only a few hundred miles of railway. It was natural that with the extension and acceleration of communications there should be greater centralization of control, making each officer in the official hierarchy less independent and more the agent of higher authority. The closer touch between Government and local officers, caused by the post and telegraph, made it increasingly necessary for the latter to solicit sanction before taking action and not to act in anticipation of it. References to higher authority consequently increased, and so did references to local officers from Governments seeking information on which to base their policy or administrative measures—in itself a natural consequence of the diversity of conditions

[1] Sir A. Arbuthnot, *Memories of Rugby and India* (1910), pp. 192–3.

in India, where uniformity cannot be imposed without due consideration of local differences and difficulties.

It is sometimes said that centralization has produced uniformity, but actually its influence in that direction has been limited, for the different provinces are distinguished by great diversities which extend even to administrative organization. Madras, for example, has its own system. There the Collector is an officer with greater authority than elsewhere; he deals direct with Government except in matters relating to the revenue administration; there are no Commissioners of Divisions comprising several districts; and their place is to a large extent taken by the Board of Revenue, each member of which deals with different subjects but with all districts. An attempt was made at one time to bring Bengal more into uniformity with other provinces. After the Orissa famine it was apparent that the standard of administration there was for various reasons lamentably low. In the Bengal Administration Report of 1871–2 it was stated that:

> "In the provinces which we have held longest of any in India we have less knowledge of and familiarity with the people than in any other province; that British authority is less brought home to the people; that the rich and strong are less restrained, and the poor and weak less protected than elsewhere."

In order to bring it into line with other provinces and raise its standard, one of the best of "the Punjab school," Sir George Campbell, was appointed Lieutenant-Governor of Bengal, and steps were taken to concentrate more power and responsibility in the hands of the District Officers by making them executive chiefs in their districts over everything except the proceedings of Courts of Justice. There, however, the process of assimilation stopped.

On the other hand, the effects of centralization were more and more apparent in the tightening of the chain of subordination of local officers to provincial Governments and of the latter to the Government of India; little effort was made to effect devolution of powers, especially in financial matters. So little was done to relax control that a local Government complained in 1908 of not having power to appoint a low-paid watchman, to sanction a small sum for the petty expenses of a lady doctor, to settle the number of orderlies in a police school, or even to decide on the situation of a staircase in a Government bungalow and the rent to be levied from its occupant.[1] The same process was repeated all down the official line, the officers subordinate to local Governments having their hands tied by financial and other restrictions, and being immersed in the details of routine.

Sufficient relief from the growing accumulation of work was not afforded by increase of the cadre of the Service. There was an increase of staff, but chiefly in lower services, and this, under the system followed in India, involved more supervision and inspection in order both to maintain and to raise the standard of efficiency: as is pithily said by the Simon Commission, "in India inspection is the Government's administrative key to advance."

[1] Lord Sydenham of Combe, *My Working Life* (1927), p. 230.

Some relaxation from the burden of work was afforded by the orders of Lord Curzon, who had a motto "*Non est scribendum sed gubernandum.*" He reduced both the number and length of reports and returns, and some devolution was effected by the work of the Decentralization Commission appointed in 1907, on whose recommendations the control of higher authorities was relaxed and administrative methods were to some extent simplified. It did not, however, effect any radical change: the Secretariats could still be described as under a tyranny of office boxes occasionally mitigated by the loss of the key. There was so little real relief that in 1913 Mr. Montagu, introducing the Indian budget in the House of Commons, said:

> "The next grievance of the Indian Civil Service is the growing complexity of the system under which they live. Half the faults which are found from time to time with the Indian Civil Service are mainly attributable to their overwork. Every year sees an increase in the inflexible rules laid down for the guidance of all grades of officers. Every year therefore decreases the responsibility of officers, which makes their task less agreeable, and who devote more of their time to reports. I have heard of an officer who said that when he joined the Service a small volume of rules was sufficient to guide him when he went into camp; now he has to pack a portmanteau with codes of regulations."

Another development affecting the work of the Civil Service was the creation of special Departments dealing with separate branches of the administration. Police, Excise, Agriculture, etc., became subject to the control of departmental chiefs with an increase of efficiency and also an increase in the number of masters to be served by District Officers. With the exception of the office of Opium Agent, the headships of Departments were not reserved for members of the Civil Service. For some special technical knowledge, which they did not possess, was an obviously requisite qualification.[1] They were, however, appointed to the charge of other Departments, such as Police, Excise, Agriculture and Settlements, on account of the experience which they had acquired in the districts, their knowledge of the customs of the people and their general organizing ability. It is generally acknowledged that their selection was justified by the success with which they laid down lines of policy and set up standards of efficiency. Of recent years the number of Civilian heads of departments has been reduced, as they have been replaced, especially in the departments of Agriculture and Police, by specialists or by officers belonging to those Departments and trained in them from the outset.

The introduction of a scheme of local self-government for rural areas was a development which might have been, but was not, a real measure of devolution. The scheme which Lord Ripon put forward in 1882 was intended to be an instrument of political and popular education. It might involve a certain loss of efficiency, but it would, he expected, bring relief to the higher executive officials, who would be freed from part at least of the ever-increasing burden of detail and routine. What he had in view was not a representative

[1] A Civilian, Mr. B. H. Baden-Powell, was, however, Conservator of Forests in the Punjab in 1876 and held that office for some years.

system of a democratic type, but the gradual training of the most intelligent and influential Indians in each district in the management of their own affairs. A necessary corollary was the dissociation of the District Officer from the active administration of the local Boards. The Boards could have real responsibility only if they could and did elect non-officials as their chairmen; official control was to be from without and not from within.

"If," he wrote, "the Boards are to be of any use for the purpose of training the natives to manage their own affairs, they must not be overshadowed by the constant presence of the *Burra Sahib*, which may be freely translated 'big swell,' of the district; they must be left gradually more and more to run alone, though watched from without by the executive authorities and checked if they run out of the right course."

Effect was given to the scheme by various Acts between 1883 and 1885, but when it came to work, it was found to be impossible to do without the help of the District Officer. The success of local government depends on the existence not only of men with public spirit and knowledge of local affairs, but also of strong and capable Chairmen. Men fit to be Chairmen were rarely available, and in default the District Officers were appointed Chairmen of the Boards. The Civil Service itself loyally accepted Lord Ripon's policy and was prepared to give full effect to it by withdrawing from the Chairmanships, but it was a usual experience that where Boards were allowed to elect their own Chairmen, they elected District Officers. In some parts no non-officials could be got to stand for election, and Boards would not elect a non-official if he did stand.[1] The net result was, as summarized in the Montagu-Chelmsford Report, that the management of local affairs remained in the hands of those who were most competent to handle them, not from bureaucratic lust of power, but because no other agency readily presented itself and District Officers neither had the leisure nor were given sufficient assistance to create one.

Even in 1915, when Lord Hardinge's Government took up the subject of a further advance, it held the view that in rural areas local bodies should still be guided by official Chairmen, owing both to the paucity of non-officials combining local knowledge with interest in local affairs and to the unique position of the District Officer. Whether British or Indian, he was the only person having the qualities essential for District Board administration. He was the only person who toured systematically through all parts of the district and so knew local requirements. He alone could assess the relative value of the claims of different departments and could impartially judge the demands of different communities, sects and classes. Consequently, the scheme of local self-government, which had been designed to remove the tutelage of the Civil Service in the administration of local affairs outside municipal areas, failed to do so.

Nor was the unique position of the Service substantially changed by reforms affecting legislative bodies until 1921. Under the Morley-Minto reforms of 1909 the elective element was enlarged, but it had a majority only in Bengal. There

[1] See L. Wolf, *Life of the First Marquess of Ripon* (1921), Vol. II, pp. 92–108.

it was expected that the Indian Civil Service would have to relinquish some of the authority and control which it had exercised, that its members would have to resort to persuasion and conciliation in place of more direct methods. They were accordingly solemnly, and unnecessarily, adjured to co-operate with the elected representatives and to work for the good of the people through them. In practice, however, the Morley-Minto reforms made very little difference to the position of the Service, which, according to Bryce, was an oligarchy of some hundreds of higher British officials with an inner oligarchy consisting of "the persons who count," who, taking the central and provincial Governments together, did not exceed thirty or forty in number.[1]

The Morley-Minto reforms were not intended in any way to transplant a European form of representative government, but to associate educated Indians more closely with Government and thus give new confidence and a wider range of knowledge, ideas, and sympathies to the holders of executive power. The existing system of government was to be maintained but improved. Any further advance towards responsible government was barred by the necessity for good government inherent in England's trusteeship for India, by the guiding principle expressed in Lord Morley's words:

"One main standard and test for all who have a share in guiding Indian policy, whether at Whitehall or Calcutta, is the effect of whatever new proposal may at any time be made upon the strength and steadiness

---

[1] *Modern Democracies* (1921), p. 595.

of the paramount power. In Indian government there is no grace worth having in what is praised as a concession, and no particular virtue in satisfying an aspiration, unless your measures at the same time fortify the basis of authority on which peace and order and all the elements of the public good in India depend."[1]

The Civil Service therefore retained its existing dual functions, being at the same time an integral part of the Government and of the legislatures and also their executive agency. Senior members of it serving as heads of provinces, or as members of legislative and executive councils, helped to shape policy, which other members carried out. The situation, however, became increasingly difficult, elected representatives having what was aptly described in the Montagu-Chelmsford Report as "power of challenge and obstruction—influence without responsibility." There was a radical change in the conditions under which the Service worked owing to the development of bitter political feeling. Mr. Allan O. Hume, in helping to found the Indian National Congress in 1885, had claimed that it would act as a safety-valve, an overt and constitutional channel for discharge of the increasing ferment which had resulted from western ideas and education. This body was for twenty years the accredited mouthpiece for constitutional agitation, but at the same time sedition was being preached actively and insidiously by a section of the vernacular Press, especially in Bengal. It had been necessary to try to counteract propaganda of this nature as early as 1878, when the Lieutenant-Governor of Bengal complained of the dangerous

[1] See *Report on Indian Constitutional Reforms*, by Rt. Hon. E. S. Montagu and Lord Chelmsford, para. 74.

tone of some newspapers. Their personal abuse of individual officers, scurrility and exaggeration might, he pointed out, be left to the action of the law courts or treated with contempt; but the actual preaching of sedition was a public danger and ought to be suppressed. In order to check it, the Vernacular Press Act was passed in 1878. This was a preventive rather than a punitive measure. Printers and publishers of vernacular papers which published seditious matter could be warned and ordered to give security: if warnings were disregarded or engagements broken, the securities could be forfeited and the printing plant confiscated. The Act proved a salutary deterrent. Seditious propaganda was stopped without stifling legitimate and vigorous criticism of Government and its measures. The Act was, however, repealed after four years under instructions from Mr. Gladstone's Government, which held that it interfered with the freedom of the Press.

The danger of a press which mistook freedom for licence was seen in 1897, when bubonic plague appeared in Bombay and unpopular measures had to be taken for its eradication, such as house-to-house visitation and the evacuation of those infected by plague. Mr. Rand of the Indian Civil Service, who was in charge of the anti-plague operations at Poona, was stigmatized in one of the vernacular papers as the tyrannical agent of an oppressive government. References were made to Swaraj, i.e., self-government, and there were ominous incitements to violence, which soon bore fruit in the assassination of Mr. Rand together with Lieutenant Ayerst, who happened to be with him at the time. In Bengal the vernacular Press went from bad to worse, and its general tone may be gathered from the words used in 1907 by Sir Harvey Adamson, who was in charge of a Bill which passed into law as the Regulation of Meetings Ordinance: "In Bengal for over thirty years sedition in the Press was neither punished nor prevented. During the whole of this time the dissemination of sedition in the Press never ceased." These words call for meditation rather than comment.

The educated classes were at this time in a state of political unrest, which was in a large measure the result of, and at the same time a tribute to, the work of British administrators, who had habituated them to settled government, schooled them in its ways, and, by means of education, opened out to them the channels of western political thought. The development of political feeling produced three schools of thought. Some were in favour of maintaining the existing constitution but of modifying it so as to give Indians a fuller voice in the councils of Government. Others favoured self-government on the model of the Dominions, i.e., Dominion status, to be acquired by constitutional means. A third party envisaged Government outside the British empire and urged that independence could and should be won by force directed towards the subversion of the existing Government. That elusive term Swaraj came into use as a political *cliché*, being variously used to mean either government by the people themselves under British sovereignty or absolute independence. The advocates of violence gained in strength and numbers during the furious agitation which followed the Partition of Bengal in 1905. Those who had sought to obtain its repeal in a constitutional manner found themselves supplanted by men working for revolution. For the first time for many years there was a spirit abroad of lawlessness and defiance of authority. It was made clear that a determined minority can dominate and terrorize a peaceful but apathetic majority. From Eastern Bengal there was what Lord Minto called " a daily story of assault, of looting, of boycotting, and general lawlessness " ; and unrest spread to the Punjab.

The calm and orderly progress of the previous fifty years was now over. From this time onwards there were intermittent periods of peacefulness with outbursts of intense violence. A new and sinister development was secret revolutionary conspiracy employing bombs and revolvers as its weapons.

> " We are," said Sir Herbert Risley, Home Member of the Government of India, in 1910, " confronted with a murderous conspiracy, whose aim is to subvert the Government of the country and to make British rule impossible by establishing general terrorism. . . . The method they favour at present is political assassination. Already they have a long score of murders or attempted murders to their account. These things are the natural and necessary consequence of the teachings of certain journals. They have prepared the soil in which anarchy flourishes ; they have sown the seed, and they are answerable for the crop. This is no mere general statement ; the chain of causation is clear. Not only does the campaign of violence date from the change in tone of the Press, but specific outbursts of incitements have been followed by specific outrages."

A number of devoted Indian police officers were murdered as the result of these outrages, and two

Indian Civil Servants fell victims, viz., Mr. Jackson, District Magistrate of Nasik (in Bombay) in 1909, and Mr. Ashe, District Magistrate of Tinnevelly (in Madras) in 1911. Others had marvellous escapes. Mr. B. C. Allen, of Assam, was shot in the back in 1907, but not fatally. In 1908 a bomb intended for Mr. D. H. Kingsford, of Bengal, was thrown into a carriage which was thought to be his, and killed two English ladies; a second bomb was sent to him enclosed in the covers of a book, which fortunately he did not open. An attempt was made in 1913 to murder Mr. Gordon, of Assam, but as his would-be murderer was approaching his house, the bomb which he carried exploded and killed him. Three attempts were made to blow up trains in which Sir Andrew Fraser, Lieutenant-Governor of Bengal, was travelling, and in 1908 a young Bengali tried to assassinate him, but the revolver twice missed fire.

CHAPTER V

THE WAR: 1914–18

IN *Germany and the Next War* (1911) General von Bernhardi expressed the opinion that if England was engaged in a protracted European war, a revolution might break out in India. He based this view on the evidence of a spirit partly nationalist and partly revolutionary which had been manifested during the unrest consequent on the partition of Bengal, and he anticipated that the combination of pan-Islamism with the revolutionary element among the Hindus might shake the foundations of British rule. Von Bernhardi failed to gauge the general attachment of the people to British rule, and his forecast, like so many others, was entirely falsified despite German efforts to bring about its fulfilment. Turkey was induced to declare a *jihad*, and this, it was hoped, would cause Afghanistan and the frontier tribes to rise. German emissaries, indeed, arrived at Kabul, but the determination of the Amir to maintain neutrality averted the danger of an Afghan invasion. German schemes to land arms in India and to subsidize revolutionary plots were also made, but were detected and frustrated. The most dangerous of these was that known as the *Ghadr* conspiracy, which was hatched by Indians in the United States supported by German agents and money. Thousands of Sikh emigrants returned to India expecting to find it in a state of chaos and ripe for revolution. Making their way back to their homes in the Punjab, they engaged during 1914 and 1915 in revolutionary activities and propaganda, which, it was authoritatively stated, came within an ace of causing widespread bloodshed; but Government and its officers, armed with new powers under the Defence of India Act (a war measure corresponding to the Defence of the Realm Act in England), were able to deal effectively with the danger.

So far from there being any general idea that England's danger was the nationalists' opportunity, the princes and people on the outbreak of war vied in offers of personal service and material help; and though the first flush of enthusiasm died away, and was followed by reaction as the long years of the war dragged on without victory crowning the allied arms, the masses remained peaceable and contented, notwithstanding the suffering which some sections endured owing to the high prices due to the war. The internal peace was only broken by the *Ghadr* movement and two local outbreaks of a different nature. The first was an agrarian rising in the south-west of the Punjab, where the Muhammadan peasants, aggravated by high prices and heavy debts to Hindu money-lenders, made a general attack on the Hindus early in 1915. The second outbreak, which was secretly engineered and adroitly organized, occurred in 1917, when the Hindus rose *en masse* over an area of 2,000 square miles in South Bihar and attacked the Muhammadans in mobs of 30,000 or 40,000 men. The resources of the civil authorities being unequal to a rising of this magnitude, they had to be assisted by a small body of troops. Order was quickly restored, but not until over 100 villages had been pillaged with murder, arson and rape. "To find any parallel to the state of turmoil and disorder," announced the local Government in a review of the outbreak, "it is necessary to go back over a period of sixty years to the days of the Great Mutiny." This was the only time during the war period of 1914–18 that military force had to be employed to put down civil disorder.

These outbreaks showed the danger, ever present in Indian administration, which is caused by the spread of wild rumours among an ignorant and credulous peasantry. In both the idea got abroad that British rule was at an end. In the Punjab it was thought that the British had evacuated the country because at one district headquarters the flag which was flown on weekdays was not flying one Sunday. In South Bihar it was common belief that Government had no longer troops with which to suppress disorder; when troops came on the scene, it was given out that they could not fire as all ammunition had been sent out of India. Other absurd rumours were current elsewhere, as, for instance, that the issue of currency notes was due to the exhaustion of Government funds; and it was by no means an unimportant duty of local officers to prevent the minds of the people from becoming unsettled and so maintain public confidence and security. This was especially the case when the fall of Kut and the evacuation of Gallipoli gave birth to suspicions of a decline of British power and when the army in India was weakened by the dispatch of troops to France, Mesopotamia and elsewhere; at one time the British portion of the army was reduced to 15,000 men. Some rumours were due to seditious propaganda, others were simply the creation of fertile imagination. Thus, to mention some personal experiences, I found in a quiet Bengal district stories of imaginary aeroplanes flying about at night and of an impending German attack on Calcutta, which had its origin in the issue by Government of a notification changing the boundaries of the port—*lucus a non lucendo.* The most curious of all the alarmist rumours in the district had its origin in a steam-roller at work on a road by the district courts and offices. Villagers coming there and seeing this strange machine imagined it to be some new-fangled kind of cannon and jumped to the conclusion that a battle was about to take place. Such alarm was created that for a short time there was a general disinclination to come near the local courts, with the result that judicial work was largely reduced, and one Magistrate suggested with a twinkle in his eye that litigation might be lessened, and he and his fellow-Magistrates relieved, if the steam-roller were kept at work on the road for an indefinite period.

Although the task of administration was not complicated by internal disorder (with the exceptions already noted), the four years of war were a time of strain and stress for the Service. It had to carry on the ordinary administrative work and to undertake many new duties consequent on the war, while the last year of the war presented new problems when the framing of a reformed constitution was mooted. So far from the staff being strengthened to deal with the increase of work, as was the case with the English Civil Service, it was reduced owing to the absence of men on military duty and the almost complete stoppage of new admissions to make up the losses due to deaths and retirements. During the years 1915–18 only twenty-nine men (seventeen British and twelve Indians) joined the Service, and the shortage after the close of the war was so great that 206 appointments had to be made in the subsequent three years. One-sixth of the total number in the Service were detached for military duty, 200 commissions in the Indian Army Reserve being given them. Others who wished to join up were not allowed to do so, as the reduced cadre was barely sufficient for current work. Most served with the Indian army in India, others with the forces in Mesopotamia either as combatants or as Political Officers, while a few who had special knowledge of aboriginal languages were in charge of labour corps. A few outstanding examples of the men who were on military duty may be mentioned. Mr. Norman Bonham Carter, who was a Commissioner in Bengal, resigned the Service and the prospects of higher office in order to take a commission, and fell in action in France, Mr. J. C. Jack, of the same province, who wrote his *Economic Life of a Bengal District* in the remarkably short space of five days as a kind of literary testament before he went to the Front, died of wounds in France after attaining the rank of Major in the artillery and being awarded the Military Cross (with bar) and the D.S.O. Sir Ernest Hotson, C.S.I., V.D., of the Bombay Presidency, saw service in Baluchistan and Persia from 1916 to 1919 with the rank of Lieut.-Colonel. Lieut.-Colonel J. C. Faunthorpe, C.B.E., M.C., A.D.C. to the King, who was Colonel of the United Provinces Light Horse, was appointed early in the war Military Director of Kinematograph Operations on the Western Front. He was also in command of the Press Camp in 1917, and a letter from the Special Correspondent of *The Times* with the British Armies in France, which was published in that paper on Colonel Faunthorpe's death in 1929, states:

"There was a certain irony in the fact that perhaps the handsomest and most soldierly man, who was also one of the finest horsemen and probably one of the first half-dozen rifle shots in the British army, was only an amateur soldier. Had soldiering been his profession, there is no saying to what distinction he would have attained."

One of those who served in Mesopotamia, Mr. E. H. Jones, of Burma, was the author of *The Road to Endor* (first published in 1920). He was among those who were besieged in Kut, starved there before the surrender, and as prisoners of war struggled, still starving, across 500 miles of desert. His book, however, is not concerned with these sufferings, but with the way in which he and another prisoner secured their freedom. Mr. Jones had, as he himself tells us, learnt human nature among the jungle folk of Burma, and his study of law and lawyers when a Magistrate in that province had helped him considerably in the gentle art of drawing a red herring across the trail. His book shows how effectually he succeeded in doing so with the Turks and what extraordinary ingenuity and perseverance he displayed in exploiting the belief in spiritualism and so securing his release.

Of those who remained in India to carry on the administration many continued, as before, in volunteer corps. It was an old tradition that the Civilian should take his part in local defence; to mention a personal experience, the writer and other Civilians of his year, on joining their first stations, found letters awaiting them from the Commissioner of the Division, saying that they would of course join the local Light Horse and that chargers had been bought for them, for which bills would follow in due course. When in 1917 the volunteer corps were merged in the Indian Defence Corps, it was a point of honour among Civilians not to seek exemption, and it was common to see High Court Judges, Members of Council, and Secretaries to Government in the ranks.

Men on leave in England put their services at the disposal of the home Government and were employed in various capacities in the English Civil Service, where, it is said, they created some surprise by their readiness to take responsibility and to pass orders on current questions without referring them to higher authority. In this way, Sir Frederic Gauntlett, afterwards Auditor-General, worked in the Board of Admiralty; Mr. R. E. Enthoven, of Bombay, was Controller of the Department of Import Restrictions in the Board of Trade; and Mr. A. W. Watson, who had been Secretary to the Bengal Legislative Council, worked under the Minister of Munitions and was transferred to the Ministry of Labour, in which he was appointed Assistant Secretary. Nor were retired members of the Service backward, such as Sir John Rees, of Madras, who was Director of the Prisoners of War Information Bureau from 1915 to 1920; Mr. L. M. Wynch, of the same Presidency, who was Deputy Commissioner of the British Red Cross in France; and Sir Patrick Agnew, who had been a Judge in the Punjab and now showed executive capacity as Managing Director and Vice-Chairman of the Central Prisoners of War Committee. Sir Walter

Lawrence, who had been a member of the Service from 1879 to 1897, became Assistant Adjutant-General on the outbreak of war and, at the request of Lord Kitchener, became his Commissioner to look after the arrangements for sick and wounded Indian soldiers; it was on his initiative that over 3,000 beds were provided in the Dome, Pavilion and other buildings at Brighton. In 1917 Sir Walter was appointed Liaison Officer between the War Office and the Ministry of Pensions; at the end of that year he was sent on a mission to America, in 1918 he was placed on the staff of the Independent Air Force, and in 1919 he was given the rank of Major-General and proceeded to Palestine and Syria.

Another somewhat remarkable example of varied activity was given by Sir Bampfylde Fuller, a retired Lieutenant-Governor, over the age of sixty, who has recently given a delightful account of his experiences in *Some Personal Reminiscences* (1930). He was ready to "do his bit" to help to win the war in however humble a capacity. Relief work among the poor of East London was followed by work in a factory at Paris for cleaning and reconditioning clothing and equipment salvaged from the Front, which, he admits, did not offer much scope for enthusiasm. He was next engaged in purchasing articles of the most miscellaneous description for the troops, together with Sir William Morison of the Civil Service in Bombay, who had retired as Member of Council in that Presidency. The sight of the two knights doing the work of commercial travellers caused some amusement, and they were known as the Knights of Paris. Sir Bampfylde was next called to England to act as Chairman of a Committee to consider the disposal of part-worn army clothing, and returned to Paris, where he organized first a factory for renovating rubber trench-boots and then an establishment for the repair of army clothing. After this he was given charge of the Army Wool Purchase operations in Ireland, which resulted in the purchase of 5 million lb. of wool. He was then sent to France to study the working of the Ordnance Department there with the idea that he might write a history of its war work, and when he declined this task, he returned to factory work in Paris. He subsequently undertook miscellaneous work under the Director of Army Contracts, and finally had work more worthy of his ability as Director of Timber Supplies, in which capacity he organized a new department for the control of timber supplies, among his assistants being two retired Civilians who had served under him in the Central Provinces—Mr. T. C. Wilson, C.I.E., and Mr. E. H. Blakesley.

In India the standard of administration had to be kept up in spite of shortage of staff and the difficulties caused by financial stringency. Economy is a necessity of the administration owing to the comparatively small revenues of the country, and during the war it was carried to an extreme length, an embargo being laid on all new expenditure which was not either directly remunerative or immediately and imperatively necessary—a formula of which the necessity was admitted but deplored by many an officer anxious to promote the welfare of the people committed to his charge, but unable to carry out schemes of improvement for lack of funds. The exigencies of war also led to many new activities in the direction of which the Civil Servants had a large share, partly because of their position as local representatives and agents of Government, and partly because they have much to do that in England would be done by local bodies or voluntary organizations. First and foremost was the recruitment of men, combatant and non-combatant, in which the civil co-operated with the military organization. Over a million men were recruited during the course of the war, viz., 683,000 combatants and 414,000 non-combatants. The Punjab alone contributed 350,000 combatants and 97,000 non-combatants, and the United Provinces 164,000 and 118,000 respectively. Various measures of State control over trade, manufactures and industries had to be applied, and strenuous efforts made to mobilize the commercial and industrial resources of the country. India supplied the requirements of all the troops serving in Mesopotamia as well as all the foodstuffs demanded for the Indian troops in France, Egypt, Central Africa, and elsewhere. Wheat purchases were brought under Government control, and foodstuffs of a value of over 40 million sterling were bought to supplement the food supply of Great Britain and her allies. Intensive activity followed the creation in 1917 of the Indian Munitions Board, which, being responsible for the supply of plant and other materials to Mesopotamia and other theatres of war, gave an extraordinary stimulus to local manufactures and industries. A Central Publicity Board was established for the purposes of war propaganda and the dissemination of reliable information to a public which is peculiarly susceptible to alarmist rumours. The Central

Food Stuffs and Transport Board took in hand the equitable distribution of supplies, which was hampered by shortage of railway rolling stock as a result of shipments to Mesopotamia and other places as well as of the stoppage of imports, and a system was introduced under which certificates were issued giving priority over ordinary traffic to goods required on civil account. Other restrictions were placed on trade so as to conserve the resources of the country and prevent diversion to use by the enemy, and the export was controlled of many articles such as hides, skins, oil, oil-seeds, and jute, the last of which was in enormous demand for the sandbags which lined the trenches.

In consequence of these developments Civilians were engaged in new and unaccustomed duties and filled posts of which the very names are strange to a later generation. To quote a few typical instances, Mr. P. R. Cadell was Controller of Prices in Bombay, Sir Charles Innes (now Governor of Burma) was first Controller of Munitions in Madras and then Food Stuffs Commissioner, Sir Arthur McWatters was successively Wheat Commissioner and Controller of Hides and Wool, Mr. C. G. Leftwich was Controller of Munitions and subsequently Director of Civil Supplies in the Central Provinces, and Mr. G. H. W. Davies (who was assassinated by a Muhammadan in 1928) was Controller of Home-Indents and Priority in Bengal. To Mr. A. J. W. Kitchin, Secretary to the Publicity Bureau in the Punjab, fell the task, unusual for a Civil Servant, of editing a weekly war journal, which was unique in being trilingual, for it was published in English, Urdu and Gurmukhi.

Unlike the English Civil Service, the Indian Civil Service received no war bonus and was content with the appreciation by the Viceroy (Lord Chelmsford) of the work done by it and other public services in British India. In a speech deliverd to the Imperial Legislative Council in February, 1919, he said:

"The Services of India have just come through a long period of exceptional strain. Their strength has been seriously depleted by the war. They have been called upon not merely to run the administration with a far weaker staff, not merely to steady men's minds during periods of depression and alarm, but they have had to organize and promote many forms of war activity. It has been out of the question to let them take leave, and so they have stayed at their posts year after year doing double work, often to the detriment of their health and commonly at the sacrifice of domestic comfort. They have been hard hit by rising prices; and they have come in for attacks arising out of the agitation in connexion with the Reforms, which have been sometimes ungenerous and unfair. But they have risen superior to all these things, and as Viceroy I am proud and glad to acknowledge on behalf of my Government the part which they have played in keeping India contented and in helping to win the war."

CHAPTER VI

AFTER THE WAR: 1919–30

LORD CURZON stated in the last speech which he made in India that he had not offered political concessions because he did not regard it as wisdom or statesmanship in the interests of India itself to do so. He also put it on record that throughout the seven years (1898–1905) during which he was responsible for the government of India he was never called upon to take measures for the repression of sedition or the restoration of order. With these statements may be contrasted one made twenty-five years later in the Report of the Simon Commission, viz. that " troops are employed many times a year to prevent internal disorder and, if necessary, to quell it." Nothing could be more eloquent of the changes which have taken place in British India since the war. There has been a radical reform of the system of government, tempests of political and communal passion have raged, sedition has been a dangerous force, and civil has often had to be reinforced by military authority.

The war was scarcely over before trouble began. In order to retain the powers which were necessary to enable it to defend its officers and the public against revolutionary conspiracies, Government introduced two Bills called the Rowlatt Bills after Mr. Justice Rowlatt, the Chairman of a Committee which recommended legislation on the lines adopted. A furious agitation and anti-Government propaganda followed, in which the object and scope of the measures were grossly misrepresented: this was not the first, and it has not been the last, time to show beyond all question that in India at least there is some truth in the jest that propaganda is the Latin for lies. The movement gained driving force and cohesion under the leadership of Mr. Gandhi, who combined political acumen with personal asceticism and had a reputation for saintliness which made him revered by the Hindus. He also obtained the support of Moslems by taking up the Khilafat cause, of which the object was to bring pressure on the British Government to restore Turkey to the position it had held before the war. It was, Mr. Gandhi declared, an opportunity of a lifetime, which would not occur for another hundred years, to unite Hindus and Moslems in a common cause.

The tactics of the non-co-operation party were much the same as, and may have been a copy of, those which had been employed by the Sinn Feiners in Ireland. It was sought to paralyse the administration by every possible means and to make British government and law unworkable. Constitutional agitation was declaimed as useless, the use of physical force was deprecated, and the weapon of offence was to be what is generally known as passive resistance, which Mr. Gandhi called "non-violent non-co-operation," but which in practice became violent illegal action. What specially differentiated the movement from previous political agitations was that it was carried from the towns to the villages and that the peaceful peasantry were rousedas they never had been before: the agitation over the Rowlatt Act, writes Mr. Ranga Iyer in *India—Peace or War?* (1930), was "the first time in the history of India when the leaders seriously approached the masses. Politics were hitherto confined to the educated classes."

Revolutionary propaganda led to risings in parts of the Punjab and Madras, where military control had to be substituted for civil administration. In April, 1919, there were outbreaks in the Punjab which the Government of India at the time characterized as "open rebellion," which it was determined to put down: they have since been euphemized as riots or disturbances. For the first time since the Mutiny martial law was declared and the rising was suppressed within a month, leaving, however, bitter memories, mainly in consequence of the action of General Dyer at Amritsar. Against the advice of the Lieutenant-Governor of the Punjab, Sir Michael O'Dwyer, the administration of martial law was in military hands and not under civil supervision, so that civil authority was superseded by military authority, with unfortunate results. After the event the Government of India laid down the principle that in future civil officers should be appointed to act as advisers to the military authorities in any area in which it might be necessary to enforce martial law.

The second rebellion broke out in August, 1921, among the Moplahs, a fanatical race of Muhammadans in Malabar. During the period of British rule there have been thirty-five outbreaks among the Moplahs, but none so fierce and formidable as that of 1921, which was due to the influence of the Khilafat agitation and aimed at the establishment in Malabar of an independent kingdom under the name of Swaraj. The rebellion was marked by outrages of the most ghastly description committed wholesale upon Hindus. Thousands of them were forcibly converted to Islam; thousands who would not give up their faith were murdered with atrocious barbarity, and were frequently made to dig their own graves before being killed. It was not till the end of February, 1922, that the Moplahs were reduced, and martial war withdrawn, after a campaign in which a small army was employed and over 3,000 Moplahs were killed in action.

There were no such outbreaks elsewhere, but the task of administration was immensely complicated by the persistent efforts made to defy and subvert lawful authority. Law and order had to be maintained, and a peaceful but somewhat supine majority protected against terrorism by an active and unscrupulous minority. It had hitherto been possible to uphold law and order without much difficulty owing to want of cohesion among the forces opposed to it, but the Civil Service and the Police now had to face a much more difficult situation owing to the organization of the movement and the activities of its agents in the villages, where a swarm of agitators advocated the payment of no rent (so as to affect the Government revenue), the boycott of liquor shops (with the same object), non-payment of the tax from which the village police are paid, and the boycott of British goods.

There was no effective anti-propaganda, and the old standards of loyalty were strained. When the present King and Queen visited India in 1906, Bengal was still in the throes of a violent agitation over the partition of Bengal, but the voice of dissension was hushed. When the Prince of Wales landed at Bombay in 1921 there was a riot in which fifty-three persons were killed and about 400 wounded.

Apart from incitements to and actual outbursts of violence, the task of maintaining peace and order was complicated by wild rumours, which, as is usually the case in times of unrest in India, excited the ignorant masses. Some were deliberately disseminated, others were apparently the creatures of untutored imagination. It was, for instance, given out that under the Rowlatt Act the income tax would be raised to 50 per cent of income—a drastic levy of capital—and the old story that the British Raj either had ended or was coming to an end was repeated. This rumour had some curious results. There was an idea that there would be a general release of prisoners to signalize the end of British rule, and in anticipation of this 660 prisoners broke out of a jail in Bengal. The aborigines in part of Chota Nagpur were deluded into thinking that a Hindu rule was to be established under which the eating of meat would be prohibited. Accordingly they crowded into the markets and sold their goats and sheep for a mere song. The sight, again, of a few elephants helped to produce a strike in one of the coal-fields, as it was given out that they were the vanguard of an army marching on Calcutta under the banner of Mr. Gandhi.

In the end the violence of the agitators defeated their objects, for they disgusted the mass of the people. A sense of disillusionment crept in, as the millennium prophesied by Mr. Gandhi failed to materialize; and horror was caused by such fiendish crimes as that of Chauri Chaura in the United

Provinces, where thirty-two policemen (regular and village) were massacred by a mob in February, 1922. In the latter province the people themselves gladly joined anti-revolutionary leagues presided over by the District Officers. Mr. Gandhi himself was almost a spent force when he was arrested (in March, 1922), tried and convicted, but his imprisonment dispelled the delusion of the masses that he had supernatural powers which no prison could restrain, and it also strengthened the hands of Government officers and the law-abiding public by showing that the patience of the Government was at length exhausted.

On the District Officers fell the brunt of the defence of authority against the attacks of the non-co-operators; and to them is justly due the meed of praise given (in 1928) to the Service at large by Lord Ronaldshay (now the Marquess of Zetland), who as Governor of Bengal had personal knowledge of the conditions under which they worked during those troubled years.

> "In the days when non-co-operation was at its height, the members of the I.C.S. fought their lone battle away in the districts, a small handful, cut off from the society and support of their own people; physically wearied in a land where the enervating climate drained a man of his vitality, mentally a prey to that brooding atmosphere of hostility and unreasoning hate which dried up the very springs of a man's joy in living. The conditions of life and service were often hard; but they had won through and had the satisfaction of knowing that their toil had not been in vain."

With the subsidence of the non-co-operation movement there was a return to more peaceful conditions, though in 1923 it was necessary to call out troops in aid of the civil authority on thirty-six occasions; the total force employed was a small army of 4 cavalry regiments, 9 infantry battalions and 7 sections of armoured cars. There was, however, an increasing tendency to communal or sectarian strife and consequent riots between Hindus and Muhammadans, occasioned by such causes as the sight of a cow being led to slaughter or a Hindu procession with music passing a mosque. It is hard to convey to English readers an idea of the murderous fury of an Indian mob carried away by religious frenzy, but the actual casualties speak for themselves, e.g. during the five years 1923–7, altogether 450 persons were killed and 5,000 injured in communal riots. For this deplorable communal strife the shifting of the balance of power due to the reformed system of Government must be held mainly responsible, and not any dereliction of duty on the part of the Civil Service and the Police: it has always been recognized that it is a more important, and often a more difficult, duty of a District Officer to prevent riots than to repress them when they have broken out. The Simon Commission, indeed, has put it on record in its Report that the presence of a neutral bureaucracy has discouraged strife and that "so long as authority was firmly established in British hands, and self-government was not thought of, Hindu-Moslem rivalry was confined within a narrower field." The true cause is, in its opinion, "the struggle for political power and for the opportunities which political power confers." Deplorable as it is, this communal strife has helped the Civil Service to retain the old confidence of the people. It has made it clear that the Service and the Police are a shield of defence against turmoil and terrorism, and that the impartial officer who can restore order is a very present help in times of violence. It is not surprising, therefore, that the Simon Commission describes the Indian Civil and Police Services as "Security Services" on which depend the organization and direction of the general administrative system and the maintenance of law and order.

Recently again British India has suffered from a spasm of intense violence. Revolutionary outrages began at the end of 1929 with an attempt to blow up a train in which the Viceroy was travelling. Since then there has been widespread lawlessness, cloaked under the name of civil disobedience, and a sustained effort has been made to shake, if not to subvert, the fabric of government, and to reduce the British Government to a mood of surrender as a preliminary to the Round Table Conference. The methods employed have included the corruption of frontier tribes, provocation to sedition and mutiny, murderous outrages, and, when more extreme measures have not been resorted to, intimidation and the weapon of social boycott which is so terrible to an Indian. As early as May, 1930, the Viceroy had regretfully to announce—"From quarters as far distant as Peshawar and Madras, Bombay and Calcutta, Chittagong and Karachi, Delhi and Sholapur, have come ominous tales of mob violence, of armed and murderous raids, and of general defiance of lawful authority." In December the Government of India summed up the situation by saying that there had been mass defiance of the law extending over eight months and affecting at one time or other every part of India.

There were two raids on Peshawar by Afridis from across the border, who had been led to believe that the days of British rule were numbered and that the people of the villages round Peshawar and the populace of the city would rise and make common cause with them. The first incursion took place in June, and the second in August, 1930, when an attack was also made on the cantonment at Nowshera. At Sholapur the situation was so serious that British women and children had to be sent out of the place and martial law declared. In Bengal there was a recrudescence of anarchical crime. A murderous raid took place at Chittagong in which the Collector, Mr. H. R. Wilkinson, narrowly escaped with his life. Later in the year the Inspector-General of Police (Mr. Lowman) was shot dead at Dacca and the Inspector-General of Prisons (Lt.-Col. N. S. Simpson, I.M.S.) in his office in Writers' Buildings, Calcutta. Mr. J. W. Nelson, Judicial Secretary to the Government of Bengal, was wounded by revolver fire at the time of Colonel Simpson's assassination; Sir Geoffrey de Montmorency, Governor of the Punjab, was similarly wounded, narrowly escaping assassination, when leaving a Convocation of the Punjab University in Lahore. Towards the end of the year the terrorist party extended its activities to Burma, where a mail train in which the Chief Secretary and other high officials were travelling was derailed, and a small rebellion was hatched, which was soon suppressed after some fighting in which nearly 600 insurgents were killed or wounded and 1,200 were captured.

It remains to add that in January, 1931, as a result of the Round Table Conference, it was announced by Mr. Ramsay MacDonald that the British Government accepted the proposal that the central Government of India should be an All-India federation, embracing both British India and the Indian States; that with a legislature constituted on a federal basis it was prepared to recognize the principle of the responsibility of the executive to the legislature; and that the Governors' provinces would be constituted on a basis of full responsibility with Cabinets of Ministers taken from the provincial legislatures, the Governors having reserved to them only the minimum of special powers necessary to secure in exceptional circumstances the preservation of tranquillity and to guarantee the maintenance of rights provided by Statute for the public services and for minorities. It is scarcely necessary to point out that if the constitution is framed on these lines, the position of the Indian Civil Service will be very materially different from what it has hitherto been.

In addition to devoting their energies to the primary duties of government, the maintenance of law and order and the protection of life and property against the forces of disorder working by means of open violence and underground conspiracy, members of the Civil Service have had no small part in preventing any breakdown of the system of representative government introduced by the Montagu-Chelmsford scheme and in making it work more or less successfully in spite of its inherent defects.

"In judging the success of the Reforms," says the Simon Commission, "it must always be remembered that the results at present disclosed are due in no small measure to the continuing influence and assistance of officers who have gained their experience under the previous system."

Again, after explaining that the organization and direction of the general administrative system, whether at headquarters or in the districts, rests upon the Indian Civil Service, and that upon it and the Indian Police Service essentially depends the maintenance of law and order, the Commission remarks:

"The existence of a highly efficient administrative machine, and the resource and energy which these two services brought to bear upon the difficult problems to which the Reforms gave rise, have contributed greatly to the large measure of success which has attended the working of the reformed Governments in the last ten years."

On the District Officers devolved the charge of the electoral machinery, which they had to introduce among a people who scarcely knew the alphabet of the new system. It was they who were responsible for preparing the electoral rolls (and incidentally dispelling suspicions that they were a prelude to fresh taxation), for receiving nominations, for conducting the elections, and for declaring the results of the polls. In provincial Governments those Civil Servants who have been appointed Governors and Members of Council have still been able to initiate and direct policy. Those who as members of the provincial and imperial legislatures have combined parliamentary with executive functions have acquitted themselves well in debate; the gibe that first-class administrators have been converted into third-class politicians has a meretricious smartness but little foundation in truth. In the Secretariats they have served different Ministers and Members of Council drawn from the Indian unofficial classes with equal loyalty, though not with equal respect, for Members have not always been men of capacity and not all Ministers have been on a par with Ministers of the Crown in England, whose previous careers give some guarantee that they have knowledge of affairs and power of conduct as well as the gift of speech. The latter have had experience of public life, and are selected irrespective of their religion; in India up to the present some of the Ministers and non-official members of Executive Councils have owed their position to the possession of qualifications other than proved capacity for the conduct of public affairs. What has added to the difficulties of working a system of what was supposed to be representative government has been the fact that Ministers have often had no parties to support them and have been able to retain office only by means of the official votes. Legislatures, as pointed out by the Simon Commission, have been produced in which the formation of political parties, in the sense in which they are understood in Great Britain, has been almost impossible and has indeed rarely been attempted.

> "There is," it declares, "no province in which the official *bloc* has not at some time or other been of decisive value to Ministers, and in some provinces there has never at any time been a sufficiently large or cohesive ministerial party to enable Ministers to ignore the assistance of their official supporters."

After this sketch of general conditions some account should be given of the changes which have taken place in the personnel and position of the Civil Service in the post-war period. Its composition has been so radically altered that it is no longer a homogeneous body such as it used to be in the Crown period from 1858 till the eve of the Great War. The process of Indianization, i.e. the admission of Indians, has progressed steadily year by year and is to go on until by 1939 the Service will be half British and half Indian. It has also been much reduced in numbers, as posts which were formerly reserved for members of the Service have been filled by members of the Provincial Services. At the same time the strength of the Secretariats has been largely increased. Large Secretariats seem to be the usual incident of democratic government—democracy apparently involves bureaucracy—but in India they have two disadvantages. The revenues of British India are limited—they amount to £130,000,000 (imperial and provincial) for a population of nearly 250 millions—and the amount available for new developments is reduced by what may be called overhead charges. It seems to take two men now to do the Secretariat work that one man used to do before the reformed Governments were introduced. Another unfortunate consequence is that not only is the work of the District Officers, heavy enough already, increased owing to the demands of Government for material for replies to questions about the minutiæ of administration, etc., but the supply of trained men available for both district and political work is reduced. Even as it is, the Indian States Committee presided over by Sir Harcourt Butler has had to suggest that owing to the Indian Civil Service being short-handed, as well as the Indian Army, the time has come to recruit separately from the universities in England for service in the States alone.

Another change of far-reaching importance has been the permission given to members of the Service who joined it before 1920 to retire at any time on a pension proportionate to the length of their service. It is merely necessary for a man to make a declaration that he desires to retire in view of the changes in the conditions of his service; and it is no longer the rule that a Civilian must serve for twenty-five years before he can draw his pension. Premature retirement has become a normal incident of service, and up to the present one man out of every ten has exercised the right to retire on proportionate pension. The number of men who retired prematurely was relatively greater during the early years of the Reforms scheme, viz., one in six up to the end of 1923; and many others who had already completed twenty-five years of service also preferred to retire rather than continue under the new conditions. The Service was consequently weakened by the loss of trained and experienced officers whom India could ill afford to spare.

Several causes have co-operated to make men prefer retirement to the active life of service. They had to live in a depressing atmosphere of bitter racial hatred which seemed to grow worse as time went on. The strain was accentuated by financial stress, for pay was not adjusted to meet the very largely increased cost of living until relief was given on the recommendation of the Lee Commission. Above all there was a feeling that good administration was being sacrificed to political expediency, that the old standards were falling, and that the welfare of the masses, which they regarded as a solemn trust, was subordinated to the clamour of politicians, and that they were powerless to prevent it.

"There are," stated the Government of the United Provinces in 1924, in a Report on the working of the Reforms, "distinct signs that the Services are losing their former keenness. Since they no longer have the power of shaping policy to the extent which they had, they no longer feel that the progress of the country depends on their efforts, nor indeed that any efforts are likely to have abiding results."

Many, moreover, chafed at the policy of Government towards the non-co-operation movement, which for a time seemed to be one of masterly inactivity. Local officers, however, were apt to consider it not masterly but weak. In India, as elsewhere, a Government is respected only as long as it commands respect, and most Civil Servants would subscribe to Treitschke's dictum, that of all political sins that of feebleness is the most contemptible and is "the political sin against the Holy Ghost."

An interesting picture of a Civilian impelled to retire prematurely by motives such as these is given in Mr. Hilton Brown's novel *Dismiss* (1923), the title of which is suggested by the parade ground and typifies the passing away of the old order. The hero is, indeed, made to say, "There is no Indian Civil Service now: the old Service is dead, and that without any very decent interment." He resigns in disgust at serving a people which, he believes, wants to get rid of British rulers and a Government which appears to him to be indifferent to its officers being the victims of mob violence.

The immediate occasion for his resignation is a murderous riot which might have been prevented had Government acted on his advice and made a demonstration of force. The imaginary hero, be it added, is not unsympathetic to Indian aspirations, and, like many actual members of the Service, is agreeable to power being handed over to Indians who command respect but not to mere politicians of no standing or influence. A pleasant little sketch is given of a Mr. Deva Doss, an Indian official, under whom it was a pleasure for Englishmen to serve, and the remark is made—"If the Progressive party were made up of Deva Dosses, we could hand over India, with reservations, to-morrow."

When the new constitution was framed, it was intended that there should be a radical change in the position of the Civil Service. Hitherto Government had, as stated in the Montagu-Chelmsford Report, been in its essentials one with the Service and the people had regarded the official as their representative in the councils of Government. The Reforms Scheme was to change all this, for the substitution of the elected politician for the Civilian as the guardian of the public interest was to be part of the progress towards responsible government. For this purpose it was necessary, as pertinently pointed out in the same Report, to tear up by the roots the people's faith in the Service as their representative, and to teach them that they must take their troubles to an elected representative. The Service was in future to fill a double part. It was to provide the executive agency of Government, though the time was envisaged when the European official would be reduced to the position of "a skilled consultant, a technical adviser and an inspecting and reporting officer." Besides performing executive duties, the Civil Servant was to assist in the political education of the people, i.e., training the rural masses for self-government, and not to leave the task of training them solely to politicians but to explain and persuade, argue and refute. He was also to be dissociated from an active part in the work of local bodies. "We can bid," it was said, "the Government official to step aside from his position as executive officer of the Boards and assume for the future the rôle of onlooker and friendly adviser." A very different idea of the future of the Service was expressed by Mr. Lloyd George, who, speaking as Prime Minister in the House of Commons in August, 1922, declared that he could conceive no period when Indians could dispense with the guidance and assistance of some nucleus of British Civil Servants. They were "the steel frame of the whole structure"; and if the steel frame was taken out, the fabric would collapse.

> "There is one institution we will not interfere with; there is one institution we will not cripple; there is one institution we will not deprive of its functions or its privileges; and that is the institution which built up the British Raj, the British Civil Service in India."

The speech caused considerable annoyance to Indian politicians, who looked forward to Dominion status with an executive entirely responsible to an elected legislature, but it made little impression on the Service itself, which was conscious of the change already made in its position and knew that in any case Mr. Lloyd George's Government could not bind its successors.

To some extent the hopes of the framers of the Reforms scheme have been disappointed, both because disorder and turmoil, and also the strength of tradition among a conservative people, have made them turn to the District Officers as their natural protectors, and also because, as pointed out by the Simon Commission, "of no country can it be said more truly than of India that government is administration" and "the great mass of the people desire personal rule." On the other hand, the people are aware of the shifting of the balance of power as evidenced by the subordination of District Officers to Ministers in some branches of work and by their removal from the Chairmanship of District Boards. Hitherto one of the most interesting and beneficent activities of District Officers had been their work as Chairmen of the District Boards. Except in the Punjab they were removed from this position in order to make room for non-official Chairmen. The object of the change is intelligible and *prima facie* reasonable. The District Officer had been a dominating personality on the Boards, the members of which left the practical work of administration to him, and it was felt that they would never learn to administer so long as he was there to do the work for them.

The result of the removal of what was called official tutelage has in many parts been most unfortunate. District Officers are no longer able to ensure the supply of local needs, such as dispensaries, schools, water supply, etc., which came to their notice when touring through the villages; and the districts themselves suffer as local needs are neglected.

The hope that the Civil Service would undertake the political education of the rural masses has not been, and is not likely to be, fulfilled, though it still seems to find favour with some. Mr. Baldwin, for instance, reiterated the idea in a speech which he delivered, as leader of the Opposition, in the House of Commons on 7 November, 1929. The education of the masses is not the duty of any Civil Service in the world, and though the Indian Civil Service has duties and responsibilities not expected from other Civil Services, it may well be questioned whether it is possible for it to engage in work of this kind without giving up the character of a non-political body which is essential to the existence of any Civil Service. A truer conception of the duties of Civil Servants in India has been expressed both by Sir Walter Lawrence and by Sir Herbert Thirkell White, formerly Lieutenant-Governor of Burma. The former, writing of the English officials who served in India during the time in which he was a member of the Indian Civil Service, i.e., from 1879 to 1897, said:

"Their mission was clear: it was to secure the welfare of the millions, to prevent corruption and tyranny, to prevent and to fight famine, plague and pestilence, and to ensure that every Indian should have the free right to enjoy unmolested the rites and the rules of his religion, his caste and his tribe." [1]

The latter wrote with reference to Burma, but his remarks are equally applicable to other parts of British India.

"Let us," he said, in *A Civil Servant in Burma* (1913), "avoid the pernicious cant that our mission in Burma

[1] *The India We Served* (1928), p. 113.

is the political education of the masses. Our mission is to conserve, not to destroy their social organism: to preserve the best elements of their national life; by the maintenance of peace and order to advance the well-being of the Burmese people."

In any case the Civil Service is far too busy doing its proper work, which is that of administration, to have time for peripatetic propaganda. The cadre is kept at a strength which is barely sufficient for current duties, and there is no reserve for extraneous work of this kind. The idea that Indian Civil Servants can be political missionaries, moreover, entirely neglects the fact that if every Civil Servant was available, there would be only one for every 1,000 square miles, i.e., for an area larger than the average English county. But every one is not available. Some are Judges and others work in the Secretariats, and are precluded by their duties from touring about the country; and a certain number are at any time on leave. The idea also rests on the assumption that the people themselves are willing to receive a political education; but this is by no means the case. The villagers, who form nine-tenths of the population, are keenly alive to questions affecting their religion or the land; otherwise their main interest is that of earning their livelihood by tilling their little fields, and unless there is some outside stimulus, such as has been supplied by the propaganda of agitators in recent years, they care little or nothing about politics.

The old-fashioned Indian gentleman also, like Gallio, cares for none of these things. To him, as Sir Alfred Lyall said in *The Life of Lord Dufferin* (1905), political agitators are new men who want to be masters; their strength, ability, and disinterestedness are not clear to him; they are likely to be affected by prejudices of race and religion; and on the whole, whatever may be his discontent with the existing regime, he does not care to join in experiments upon the constitution of a Government that rules with strength and impartiality. These views are not shared by the more modern educated Indians, of whom some have the keenest interest in politics and have eagerly taken to a political life. But even these latter do not welcome outside tuition and resent the idea of being pupils to be taught. Their attitude and the general effect on district work are summed up as follows in a report on the working of the reforms made by the Government of Bihar and Orissa in 1927:

"The position of the District Officer has definitely changed for the worse; it is true that the poison gas let loose by the non-co-operation movement has ceased, and in many districts the personality of the District Officer has reasserted itself; but the new system has inevitably diminished his efficiency. In the pre-reform days the District Officer was actuated by the guiding principle of improving the district of which he was in charge, and he had power in his manifold capacities to give effect to his ideas. But this idealism cannot survive the complete transfer of his responsibilities in the sphere of self-government, and has to some extent been replaced by an attitude of half-cynical criticism. The prophecy of Mr. Montagu that the District Officer would find a worthy substitute for his past position in the training of men who can relieve him of much of his burden is far from realization. The modern politicians, as elected to the District Boards and Municipalities, have no desire to be trained. They resent interference, and it is not possible for the District Officer to continue making futile efforts to improve matters. This is where the Reforms touch him most nearly, and as he sees the structure built up by his predecessors in the District Boards and Municipalities travelling down the easy road to chaos and bankruptcy,[1] he has strong doubts of the wisdom of the policy that the people should learn by their mistakes. The people who pay the cost of these mistakes have not the remotest conception that they have even had the opportunity of making mistakes and pathetically reproach Government and its officers for allowing these things to be."

[1] The same Government, in a report (1927) on the working of the new constitution, remarked, in regard to local bodies: "The misappropriation of public funds is generally regarded more as a subject for mirth and envy than reprobation."

CHAPTER VII

A BUREAUCRACY

TO speak of Indian Civil Servants as " sun-dried bureaucrats " is a common *cliché* of Indian politicians and journalists, who frequently also refer to the whole system of government in India as bureaucracy.[1] The term is sometimes used to create prejudice or enlist English sympathy, in the belief that officialdom and bureaucracy are synony-

[1] The Swarajist party in August, 1924, defined its policy as follows :

" Whereas by the programme adopted at Allahabad, on February 23, 1923, the party declared that its policy shall include on the one hand all such activity as stands to create an atmosphere of resistance making government by *the bureaucracy* impossible with a view to enforce our national claims and vindicate our national honour, and on the other hand shall include for the said purpose all steps necessary for the gradual withdrawal of that co-operation by the people of this country without which it is impossible for *the bureaucracy* to maintain itself.

" And whereas the application of the said principle to the existing facts of our national life, with special reference to the varying attitude of *the bureaucratic government* which rules that life, demands that such principle must include self-reliance in all activities which make for the healthy growth of the nation and resistance to *the bureaucracy* as it impedes our progress towards Swarajya . . .

" Now the Swarajya party declares that the guiding principle of the party is self-reliance in all activities which make for the healthy growth of the nation, and resistance to *the bureaucracy* as it impedes the nation's progress towards Swarajya." The italics are mine.

mous terms and that the English are apt to regard officialdom with suspicion or distrust. Some, however, have no clear idea of the meaning of bureaucracy, but believe it to be a derogatory, almost opprobrious, name. The Indian Civilian himself has no objection to being called a bureaucrat. He regards it not as a discreditable designation but as a correct definition of what he is, viz., a salaried official engaged in civil administration: "sun-dried" he accepts as a picturesque touch of local colour.[1] He knows that a bureaucracy, in its true sense of a body of trained administrators, is necessary for the conduct of administration in a modern State; and he is aware of the truth of the dictum of John Stuart Mill, that no progress at all can be made towards obtaining a skilled democracy unless the democracy is willing that the work which requires skill should be done by those who possess it. Many Indians have not yet grasped this principle, as they have no idea of the complexity of administration and imagine it to be work which the amateur can do as well as the professional, who has had a long apprenticeship and specialized training.

As a bureaucracy the Indian Civil Service differs in several important respects from the English Civil Service. It is not a purely executive agency acting under the direction of a Parliamentary Chief. Some members of the Service are Gover-

[1] Sir Walter Lawrence, who was at one time a "sun-dried bureaucrat," writes: "It is impossible to learn the real facts of India without toil under the sun; and the epithet 'sun-dried' conjures up to me the good, keen men who scorned the fierce Indian sun when there was duty to be done." *The India We Served* (1928), p. 276.

nors of Provinces, members of Executive Councils and members of Legislative Councils, and as such have a voice in directing policy, though the greater number merely execute it. Under the dyarchic system, moreover, one branch of provincial government has been responsible not to a body of elected representatives of the Indian people, but to the Secretary of State for India, and ultimately to Parliament. Another part of the administrative work has been done under the control of elected Ministers, who, however, have not had the power of appointing and dismissing members of the Service. On account of these anomalies dyarchy has been variously compared to a Janus with one face looking eastward and the other westward to Whitehall, to a Siamese twin with the Governor serving as a connecting cord, and to two teams harnessed to the car of State and pulling in opposite directions.

Apart from this radical difference, the Indian differs from the English Civil Service in composition, duties and size. The English Civil Servant is a servant of the Crown who is not the holder of a political or judicial office and who is employed in a civil capacity. As thus defined the English Civil Service numbers over 400,000, or, if industrial workers are excluded, over 300,000, of whom between 1,100 and 1,200 belong to the controlling grades and form what is called the Administrative Class. This class is concerned with the formation of policy, with the co-ordination and improvement of Government machinery, and with the general administration and control of the departments of the Public Service.

The Indian Civil Service, on the other hand, has

a little over 1,000 members—the actual number on 1 January, 1930, was 1,014—and it is not divided into superior and inferior services. All belong to one service and, with the exception of junior members serving in lower posts for the purpose of training, all fill posts in which they exercise powers of superior control. Its members serve in three main Departments, viz., Political, Judicial and Executive. The Political Department is manned partly by Civil Servants and partly by officers of the Indian Army. The work connoted by the word Political is entirely unlike that which would be inferred from its English sense, for it is chiefly diplomatic and includes political work (in the Indian sense), i.e., diplomatic work in the Indian States, and foreign work on or beyond the frontier. Some idea of it may be gathered from the description given by Lord Curzon just before leaving India in 1905:

> "The public at large hardly realizes what the Political may be called upon to do. At one moment he may be grinding in the Foreign Office, at another he may be required to stiffen the administration of a backward Native State, at a third he may be presiding over a *jirga* [assembly] of unruly tribesmen on the frontier, at a fourth he may be demarcating a boundary amid the wilds of Tibet or the sands of Seistan. There is no more varied or responsible service in the world than the Political Department of the Government of India. I commend the Political Department of the Government of India to all who like to know the splendid work of which Englishmen are capable."

Members of the Judicial Department serve as Judges in the districts, and a few of seniority and ability as Judges of the High Courts. It is provided by law that one-third of the High Court Judges should be Civil Servants and one-third barristers, leaving Government free to choose the remaining third from either of these classes or from outside them ; the object is to unite the training and legal knowledge of the barrister with the intimate knowledge of the customs, habits and laws of India possessed by Judges belonging to the Civil Service. The fact that members of the Service are employed in a judicial capacity alone differentiates it from the English Civil Service. Men are asked after they have served a certain number of years whether they desire to serve on the judicial or the executive side and are allotted to one or the other.

Executive officers may serve in the Secretariats of the different provincial Governments or of the Government of India, but the great majority remain in the districts. The Secretaries to the provincial Governments, most of whom have hitherto been members of the Service, occupy a peculiar position, as they have dual functions. They supervise on behalf of Government the different administrative Departments, and in this respect they correspond to permanent Under-Secretaries of State. They are also members of the legislatures, in which they deal with matters affecting their Departments, and in this respect resemble parliamentary Under-Secretaries of State.

The other executive officers are stationed at different places in the interior but cannot be said to be altogether concentrated there, for they are travelling officers and spend a considerable portion of the year going from place to place within their charges, inspecting, holding inquiries, etc. One very important distinction between them and Civil

Servants elsewhere is that they are the local representatives of a Government which is not only the supreme administrative authority, but also the supreme landlord. Its position as such has been inherited from previous Governments. In India the right of the State to a share in the produce of the soil has been recognized from time immemorial. This right takes the form of payment of land revenue, which historically is older than private rent. The land revenue has to be assessed (except where it is permanently settled), and the officers of Government have consequently an intimate connexion with the land and a close concern with matters affecting the cultivators. In some areas also Government is the actual proprietor of estates, which are accordingly known as Government estates. The management of these estates devolves on the local officers, who on behalf of Government discharge the duties of estate agents in regard to them.

The burden of administrative work in the districts is borne by the District Officer, of whose position it is difficult to give an adequate conception to English readers. He is in charge of a district, i.e., an area averaging 4,430 square miles or four and a half times the size of an English administrative county, and he is both District Magistrate and Collector. As District Magistrate he is responsible for the maintenance of law and order, for the prevention of disorder as well as its suppression—one test of a good officer is his capacity for keeping things quiet—for the proper working both of the local police and of the jails; both police and jails are under their own officers, and the District Magistrate exercises only a general supervision over them. He has control over the administration of criminal justice by the subordinate magistracy, and he has appellate powers in minor cases and may himself try a case if it is of special importance or if there are any reasons why the accused should not be tried by a subordinate magistrate. As Collector he is responsible for the collection of the land revenue and other revenues, some of which correspond to what is called inland revenue in Great Britain ; and he has to a greater or less extent to supervise the work of the different executive departments of the civil Government in his district. Authority is concentrated in him, but he is not a super-man and does not therefore deal with the minutiæ of administration, which he leaves to the officers under him ; his part is that of a controlling and directing authority, seeing that others do their duty as well as doing his own.

Milton was once impelled by national pride to say that when God wishes to have some hard thing done, he sends for His Englishman. In India it may more truly be said that when the Government wants a hard bit of work done, it calls on the District Officer. He is the man to whom fall all sorts of miscellaneous jobs, such as the taking of the census, preparing an electoral roll for his district, providing supplies for troops marching through it, etc. He has not only to discharge the everyday duties of administration (many of them dull, petty and uninteresting), but also to cope with sudden emergencies of extraordinary diversity. He may sometimes, when overburdened with work, grumble that he has the life of a dog, but he knows that he has the work of a man.

Murderous riots sometimes break out with little

warning and have to be suppressed by force—a contingency of increasing frequency in late years. The relief of the distressed has to be organized in times of famine, which, on the contrary, are decreasing in frequency owing to the protection afforded by the spread of railways and canals; or disaster may come, sudden and terrible, in the shape of floods and cyclones, when measures of relief have again to be organized: it has been said somewhat cynically that in times of disaster the people expect either God or the Government to come to their rescue. Crises such as these cannot be met by the rule-of-thumb procedure which is ascribed to a routine-ridden bureaucracy, but call for, and bring out, the higher qualities of leadership and resource. The subordinate staff has to be stimulated by personal example, the people have to be made to keep up their courage and vitality. It is this which has led to quiet acts of heroism like that displayed by R. B. Stewart and Martin Wood in the Bombay Presidency. During a cholera epidemic the former buried the corpses of those who had died when the terrified sweepers had fled. The latter, a young officer under him, ate his meals among the sick and dying in hospital in order to put heart into the people, and by force of his example succeeded in staying their panic.

Owing both to the variety of the work which it has to do and to its small numerical strength, the Service is very different from other Civil Services, which consist of different departments, each with a staff of men who are experts in one particular branch of work. Its members are called upon to fill different offices in succession, largely as a result of illness, leave and transfers, e.g., a man may serve as a District Officer, as head of a Department, such as Agriculture, Excise or Police, and as a Secretary to Government; or he may be required to organize and develop new branches of work, such as, in recent years, co-operative credit societies. It has been said in jest that a Civilian should be ready to take on any job from Chief Justice to Bishop. He is not, and does not pretend to be, a specialist in all, but is more of an administrative handy man. There have been failures, but the Civilian, as a rule, has succeeded because of natural ability and acquired training, organizing power and a certain versatility. Want of previous specialist knowledge has been got over by close study ending in practical knowledge, by the assistance of experts, and by the application of Bacon's maxim, "Preserve the rights of inferior places and think it more honour to direct in chief than to be busy in all."

In England the term bureaucracy seems at present to be used most frequently, and with the most unfavourable implications, in connexion with the issue of statutory rules and orders by Government departments. As is well known, it has become customary, owing to the demands on the time of Parliament, for statutes to be confined to the formulation of principles and the creation of the administrative machinery required for their working and to leave matters of detail to rules and regulations to be made by Ministers acting on the advice of their departments. It is complained that these regulations are made in departmental seclusion, that those interested have not sufficient opportunity to examine them with a view to revision before they become valid, and that they interfere unduly with personal matters and encroach on the rights of individuals: a stock example is a rule that everyone must wash his or her hands before milking a cow. In India up to the present there has been nothing of this kind of bureaucracy. The country is not highly industrialized or economically developed like Great Britain. Legislation has neither the same volume nor scope, and the Government there does not extend its activities into the sphere of private interests and personal relationships as it does in England. Moreover, steps are taken to give publicity to, and to secure opinion on, statutory rules before they are finally approved. The practice is not only to publish draft rules in the official Gazette but also to circulate them for criticism. All opinions received are carefully considered and the draft rules are revised, if necessary, to meet valid objections, remove defects, and embody improvements before being issued in a final form.

The legal liability of the Crown in India is a check on bureaucratic action which has no exact parallel in Great Britain. In the latter country an action does not lie against the Crown, and it is only possible for a private person to proceed against it by petition of right. In India, on the other hand, though suits cannot be brought against the Secretary of State for India, as representing the Crown, in respect of acts done in the exercise of sovereign powers, they can be brought in respect of other acts or undertakings. This anomaly is due to the fact that the Crown is the successor of the East India Company, which could be sued as a commercial body, but not in regard to anything done in exercise of the sovereign rights delegated to it by the Crown.[1] Private persons consequently have a right of legal

[1] Sir C. P. Ilbert, *The Government of India* (1915), pp. 196–7.

action against Government which is not yet possessed by the British public. Except where the exercise of sovereign powers is involved, Government may be sued in the same way as a private person by anyone who considers himself aggrieved by its proceedings. In addition to this general liability to legal action, the powers of Government and its officers are regulated by specific provisions of statute law, which are made effective not only by judicial courts and the astute lawyers practising in them rigidly demanding legal warrant for official action, but also by the knowledge which Indians possess of their legal rights and by their readiness to apply to the courts for their enforcement. There is no hesitation about disputing the legality of official acts and about appealing to judicial against executive authority. The latter propensity sometimes manifests itself in unexpected ways. A few years ago, for example, some District Boards in one province directed that the day's work in elementary schools should begin with the scholars singing a seditious song. When the Government prohibited this practice, an appeal was promptly made to the High Court for a reversal of its order. The right of appeal to the judicial courts gives a stimulus to accuracy and circumspection ; an executive officer has to know the law thoroughly and to be careful to keep within it when an indiscretion may result in legal proceedings. A further check on bureaucratic action is afforded by the right of appeal to higher executive authority. Executive proceedings are open to appeal and revision no less than judicial proceedings, and the right is freely exercised.

The checks on bureaucratic action in England are control by Ministers who are responsible for their departments, debates and questions in Parliament, and the force of public opinion. Ministerial control over the Indian Civil Service is, as already shown, limited in extent, but its proceedings are the constant subject of criticism and questions in the Legislative Councils. The right of asking questions about administrative matters seems, indeed, to be exercised more freely than in Great Britain. Members of the legislatures have a thirst for information about the petty details of administration which is embarrassing to busy officers who have to supply the materials for replies. Public opinion is also freely expressed in the newspapers, especially those published in the vernacular, which are eager to detect any shortcomings on the part of Government or its officers and to find grievances against them; indeed, their view often seems to be that any stick is good enough to beat a dog with.

The Indian Civil Service is, in fact, more in the public eye than the English Civil Service, of which, with the exception of the Post Office, little is known outside: the public scarcely knows who are its members or what their duties are. They are regarded as outside politics and, as a rule, are free from attack and hostile criticism, though there may be a general grumble about bureaucratic methods. The Indian Civil Service, however, is very much in the limelight. Its personnel is well known: a Civil List showing its members, their length of service, their appointments and their pay, is published quarterly, and can be bought by anyone. It is exposed to constant criticism, largely no doubt because, having long helped to direct as well as to execute policy, it has been identified with the government of the country. Like the Civil Service in England it is a silent service, and this is a disadvantage in a country where statements are assumed to be true if they are not contradicted, and sometimes even when they are.

It suffers also from a tendency not to give sufficient publicity to the reasons for its actions and to satisfy the public, or that section of the public which is interested, as to their soundness. This attitude of reserve is apt to lead to misunderstanding or lack of appreciation of its motives.

The charges most commonly made against bureaucracies are that they make a fetish of efficiency, that they do not sufficiently realize the importance of measures being acceptable to the people, and that they suffer from rigidity. No one doubts the value of efficiency, especially in India, where, as said by the Simon Commission, government is administration. But there is a danger in pushing efficiency too far. A zealous public servant, unless he has good judgement and common sense to temper his zeal, may harass the people under his care by irritating restrictions and orders which, though lawful, are not expedient; a Civilian, whom no one would accuse of ultra-efficiency, once said that the ultra-efficient ruler causes misery to millions. It is chiefly a question of the personal equation. Some men err in this direction; others, and those the great majority, are too busy doing their work to look for trouble in this way.

The second charge has often been levelled against the Service, and one of its former members, Sir Robert Montgomery of the Punjab, even said in 1871: "In India we set aside the people altogether; we devise and say that such a thing is a good thing to be done and we carry it out without asking them very much about it." It is so far true that, as already stated, the Service is apt to let a good case go by default by not taking the public sufficiently into its confidence; but it would be a mistake to suppose that measures are imposed on the people without their having an opportunity to express their views or without any consideration of them. Sir Robert Montgomery's statement dates back to the days of paternal government, and at the present day there are many channels by which public opinion can be and is expressed, such as the different legislatures, the newspapers and the National Congress; and they are strongly vocal, not to say vociferous. The Governments in India generally are nervous of undertaking new measures unless they are assured of support, though individual instances might be quoted to the contrary, such as the Rowlatt legislation mentioned in a previous chapter. So far from acting without regard to popular sentiment, they are frequently accused, especially in regard to questions of social reform, of not being progressive enough. It is, however, true that individual Civil Servants are apt to think that they know what is good for the people better than the people themselves; and there is this much to be said for their thinking so, that the masses are either inarticulate or incoherent, and their views are often sectarian in character or parochial in scope, while the Civil Servant in India has some right to an independent judgement, as he is disinterested and not affected by the religious, social and economic lines of cleavage, e.g., Hindus and Muhammadans, high and low castes, landlords and tenants.

The third complaint, which is commonly made by

educated Indians, is that administration is becoming too impersonal, that there is a lack of the human touch, in short, that government is becoming dehumanized. This criticism is, I believe, largely due to Indian psychology. The average Indian seems to prefer flexibility to uniformity, and even sometimes, as he has something of the gambler's spirit, chance to security. He certainly does not relish the fact that English administrators adhere to their own standards of conduct, are not susceptible to influences which might, or might seem to, undermine them, and are unwilling to yield to solicitation on questions of principle. It is this which is often the ground for complaints about rigid uniformity: and it is largely the result of India being under the rule of law. The man who administers the law is bound by its provisions and cannot deviate from them. Where an officer can exercise his own discretion, the case is different. An inferior officer may play for safety by slavishly following precedent; he may even be a legal pedant and apply rules without having the intelligence to see when there are exceptions; but a good officer knows when to depart from precedent and when to put the telescope to the blind eye.

Rules and regulations have their value because they are the product of accumulated experience, but their mechanical application is a danger to be guarded against, though it is not always easy to do so, because the staff is so small and the mass of work so great that it is not always possible to make personal inquiry. Under such conditions the principle that the letter killeth and the spirit giveth life may be forgotten. But the varied nature of the work to be done and the new problems constantly arising do much to counteract any tendency to mechanical routine. Personality, as always, is a dominating factor in district work, and great as may be the mass of precedent and prescribed routine, this work calls for the display of such qualities as independence of judgement, self-reliance, resourcefulness and tact. A man who is in charge of the administration of an area with two or three millions of people must constantly be called upon to exercise and rely on his personal judgement and discretion. Nor need he fear undue interference by Government. The last thing Government wishes to do is to intervene unnecessarily in the conduct of local affairs, and so long as the District Officer does his duty efficiently and well, he may rely on its confidence and support.

The Simon Commission has found that official work is more impersonal than it used to be, and this is for many reasons inevitable; but at the same time it has made it clear how strong the personal element still is.

> "The Services," it remarks, "grew up under a regime which permitted, and even fostered, initiative and resource to an extent unknown, and indeed impossible, in the civil service of a concentrated democracy like our own. The isolation of the individual official—the sudden call for personal decision—the special knowledge of local conditions possessed by the officer on the spot—the trust of the mass of the population in the person they know—all these have made civil administration in India depend on the man, rather than on the machine." [1]

Those who have been in a position to observe and judge of the work actually done have borne

[1] Report, Vol. I, paras. 307, 321.

consistent testimony as to its merits and general freedom from the vice of formalism and mechanical routine. Sir Henry Maine declared :

"The 'Indian bureaucracy' is merely a barbarous foreign phrase applied with gross inaccuracy to as remarkable a group of public servants as any country has produced, engaged in administering the affairs of a vast population under perfectly definite and intelligibly stated rules."[1]

Lord Dufferin, Viceroy from 1884 to 1888, wrote to M. Joseph Chailley :

"You ask me to tell you the plain truth regarding the skill, experience, and, in more general terms, the moral worth of the officials of our Indian Civil Service. I reply without hesitation : *There is no Service like it in the world.* For ingenuity, courage, right judgement, disinterested devotion to duty, endurance, open-heartedness, and, at the same time, loyalty to one another and their chiefs, they are, to my knowledge, superior to any other class of Englishmen. They are absolutely free from any taint of venality or corruption. Naturally, they are not of equal worth, and so I am merely speaking of them as a whole. And moreover, if the Indian Civil Service were not what I have described it, how could the government of the country go on so smoothly? We have 250 millions of subjects in India and less than 1,000 British Civilians for the conduct of the entire administration."[2]

M. Chailley, fearing that his French readers might regard English opinions as not disinterested, also cited the enthusiastic remarks made by M. de Hübner, an Austrian, in *Voyage à travers l'Empire*

[1] T. H. Ward, *The Reign of Queen Victoria* (1887), Vol. I, p. 524.

[2] *The Colonization of Indo-China* (1894), p. 261.

britannique, about the miracles of British administration in India.

"To what are these miracles due? They are due to the wisdom and intrepidity of a few leading statesmen, to the bravery and discipline of an army composed of a small number of British and a large number of natives, and led by heroes; lastly, I may say, almost chiefly to the intelligence, the devotion, the courage, the perseverance, the skill, combined with an integrity proof against everything, of the handful of officials and magistrates who govern and administer the whole of India."

To come to more modern times, Lord Bryce wrote in *Modern Democracies* (1921) in the pre-Reform days of "an enlightened, hard-working, disinterested, very small official class ruling a great country"[1]; and Lord Curzon declared: "In India I was magnificently served. The whole spirit of service there was different. Everyone there was out to do something."[2] Lord Morley might, half in jest, gird at Civilians as "over-confident and over-worked Tchinovniks" when he feared they might oppose his policy, but he recognized their "splendid devotion to duty"[3] and declared in the House of Commons, "I have seen what is called the 'sun-dried bureaucrat,' and I have seen that what is meant by that phrase is a man eminent for experience, for knowledge, and for responsibility, faithfully and honourably discharged." The last statement was made in Lord Morley's Indian budget speech of 1906. Two years later it was stated in the proclamation of King Edward VII to the Princes and peoples of India, which was issued to commemorate

[1] Vol. II, p. 595.
[2] Lord Ronaldshay, *Life of Lord Curzon*, Vol. II, pp. 3–4.
[3] Lord Morley, *Recollections* (1918), Vol. II, p. 265.

the fiftieth anniversary of the assumption of the government of India by the Crown and which was intended to be a manifesto not only to India but to the whole world :

> "Difficulties such as attend all human rule in every age and place have risen up from day to day. They have been faced by the servants of the British Crown with toil and courage and patience, with deep counsel, and a resolution that has never faltered nor shaken. If errors have occurred, the agents of my Government have spared no pains and no self-sacrifice to correct them : if abuses have been proved, vigorous hands have laboured to apply a remedy."

These words have all the greater value, both because they admit the possibility of mistakes and their correction in no hide-bound spirit, and also because they apply generally to the public services, which, in the considered judgement of the Joint Select Committee of Parliament on the Government of India Bill of 1919, "have deserved the admiration and gratitude of the whole Empire."

Of more particular application to the Civil Service is the opinion expressed by Lord Sydenham of Combe, who was Governor of Bombay from 1907 to 1913 :

> "Of the hide-bound bureaucracy which voluble politicians professed to discover I found scarcely a trace. For five or six months in each year the District Officers toured throughout their areas inquiring into grievances, settling disputes, and assimilating the lore of the countryside. Nowhere was the contact between the cultivators and the administration more close than in Bombay in my time. All Secretariats tend towards bureaucracy ; but this—in India—could be prevented by constantly bringing in new blood from the districts, which I was

careful to arrange. There are no officials in the world less bureaucratic than the Indian Civil Servants where this provision is insisted upon."[1]

It would be easy, but it is neither necessary nor desirable, to add to these eulogies: the story of Aristides has its moral. For their part members of the Service are fully conscious of the fact that their work depends on the co-operation of other public services, which are also inspired by a spirit of devotion both to duty and to the welfare of the people of India. This spirit cannot be expressed better than in the words once used by Sir George Grierson, a retired and honoured member of the Civil Service.

"How can I help India? This is a question which we Westerners who have gone to India in the service of His Majesty have each in his own way done our best to answer. Among us have been great administrators, great soldiers, great scholars, great teachers, masters of the healing art. There have been diversities of gifts but the same spirit—a spirit of devotion to duty and of sympathy with the millions among whom our lot was cast."

---

[1] *My Working Life* (1927), p. 229.

CHAPTER VIII

THE SERVICE AND THE PEOPLE

"I mourn the rule the Magistrate of yore,
A fostering despot, o'er his people bore:
He reigned supreme within his little State,
His smile shed honour, and his frown was fate.
Prompt with the rifle, niggard of the pen,
By manly deeds he won the hearts of men.
Friend of the people, in their midst he moved,
To all familiar and by all beloved." [1]

IN these words a Bengal Civilian, Thomas Francis Bignold, depicted the life of an early Civil Servant, who fulfilled the traditional Indian ideal of being the "father and mother" of the people and the "cherisher of the poor." It was not an imaginative picture. The account of his work given by Thomas Twining, who served in India at the end of the eighteenth and the beginning of the nineteenth centuries, shows clearly enough that the description of the "fostering despot" was true to life.

"I moved about with the parade and display of former times, being accompanied with a large number of attendants, civil and military. Wherever I encamped I held a court; received the homage of the principal inhabitants; the petitions and complaints of all; granted redress; distributed pensions; ordered the execution of public works, and the formation of villages for the recep-

[1] *Leviora*, a collection of poems published at Calcutta in 1888.

tion of retired sepoys from our army, whom Lord Wellesley had been pleased to place under my protection." [1]

Owing to poor communications and the heavy expenses of voyages, men spent long periods of service in India, extending to forty, fifty or even sixty years, with few interruptions for leave. William Augustus Brooke, who joined the Company's Civil Service in 1769, served continuously for sixty-four years, dying at Benares in 1833. As Collector of Shahabad in 1789 he forcibly prevented a suttee, this being the first recorded case of such action on the part of a Civil Servant, and it was said in 1794 that he "seemed to have the state and authority of a prince, while the name of the Governor-General was scarcely known, and his power scarcely felt, in these distant parts." [2] His obituary notice in *The Gentleman's Magazine* of May, 1834, described him as "one of the few instances of that complete alienation or expropriation of mind and indifference to their native country which have sometimes appeared in persons long resident in India." Jonathan Duncan, whose service ran to thirty-nine years, was similarly said to have been Brahmanized by long residence in India. It is not surprising that men became habituated to Indian manners and customs, religious as well as social. Government, moreover, did not stand altogether aloof in matters of religion. In 1811, for example, the Board of Revenue in Madras moved Government to sanction the expenditure by a Collector of 150 pagodas on Hindu

[1] Thomas Twining, *Travels in India a Hundred Years Ago* (1893), p. 520.

[2] Article on Suttee in *Calcutta Review* of 1867 (in which his initials are incorrectly given) and Twining's *Travels*, p. 141.

ceremonies, which were performed in order to bring down rain.[1] The Serampore missionary Ward in 1802 mentioned the fact that in Calcutta

"a deputation from Government went in procession to Kalee Ghaut—the most opulent and popular shrine of the metropolis—and presented 5,000 rupees to the idol in the name of the Company for the success which had attended the British arms."[2]

Gifts were made by individual members of the Civil Service to Hindu temples: a bell may still be seen in the Vishnupad temple at Gaya with an inscription showing that it was presented by Francis Gillanders, the local Collector of the pilgrim tax; a pair of golden stirrups given by Peter Rous, Collector of Madura from 1812 to 1828, is treasured at the Madura temple[3]; a Vaishnavite shrine in Conjeeveram contains jewels which were presented by a Collector, Place, who induced Government in 1796 to take over its administration. In 1806 an Act was passed enabling Government to assume the control of the famous Jagannath temple at Puri, and in 1833 the Madras Government was responsible for the administration of 7,600 Hindu shrines.[4] Officers of the Civil Service were accordingly in the anomalous position of being in control of Hindu temples, though their action was limited by the Directors' orders to the protection of pilgrims, the preservation of the public peace, and the collection of the

[1] W. Hamilton, *Hindostan*, Vol. II, p. 342.

[2] J. C. Marshman, *The Story of Carey, Marshman and Ward, the Serampore Missionaries* (1864), pp. 74–5.

[3] J. C. Molony, *A Book of South India* (1926), p. 228.

[4] A. Mayhew, *Christianity and the Government of India* (1929), p. 150.

pilgrim tax, the proceeds of which were devoted to temple repairs and provision for the comfort of pilgrims, so that the Company was described as being "the Churchwarden of the idol." Objections were raised to this system as giving State sanction to idolatry, and eventually the Directors sent out orders in 1833 that the servants of the Company should cease to take any part either in the management of temples or in religious ceremonies and festivals, while the pilgrim tax was to be abolished—a change legally sanctioned by an Act passed in 1840. Instructions were also issued that no troops or military bands of music should be called out, nor salutes fired, in honour of Indian festivals (e.g., among other things a military salute was fired to announce the appearance of new moon which ushers in the Muhammadan fast of Ramzan),[1] but these orders were not passed until after Sir Peregrine Maitland, Commander-in-Chief of the Madras Army, had resigned his command (in 1838) by way of protest against the troops assisting in Hindu celebrations.

In the early days of British administration a problem of a peculiar nature was the pacification and civilization of aboriginal tribes. Among the first of these tribes with whom British officers came into contact was the wild race known as the Sauria Paharias of the Rajmahal Hills, who had an evil reputation as marauding savages. The Muhammadan Government treated such races as Ishmaelites, and the Sauria Paharias were shot down like dogs. Their pacification was finally effected by Augustus Clevland (often wrongly written as

[1] A. Mayhew, *Christianity and the Government of India* (1929), p. 147.

Cleveland), a young officer of the Civil Service, who died in 1784 at the early age of twenty-nine. The work done by him in the preceding six years is commemorated by the inscription on his tomb, erected by Warren Hastings and his Council, which tells how Clevland

"without bloodshed or the terror of authority, employing only the means of conciliation, confidence and benevolence, attempted and accomplished the entire subjection of the lawless and savage inhabitants of the Jungleterry [Jungle Tarai] of Rajamahall, who had long infested the neighbouring lands by their predatory incursions, inspired them with a taste for the arts of civilized life and attached them to the British Government by a conquest over their minds—the most permanent as the most rational mode of dominion."

The secret of his success was simply that he conciliated and won the confidence of a wild people. He went among them unarmed, presided at their tribal feasts, respected and preserved the authority of their chiefs, encouraged agriculture and started markets for the sale of their produce. Clevland has accordingly been generally, and also officially, credited with being the originator of the policy of making aboriginal tribes the agents of their own civilization and of turning their spears into ploughshares by moral suasion rather than by force. The Directors of the East India Company in 1836, referring to the efficacy of conciliatory methods in reducing uncivilized and predatory tribes to order and obedience, said that this wise and beneficient policy was first adopted by Clevland. The memorial of the East India Company submitted in 1858 also stated that he was the first person who was known to have tried the effect of justice and conciliation on any of the hill tribes and recorded the interesting fact that the feelings which he left behind among the ruder people of the district were such, that they long continued to pay religious honours to his tomb. In justice, however, to others it should be recorded that a similar policy had been followed, before Clevland, by two military officers, Captain Brooke and Captain Browne, with such success that in 1774 Warren Hastings wrote that the country of the Sauria Paharias, which had only served as a receptacle for robbers, had been reduced to government and its inhabitants civilized.

It is unnecessary to dilate on the civilizing work done among other aboriginal tribes, e.g., in Assam, Chota Nagpur, the Central Provinces and Bombay, and on the humane services rendered not only by Civilians, but also by military officers, such as Outram among the Bhils, General Hall among the Mhairs, Major S. C. Macpherson and Sir John Campbell among the Khonds : to the last two is due the credit of putting an end to the barbarous practices of human sacrifice and female infanticide which were customary among the Khonds. Equally savage was the practice of headhunting among the Nagas of Assam : in reviewing the results of the census of 1921 the Government of Assam stated that in the Hills it is not so long since head-hunting was considered to be the only proper occupation of man, and that the country at the foot of the hills suffered too much from the raids of the neighbouring hill tribes to be inviting places of residence. Three Civilians in Assam have lost their lives in dealing with its races. Mr. Damant was killed by the

Nagas in 1879 with thirty-five men of his escort. In 1891 Mr. Quinton, the Chief Commissioner, and four other officers were treacherously put to death in the State of Manipur—a ghastly tragedy, for all five were beheaded by the public executioner. In 1911 Mr. Williamson, Assistant Political Officer at Sadiya, was murdered by the Abors together with Dr. Gregorson, who was accompanying him, and forty-two followers.

In our relations with the aboriginal tribes mistakes have undoubtedly been made. In a few cases it was not realized that they were being oppressed by Hindu and Muhammadan outsiders until they had been goaded into rebellion in the hope of preserving their traditional rights. Thus, in 1831 the Mundas and Hos of Chota Nagpur rose in a revolt called the Kol Rebellion, because their villages had got into the hands of alien lessees in supersession of the tribal headmen, and the Santal War of 1854 was caused by the oppression of the Santals both by landlords and moneylenders. Mistakes of this kind were, however, remedied, and the whole history of our relations with aboriginal tribes is one of legislative and other measures designed for their protection against more civilized neighbours.

It is necessary now to turn from this fringe of barbarism to the more highly developed races which inhabit the greater part of British India. Here the Service has shown constant sympathy with, and solicitous care for, what may be called the under-dog, such as the tenantry oppressed by their landlords. Agrarian legislation and executive proceedings have done much for the uplift of the tenantry, often a depressed class like that of Bihar, which was described in 1878 as "poor, helpless, discontented, bound down to a state of extreme depression and misery, the poorest and most wretched class we find in the country, entirely at the mercy of their landlords." No one at the present time would describe them in these terms, for they, as well as cultivators elsewhere, have been given what in Ireland are called the Three F's, i.e., fair rents, fixity of tenure, and freedom of sale (of landed rights). This protective attitude towards the cultivating classes has had its drawbacks, for the idea that Service is their representative in the councils of Government has tended to alienate the powerful landlord class. Protection from the exactions of money-lenders has been no less necessary in many parts and has been afforded by specific measures like the Land Improvement and Agriculturists' Loans Acts, the Deccan Agriculturists' Relief Acts and the Punjab Land Alienation Act, as well as by the co-operative credit system.

Active work for and among the villagers (who form nine-tenths of the whole population) has endeared to them many members of the Service, such as Sir Frederick Lely, who joined the Service in 1869 and retired in 1905 after thirty-six years' service, mostly in Bombay and partly in the Central Provinces, of which he was Chief Commissioner. His work in Gujarat is commemorated by a jingle "Lely, Lely, *raish no beli*," i.e., "Lely the protector of the people," and a charming story, told by Sir Evan Maconochie, shows how he deserved the name. A missionary who was preaching in Porbandar, where Lely had served twenty years previously, described the life of Christ, how he went about doing good and was always ready to help those who were in need. An old villager came up after the missionary had ceased to mention the name of Christ. He listened with keen interest and before long his face lit up. He knew who the "He" was, and kept nodding his head and saying "Lely, Lely, Lely."[1]

Similar fame was attained by Colonel L. J. H. Grey, a Military Civilian, who in 1874–6, when Deputy Commissioner of Firozpur in the Punjab, created a system of canals (now merged in the Sutlej Valley system), which were called the Grey Canals after him. This was a remarkable achievement. Colonel (then Captain) Grey had no funds nor expert staff beyond two surveyors lent by the Bahawalpur State, where he had already started an irrigation system; but he succeeded in getting thirteen canals constructed, and over a quarter of a million acres irrigated, without Government having to spend a penny. He succeeded by reason of his influence with the people of the district, whom he induced to work on a co-operative system operating on a huge scale. The canals were designed by Colonel Grey; the work, including vast excavation and the construction of dams and embankments, sluices and aqueducts, was carried out by the people, whom he taught and supervised. It meant immense labour for Colonel Grey and his Assistant, Mr. H. C. Fanshawe of the Indian Civil Service (afterwards Commissioner of Delhi), for, in addition to ordinary revenue and judicial duties, they themselves worked with chain and tape, teaching an improvised staff how to survey, superintended the actual work of construction, and toiled with the people in the repair of

[1] *Life in the Indian Civil Service* (1926), pp. 243–4.

breaches made by floods—on one occasion for eighteen hours on end. Colonel Grey had his reward in the gratitude of the people, as well as in the knowledge that he had spread plenty over a smiling land. The Jats of Firozpur claimed him as one of themselves, saying that he

> "must have been one of our ancestors in his former life, and must have suffered a great deal from want of water in the old days, when he was a Jat; so, after his death he thought of doing good to his children, and was therefore born this time in the house of a Sahib, and at last came to this land again and has done all this for our generation; otherwise why should a Sahib take all this trouble?" [1]

Till at least thirty years afterwards his praises were sung in popular songs with the refrain "All praise to Grey Sahib. Never will there be another like him." [2]

Men who have been in India can name others of this type, men who devoted their lives and, in many cases, sacrificed their health to the country, who were personally attached to the people among whom their work lay, and who laboured wholeheartedly for their welfare. Not all have been personally popular. Popularity, like success, cannot be commanded, though it may be deserved, and it is perhaps the exception rather than the rule to obtain it in administrative work; but it may fairly be stated that members of the Service have generally commanded not only respect, but also a certain admiration. The attitude of the

[1] G. R. Elsmie, *Thirty-five Years in the Punjab* (1908), p. 285.

[2] F. and C. Grey, *Tales of Our Grandfather* (1912), pp. 218–33, 240–3.

people to those who have been least popular has been compared, not unaptly, to that of the schoolboy who is said to have described William Temple, the Head Master of Rugby, as "a beast, but a just beast."

It has not been possible to intervene in regard to the caste system, which is a matter for the Hindus themselves, beyond securing for the low castes equality of legal status and equality of opportunity in Government service. Nor has it been possible to be very progressive in questions of social reform. Politicians and advanced thinkers in India have made it a reproach against Government that it has been slow to tackle thorny problems of this nature, but caution has been dictated by the feeling that reform should come from within and not be imposed from without. It has been a fixed principle that, where the personal laws and customs of the people are concerned, legislation should be in response to and not in advance of public feeling, and there has been unwillingness to place on the Statute Book measures which without the co-operation of the people themselves would remain a dead letter. Eyewash is abhorred by the British administrators in India, who are trained on the principle that it is no use passing an order unless one knows, or can ensure, that it will be carried out. Many Indians, on the other hand, have a predilection for paper schemes and often seem to adopt an attitude like that of Koko in *The Mikado*. It will be remembered that Koko says to the Mikado, "It's like this, when your Majesty says 'Let a thing be done,' it's as good as done. Practically, it *is* done because your Majesty's will is law." This cautious policy has been justified by recent experience in connection with the Sarda Act prohibiting the marriage of girls under fourteen and of youths under eighteen years of age. Government was blamed for delay in its enactment; when it was enacted, it was used as a weapon with which to attack Government. The frontier tribes were incited by misrepresentations about its objects to attack Peshawar, and already there seems a prospect of the Act becoming a dead letter.

Since the British connexion with India began there has been extreme reluctance to do anything which might be possibly construed as an interference with religious beliefs or customs based on them, except in regard to practices abhorrent to humanity, such as suttee, female infanticide and human sacrifice. These have been stopped by legislation, in advance of which individual efforts were made without recourse to legal powers. Before the Regulation for its suppression was passed, suttee was stopped in one district of Bengal by the Magistrate, Mr. Pigou, without any public remonstrance. When he followed the same course in another district, his humane zeal had to be checked because it went beyond the law. At Delhi also Sir Charles Metcalfe never permitted a suttee to be performed.[1] In the States of Kathiawar female infanticide was stopped by the politic measures of Sir J. P. Willoughby, who was Political Agent there from 1831 to 1835. He rewarded those who preserved the lives of their infant daughters, fined those who did not, and credited the fines to a fund called the "Infanticide Fund," from which dowries were

[1] A. B. Keith, *Speeches and Documents on Indian Policy* (1922), Vol. I, p. 217.

assigned to brides in need of them. By tact alone Mr. Colvin, Magistrate at Allahabad, stopped a curious custom of self-immolation. Every year a Hindu *sadhu* announced that he would throw himself into the Ganges with a stone tied round his neck and another round his feet; such self-sacrifice was regarded as a highly meritorious act ensuring his bliss hereafter. Hindus used to gather to witness the act of self-sacrifice in such vast crowds that many were crushed to death. Mr. Colvin issued an order explaining that he did not desire to interfere with the people's religion, but in future anyone who wished to drown himself must first send in his name to the Magistrate, who would command the people to remain in their houses so that the man might be able to drown himself undisturbed. The ceremony ceased as soon as it was deprived of publicity.

The fact that the Service has until recent years consisted almost entirely of British officers having neither language nor religion nor customs in common with the people of India has admittedly made it slow to intervene in religious and social matters. On the other hand, the very consciousness of being aliens has had its counterbalancing advantages. It is a general principle that members of the Service should not drive the people, but lead them with their own free will and consent. Studious respect, almost tenderness, is consequently shown for the beliefs and susceptibilities of the people under their care, as may be seen from two instances. The first is a personal experience of Mr. Grant Brown which he relates in his book *Burma as I Saw It*. In 1907, when he was in charge of a district, the Civil Surgeon, who was an Arakanese, died. His wife came and told Mr. Grant Brown that the ghost of her husband was haunting the hospital and disturbing the patients, because he had not been given an order of discharge from Government service; his spirit, therefore, as in life, frequented the hospital. She begged Mr. Grant Brown to sign an order of discharge. This he did, and the ghost was laid. The other instance is of more recent date, for it is connected with an anti-malarial campaign undertaken in the city of Bombay in 1928. Certain private wells were found to be breeding-places of malaria-bearing mosquitoes, and proposals to cover them over were opposed on religious grounds. These had to be met in various ways, e.g., by providing brass taps without leather, rubber, or other materials objectionable to Hindus, and by plate-glass tops to meet the scruples of Parsees who desired that the water should be open to the sun's rays. Others objected that covers over the wells would prevent the passage of spirits in and out of them, and this difficulty was met by brass plates with holes in them not more than one-twentieth of an inch in diameter.

Sir Charles Aitchison, describing the early days of his service in the Punjab, wrote in 1892:

> "Looking back at them after an interval of five-and-thirty years, I seem still to have a sort of feeling of ubiquity. A good stable was an essential equipment. If in the remotest corner of the District there occurred a cow-riot or an affray or a murder or a big burglary, the Deputy Commissioner or an Assistant had to be on the spot. If cholera broke out, every village affected had to be visited. No remission of revenue was ever granted without a personal inspection of the land and

the crops. Nothing that affected the welfare of the District or the contentment of the people was too insignificant for personal attention. It was an unwritten law that the Civil Officers should see things with their own eyes, do things with their own hands, and inquire into things for themselves. Thus they came to know the people, the people learned to know them, and a grip was got on the country which the Mutiny of 1857 did not loosen." [1]

This is a description of paternal rule in a province where districts were adequately staffed and personal activity was not trammelled by the ties of judicial and other sedentary work. The time to which it refers was the pre-railway period, and the Punjab was particularly a province where activity was a *sine qua non.* It is said that John Lawrence disliked having young married officers because of their encumbrances. They were accompanied, he said, by a wife, a baby and a

[1] *Lord Lawrence* (1897), pp. 62–3. It was not always possible to keep up to this standard. Colonel Grey, himself a Punjab officer who never spared himself, wrote : " ' Listen to every one ' was the order of the John Lawrence days in the Punjab—an order which broke down those who were not as tough as our famous John. . . . I remember, in 1860, seeing a District Officer start for his office, only a few hundred yards from his house. He never got there. First one old woman, then some importunate man, then this, then that. How about the suitors who were waiting in his court ? " F. and C. Grey, *Tales of Our Grandfather* (1912), pp. 301–2. Mr. G. R. Elsmie, again, when Deputy Commissioner of Jullundur in 1866, said that he was beginning to agree with Sir Douglas Forsyth that " the Punjab system of overwork is a great mistake " and to vote it " a miserable economic dodge." His despondency, he wrote later, was the result of " a state of things which in those days used sometimes to produce what was called ' a Punjab head.' " —*Thirty-five Years in the Punjab* (1908), p. 118.

piano: and they were transferred from place to place, with the result that first the piano went, then the baby was sent away, and last the wife went also, and a mobile officer remained. A good rider with a good stable had not only a wide sphere of action, but also an extraordinary influence, as no one knew when or where he might turn up. One such was Sir George Clerk, whose powers of horsemanship earned him a singular reputation among the Sikhs. They believed that he had 100 horses and that some of them were always posted in relays in different parts of the country, so that he might be in their midst before they could hear of his having left headquarters; and the actual news that his horses had been sent out prevented many a fight.

Horses were still relied on for locomotion even after railways were introduced, because most villages are remote from the railway and a large proportion from the roads as well. The system of *dāks*, i.e., of relays of horses or ponies to enable long journeys to be made, was general when the writer first went to India and for many years afterwards: as much as seventy miles could be covered in the day in this way. In time the horse was supplemented by the bicycle, and greater mobility gained by the combined use of both; and we are now in the age of mechanization when motor-cars are extensively used in districts with a good system of roads; in water districts, like those in Eastern Bengal, their place is taken by steamers and boats. The great mobility afforded by the motor has, however, its defects, for touring is apt to become a series of rapid excursions instead of the former more leisurely progress from camp to camp and from village to village, which enables the villagers to meet and talk with their District Officer. Rapid excursions are of use for surprise inspections, but an officer who habitually rushes over his district, like the Red Queen over the chess-board in *Alice Through the Looking-Glass*, can see little of village life. Horses are as necessary as ever to reach the villages, and riding is still a compulsory subject which probationers have to pass before they can enter the Service—a test which incidentally differentiates it from a sedentary Civil Service.

Touring in the districts has been closely affected by the increase of office work and the growing pressure of official duties without the relief which might be afforded by a larger cadre or by devolution. It must not be imagined that office work is a plant of recent growth. Over sixty years ago an English writer roundly declared that what is known as "duftur," i.e., office work, was the curse of India, while an Indian writer observed quaintly and simply:

> "The Commissioners, Deputy Commissioners and Collectors are chiefly for protecting the people. If these officers are engaged in writing proceedings, etc., they will not have time to know personally the state of the ryot. Such officers, therefore, should have less business of writing proceedings, etc. By this means they will have time to speak with the ryots and know their intentions and wishes." [1]

The amount of work at that time was, however, small compared with what it became later. Not only can less time be spared than formerly for

[1] Hon. T. J. Hovell-Thurlow, *The Company and the Crown* (1867), pp. 94–5.

lengthy tours in leisurely contact with the people in the villages; but there may be pressure of work in camp tents as well as in the office room. Files follow a touring officer from camp to camp, so that at each remove he drags a lengthening chain. A story told by an ex-sepoy gives a naïve account of a day spent by an overworked officer in camp.

"He arrived with his attendants. He went into his tent. He immediately began to write. He went on writing. We thought he had got very urgent business to do. We went away. We arrived in the morning soon after dawn. He was still writing or had begun again; and so concerned was he, both in the evening and in the morning, with his writing that we really had nothing from him but a polite salaam." "This," he said justly, "is an odd state of things." [1]

This cannot be regarded as a normal case: indeed, it is most probable that the officer in question had gone into camp for a few days so as to be free from the routine work of headquarters and clear off arrears or write some important report without interruption.

There has been a certain amount of exaggeration about the reduced amount of time available for touring with its opportunities for contact with village life; and it is not generally known that a minimum number of days to be spent on tour is prescribed for each District Officer; in the provinces with which I am acquainted it is ninety days in small and 120 days in large districts, which, after all, amount to one-fourth and one-third

[1] Quoted in a speech of Lord Morley to the Indian Civil Service Probationers at Oxford, 12 June, 1909.

respectively of the year. The District Officers themselves are anxious to be on tour as much as possible, for they know that this is the only way to get into touch with the villagers and to get first-hand knowledge of their needs. It has been said that when he is a witness in the law courts, no villager seems to be able to tell the truth, but that in his own village he seems to be unable to tell an untruth, for everyone knows his neighbours' affairs and a lie is greeted with derision; an exception must be made of communal and religious matters, e.g., when tenants combine against landlords or Hindus are at feud with Muhammadans.

The value of personal visits cannot be exaggerated, for they serve as a tonic to the District Officer by substituting favourable impressions for the unfavourable views he may derive from work at headquarters, and they are highly appreciated by the villager, who has a prepossession for personal government. He wants to see and talk to the representative of Government, and to know that he is actually heard; he suspects that a written petition may never reach the District Officer for whom it is intended; and the pen in any case is a poor substitute for personal access. There are also the good fellowship and *camaraderie* of sport, in which the villagers and local land-holders are glad to join; sport has also a practical use, for the man who kills the tigers or leopards that prey on the cattle, or the wild pigs that destroy the crops, is a public benefactor. District Officers are fully alive to their opportunities in this direction, and even in modern times the Service has had its Nimrods, such as the late Colonel Faunthorpe, who on one occasion when out pig-sticking speared a full-grown leopard, and Sir Charles Cleveland, a man of great strength, who when attacked by a wounded panther swung it round and round till his shikari came to the rescue. The real difficulty is that there are so few men and the areas to be covered are often so vast. The Bengal District Administration Committee found in 1913 that in eight districts there were only thirty-nine Indian Civil Servants, of whom nine were young officers without full magisterial and executive powers. This left only thirty competent officers for an area of 28,000 square miles and a population of 15½ millions, with poor communications, 1,000 square miles being occupied by rivers and swamps.

"The people," said a non-official to the Committee, "don't see enough of Englishmen. They don't see enough of the District Magistrate or of the Superintendent of Police. When they do so, and know them, and are on pleasant terms with them (and pleasant terms can only come from seeing and knowing), all goes well."

Still, the old contact with the villager is maintained, though it is not as close as it used to be. According to the Simon Commission, official work has become more impersonal and

"the probability of long service in a district with the intimate knowledge and personal friendship with men of all classes which it brings, is much less to-day than before," but "it is not generally true that the attitude of the villager has changed or that the satisfaction which comes from close and continuous association with him and his daily cares and interests is now denied to the British official." [1]

---

[1] Report, para. 321.

During recent years political propaganda has infected even the villagers with racial bitterness, but when the waves of passion subside, genial relations are soon re-established. Even in the unrest of 1930 there was a pleasing example of this in the Satara district of Bombay. There some thousands of villagers, deluded by reports that the British Raj was at an end, rebelled against the forest laws, defied authority, and consequently came into conflict with the police. When the little outbreak died out, the District Officer held a *durbar* at which he addressed the people, and the day ended with sports in which the police and villagers took part—a truly idyllic scene.

I think that, so far as it is possible to generalize, it may fairly be stated that the Service has never been in such sympathy with the educated classes as with the simple villagers. The evidence of a thoughtful Indian, Sir Saiyid Ahmad, on the relations between the two is of particular value as showing what were the feelings of Indians at the time when the Company's rule came to an end. In 1858, while admitting the good qualities of some British officials, he deplored the attitude of others. There were many, he said, who were well known for their kindness and friendly feeling towards Indians. "These are in consequence much beloved by them, are, to use a native expression, as the sun and moon to them, and are pointed out as types of the old race of officials." [1]

[1] If Sir Richard Temple's experience may be taken as typical, friendliness and sympathy were inculcated from the outset of a Civilian's career under the Company. In 1847, before leaving for India, he and other men of his year went to the East India House for a formal leave-taking and

On the other hand, he thought that there was a general tendency to treat Indians with contempt and a want of good feeling on their part towards officials. The root cause was, he considered, that there was

"no real communication between the governors and the governed, no living together or near one another, as has always been the custom of the Muhammadans in countries which they have subjected to their rule. Government and its officials have never adopted this course, without which no real knowledge of the people can be gained." [1]

It is interesting to note the eulogy of the old type of official. Year after year the same thing goes on, the old type being praised and held up as an example; and one is inclined to suspect that one generation of officials is much the same as another.

The Mutiny, with the atrocities committed on the one side and stern, sometimes ruthless, repression on the other, left bitter memories which did much to estrange the two races. The Civil Service, however, was free from the racial animosity displayed at that time by non-official Europeans and kept the scales of justice even, particularly in protecting cultivators in Bengal against rack-renting by European planters: Lord Canning

were entreated by one of the Directors "to think kindly, even fraternally, regarding the natives of India"; and his first District Officer strove to make his Assistants "care personally for the natives, guard their interests, and enter into their troubles and anxieties." Sir R. Temple, *Men and Events of My Time in India* (1882), pp. 19, 34.

[1] See Sir Verney Lovett, *History of the Indian Nationalist Movement* (1921), p. 40.

said that the situation there in 1860 caused him, for about a week, more anxiety than he had since the fall of Delhi during the Mutiny. On account of its attitude the Service was exposed to odium in European circles: equity and fair dealing were sneered at as "the principles and maxims of civilianism." [1]

Within a few years after the Mutiny kindly relations between the Service and the Indian upper classes were resumed. Although they did not have the advantage of family connexions with India possessed by many of the Haileybury men, the new class of Civilian recruited by competition brought to India a spirit of goodwill and broad-mindedness. Recalling the early days of his service, Mr. C. J. O'Donnell, a Bengal Civilian, who began his service in 1872, remarked:

> "When I went to India first, I was much struck by the sincere friendliness that existed between Indian gentlemen of position and the European servants of the Crown. They often went out shooting together, and the Magistrate and the Judge were frequent visitors at the houses of the gentry during native and religious festivals. Intercourse was, in fact, as intimate as widely differing domestic customs would allow." [2]

The spirit of understanding and goodwill was clouded over for a time by an outbreak of racial passion over the Ilbert Bill of 1883, which was designed to remove a judicial disability under which Indian members of the Service lay. Outside the Presidency towns none but judicial officers

[1] Sir G. O. Trevelyan, *Letters from a Competition Wallah*, Letters V and IX.

[2] *The Cause of the Present Discontents in India* (1908), p. 115.

who were both Justices of the Peace and European British subjects could try criminal cases brought against European British subjects. Indian Judges and Magistrates had no jurisdiction in such cases, though in the Presidency towns Indian Presidency Magistrates had such jurisdiction and exercised it without objection or complaint. Attention was drawn to this anomaly by Mr. Bihari Lal Gupta, who was at the time a Presidency Magistrate in Calcutta; and in 1883 the Government of India brought in a Bill (named the Ilbert Bill after its mover Mr. (afterwards Sir) Courtenay Ilbert, then Legal Member of the Government of India) not only conferring jurisdiction in such cases on all District Magistrates and Sessions Judges by virtue of their office, but also empowering local Governments to confer similar powers on any officer of the Indian Civil Service, Statutory Civil Service and Non-Regulation Commissions who was already exercising first-class magisterial powers.

The Bill gave rise to a furious and totally unexpected agitation on the part of the European community, which aroused an antagonism between it and the educated Indian community such as had not been known since the Mutiny. The cry was raised that liability to trial before Indian Magistrates was a danger to European women in remote districts; the Bill was fiercely denounced on the platform and in the Press; a body called the Anglo-Indian and European Defence Association was formed. Lord Ripon's Government was taken by surprise and bowed to the storm. It compromised by withdrawing its original proposals and substituting provisions, which were passed into law, that European British subjects when brought for trial before a District Magistrate or Sessions Judge, whether British or Indian, should have a right to claim trial by jury. They were thus given the same judicial security as in Great Britain, and the judicial disability of Indian officers serving as District Magistrates or Sessions Judges (but not that of officers of lower rank) was got over by placing them on the same footing as British officers of the same status.[1]

This agitation created bad feeling and did much to estrange Indians from Europeans, more especially in Bengal. In the words of Sir Ashley Eden, then Lieutenant-Governor of Bengal, it

> "excited a fiercer and more perilous conflict of races than was witnessed after the Mutiny of 1857. And so the work of twenty-six years, in which every true Englishman and native has welcomed the growth of a stronger mutual regard and toleration for each other, and in which a spirit of charity and forbearance was winning its way to a better understanding of each other's wants, has to be begun over again."

The bitter feelings which it aroused gradually died down, however, as the result of time and the good sense of the two communities. A leading Calcutta newspaper, *The Englishman*, remarked in July, 1906, that it was extraordinary how amicable the relations between Europeans and the educated class of Bengalis had become. "The spirit of friendliness," it declared, "is growing and its trend is toward that happy sympathy which

[1] See L. Wolf, *Life of the First Marquess of Ripon* (1921), Vol. II, pp. 118–50. In 1923 a Bill, generally called the Racial Distinctions Bill, was passed into law, with scarcely a dissentient voice, which removed the more important distinctions between the trials of Europeans and Indians.

should, and does in many cases, exist between men of different races."

Since then there has been a change. There has been a surge of nationalist feeling, which increased in volume and strength after the victory of Japan in the Russo-Japanese War created the impression that an eastern David could hold his own, and more, against a western Goliath. It has been accompanied by an antagonism to western influences, and some of the educated classes appear to have been affected by a struggle against what is nowadays called the inferiority complex, which at times has manifested itself in an extreme sensitiveness and a certain aggressiveness; a symptom is the way in which the song *Bande Mataram*, which is a pæan of national pride, is sometimes sung as if it were a hymn of hate. Great mischief has also been done by a section of the vernacular Press, which has long endeavoured to create hostility towards the Government and its officers. Many vernacular papers have for the last half-century carried on a vendetta against them, no incident being too trivial to be twisted into a grievance. It is difficult for persons accustomed to the restraint and sobriety of the English Press to realize the irresponsibility of some Indian newspapers, but some idea of their malicious mendacity may be gathered from a recent case. A railway accident occurred near Calcutta in which twenty-two persons met their death. A Calcutta newspaper published a letter purporting to come from a passenger in the train, who declared that over 300 persons had been killed, of whom half could have been saved but were bludgeoned to death by British railway employés. To give verisimilitude to this monstrous statement, he wrote : " The wounded were searched for and killed—mind you, killed—not saved. When a cry rose, a Sahib came with a light, and somebody delivered a blow, and the Indian spoke no more." Needless to say, heavy damages for libel were awarded against the paper in question, but in the meantime the lie had spread among a credulous people.

The campaign of calumny, designed to produce racial hatred against the British, is the work of a small minority with little stake in the country, which is not in any way representative of the people. But its organization, virulence and persistence, together with the ignorance of the masses, make it formidable. Its subversive efforts have been continued for two generations, and their cumulative effect is obvious. In the Administration Report for 1928 issued by the Bengal Government it was stated :

> " The evil results of a campaign of persistent vilification on an ill-balanced community have already manifested themselves in ugly and ominous forms, and the reputation and prestige of the official classes and of Government have been seriously undermined by the unending repetition of falsehood."

The present Viceroy, Lord Irwin, also said in 1929, in an address to the Indian Legislature, that an atmosphere conducive to acts of lawlessness had been created by the incessant stream of mendacity directed against the Government and its officers ; the minds of the youth of the country were being poisoned by the constant repetition of grotesque slanders and cruel falsehoods. " Here, indeed, is the fountain-head of the trouble."

The Indian Civil Service is not the only public service attacked, but it is the chief target because it is so largely identified with the British government, and it is believed that its existence prevents the concentration of power in the hands of an Indian governing class. As expressed by one Indian politician, " the Government is in the hands of the British bureaucracy. And so long as this bureaucracy continues to be in power, so long there cannot grow an indigenous ruling caste." The objection therefore is to the Service as an institution, as part of the system of government, and not to its individual members. There is rarely personal animus. On the contrary, there is generally good feeling between Indian politicians and those members of the Service with whom they come into contact; Pandit Moti Lal Nehru, the late leader of the Swarajist party, himself acknowledged in a published letter:

> " Strange as it may seem to some, I have found the sun-dried bureaucrat to be the most charming fellow in the world once he has put off the bureaucratic mask which is so indispensable a part of his official kit." [1]

To some Civilians, indeed, Indian politicians will pay the compliment of saying that they " get into the skins " of Indians or at least try to do so. This is a favourite phrase among educated Indians: it was first used by General Gordon, who wrote in a letter: " To govern men there is but one way, and it is an eternal truth. Get into their skins. Try to realize their feelings."

[1] Letter of 12 March, 1926, to *The Hindustan Times*, quoted in J. A. Spender, *The Changing East* (1926), p. 152.

CHAPTER IX

INDIANIZATION

SO long as the East India Company was associated with the government of India the Civil Service was exclusively British. Warren Hastings had been in favour of employing Indians in the administration, both revenue and judicial, but an opposite policy was followed by Lord Cornwallis. The effect was to exclude Indians from offices of trust and power in British India. The field open to them was, moreover, narrowed by the expansion of British power and the absorption of territory which had been under Indian Governments. When an Indian State was taken over, the ruling Chief, his ministers and other officials, were replaced by a few British officers ; his court disappeared and a small but efficient British staff controlled the administration instead of a crowd of Indian functionaries. The people, it is true, were protected from oppression and enjoyed many advantages of which they had not dreamt under their own rulers ; but if they had nothing to dread, they had little to look forward to, for, though Indians held subordinate posts, they were not admitted to high office. The Government had, in the words of Lord William Bentinck, " the iron hand of power on the one side, monopoly and exclusion on the other." Lord William Bentinck himself was able to associate Indians more closely with the Government ; in 1831 he created a higher grade of Indian civil judges, and two years later he threw open the office of Deputy Collector to Indians, who were thus inducted to responsible, but still subordinate, office in the executive branch of the administration. The system naturally created discontent among Indians of the better class with memories of past power and was felt by many to be politically dangerous. It was also deprecated on financial grounds, viz., that the exclusive employment of Europeans in the higher branches of administration involved an ever-increasing cost as the extension of governmental activities demanded a larger staff.

The need for a change was pointed out by the Parliamentary Committee which held an inquiry into the administration of India before the renewal of the Company's Charter in 1833.

"At present," it remarked, "natives are only employed in subordinate positions in the revenue, judicial and military departments. They are said to be alive to the grievance of being excluded from a larger share in the executive government. It is amply borne out by the evidence that such exclusion is not warranted on the score of incapacity for business or the want of application or trustworthiness; while it is contended that their admission, under European control, into the higher offices would strengthen their attachment to British dominion, would conduce to a better administration of justice and would be productive of a great saving in the expenses of the Indian Government."

These views were accepted by the British Government, and statutory recognition of the eligibility of Indians to responsible office was given by the Charter Act of 1833, which expressly enacted that no native of the British territories in India, nor any natural-born subject of His Majesty resident therein, should, by reason only of his religion, place of birth, descent, colour or any of them be disabled from holding any place, office or employment under the Company. The object of the Act was to remove the disabilities of Indians: as pointed out by the Directors themselves, there was to be "no governing caste in India." Indians, they declared, should be admitted to places of trust as freely and extensively as a regard for the due discharge of the functions attached to such places would permit. Fitness, wholly irrespective of racial distinctions, was henceforth to be the criterion of eligibility.

Aptly and accurately as the Directors could interpret the Act and expound the principles which were to be observed by the Government of India in making appointments to the public services, they did not dream of appointing Indians to the Covenanted Civil Service, over which they alone had patronage. They candidly believed that owing to defective education Indians had not yet attained a level which would make them fit for membership of the Service. Less than two years later Lord Macaulay himself, who had proclaimed his pride in being one of the framers of the Bill containing "that wise, that benevolent, that noble clause," was to write his famous minute denouncing the existing system of education in India and urging the need of English education in order to form a class who might be interpreters between Government and the governed. The Directors felt that their primary duty was to maintain good government, which might be endangered by premature admission of Indians to the Civil Service. As they pointed out to the Government of India:

"Facilities for official advancement can little affect the bulk of the people under any Government, and perhaps least under a good Government. It is not by holding out incentives to official ambition, but by repressing crime, by securing and guarding property, by ensuring to industry the fruits of its labour, by protecting men in the undisturbed enjoyment of their rights and in the unfettered exercise of their faculties, that Governments best minister to the public wealth and happiness."

The Directors therefore held that the first essential was to train Indians to fitness for public service by means of education. For this purpose, and in order that they might be qualified for competition, every design tending to their improvement must be promoted. The upshot was that Indians were not appointed to the Covenanted Civil Service, but were employed in increasing numbers in other public services, and in 1843 were admitted to the criminal branch of the judiciary by an Act authorizing the appointment of uncovenanted Deputy Magistrates. This was done partly in pursuance of the liberal policy inculcated in the Charter Act, partly because of the expense of a European staff.

In consequence of the Directors' patronage being confined to young men of British parentage, the Covenanted Civil Service continued to be closed to Indians until the Government of India Act of 1853 abolished nominations and threw open the Service to competition among all natural-born subjects of the Queen. Indians thus had equality of opportunity subject to the handicap imposed by the examinations being held in London under the direction of the Civil Service Commissioners. This limited the number of candidates, for only well-to-do parents could afford to send their sons to England, while orthodox Hindus had strong religious objections to the voyage overseas. Too much stress should not be laid, however, on these considerations, for exactly the same difficulties were met with in the case of the young men who proceeded in increasing numbers to England to read for the Bar or to study for the medical and other professions. A Committee appointed by the Secretary of State in 1860 was in favour of simultaneous examinations in England and India, but its recommendation was not accepted. Up to 1870 there was only one Indian among the 916 members of the Service: this was Mr. Satyendra Nath Tagore, a member of a well-known Bengali family, who joined the Service in 1864 and was posted to the Bombay Presidency. The year 1871, however, might almost be described as a vintage year for Indians, for in it three (all Bengalis) joined the Service—an achievement which was regarded as so remarkable that on their arrival they were given a public reception by the people of Calcutta.[1] All three became distinguished men. Mr. Ramesh Chandra Dutt became a Commissioner in Bengal, was Prime Minister in Baroda after retirement, and was well known for literary work. Mr. Bihari Lal Gupta, after being Legal Remembrancer in Bengal,

[1] They also had an extraordinary experience on their way back to India, being arrested at Versailles on suspicion of being Prussian spies, apparently because they wore Indian dress and spoke a foreign language: a spy mania was raging at the time in Paris and all who did not speak French were suspect.

officiated as a Judge of the Calcutta High Court and was also Prime Minister of an Indian State after retirement. Mr. Surendra Nath Banerjea had only a short official career. He was dismissed from the Indian Civil Service on account of some delinquencies, for which dismissal was *prima facie* a severe penalty, and became a newspaper editor in Calcutta and a political leader with an influence so great as to earn him the name of the uncrowned King of Bengal; he was eventually knighted and appointed one of the first Ministers in Bengal on the introduction of the Reforms scheme in 1921.

Educated Indians were generally disappointed by the working of the competitive system. Their hopes had been raised by the declaration made by Queen Victoria on the transfer of the government of India to the Crown that it was her will that "so far as may be, our subjects, of whatever race or creed, be freely admitted to office in our service, the duties of which they may be qualified by their education, ability, and integrity duly to discharge." Their ambitions and aspirations had been stimulated by education and the influx of European ideas; the demand for a greater share in the administration of their own affairs was growing in strength and frequency of expression. The great bulk of judicial and revenue work was discharged by services manned by Indians with a small sprinkling of Europeans, but the premier service, which monopolized the higher offices, remained almost entirely British.

The question of Indianizing the service became the subject of agitation both in India and England. In India it was joined in chiefly by educated Hindus of the higher classes, who pressed for simultaneous examinations in India and England as a means of giving them real equality of opportunity. Muhammadans, under the guidance of Sir Saiyid Ahmad, held aloof from it, for they realized that they were still backward educationally and were no match for the nimble-witted Hindus in examination tests of knowledge. In England the agitation found a leader in a Parsi gentleman, Mr. Dadabhai Naoroji (the first Indian Member of Parliament), who founded the East India Association. That body in 1867 memorialized the Secretary of State, asking not only for simultaneous examinations, but also for the institution of scholarships to be held by young Indians in Great Britain. Next year Mr. H. Fawcett, M.P., moved, but did not carry, a resolution in the House of Commons that simultaneous examinations should be held in London, Calcutta, Bombay and Madras. In response to the demand which had been expressed, the Government of India, under Lord Lawrence, in 1868 established nine scholarships, each of £200 a year, to enable Indian students to go to Great Britain and study for the learned professions or for the Indian Civil Service and other public services in India. This meagre scholarship scheme was discontinued by the Duke of Argyll, Secretary of State for India in Mr. Gladstone's first Government, which came into office in 1868.

That Government, however, took up the general question of the recruitment of Indians, and in 1870 an Act was passed by Parliament which declared that it was expedient to afford "additional facilities for the employment of Indians of proved merit and ability in the Civil Service," and that the Act of 1861, reserving specified appointments for the Service, should not debar the Government of India from appointing Indians to any post in the Service even if they had not been admitted to it by the competitive examinations held in England. It was, at the same time, provided that Indians could only be selected under rules prescribed by the Government of India and sanctioned by the Secretary of State. It was not intended to appoint more than a limited number of Indians, the Duke of Argyll (then Secretary of State for India) pointing out to the Government of India:

> "It should never be forgotten, and there should never be any hesitation in laying down the principle, that it is one of our first duties to the people of India to guard the safety of our own dominion. In the firm belief of the beneficent character of our administration and of the great probability that on its cessation anarchy and misrule would reappear, the maintenance and stability of our rule must ever be kept in view as the basis of our policy, and to this end large proportions of British functionaries in the more important posts seem essential."

Two years later (1872), in pressing the Government of India to issue the rules on which the operation of the Act depended, he suggested that a definite proportion of appointments should be reserved for Indians, that these should be mainly judicial, on the ground that Indians were better adapted for judicial than for executive duties, and that Indians should receive less pay than European members of the Service.

Rules were drawn up in 1873, which were based on the assumption that previous service was the best criterion of "proved merit and ability." Service in the higher ranks of the subordinate service was therefore to be the main qualification for appointments under the Act. These rules were disallowed, however, on the ground that they unduly limited the field of selection. Approval was next given tentatively in 1875 to a new set of rules which were simple and elastic enough, for they merely declared that provisional appointments were to be given to Indians of proved merit and ability nominated by the Government of India or local Governments. Only one or two appointments were made under these rules, which were kept in abeyance owing to a new proposal made by Lord Lytton in 1877. This was that a close service should be created for Indians to which appointments should be made by nomination. For this purpose a certain number of posts hitherto reserved for the Covenanted Civil Service should be allocated to the proposed new Service, together with some which had been held by the Uncovenanted Service, the number of admissions to the Covenanted Service being reduced *pro tanto*. Lord Lytton, while anxious to carry out the purpose of the Act, was impressed with the necessity, acknowledged by the Duke of Argyll, of ensuring the stability of British rule by reserving the more important executive posts for Europeans and also of preserving the rights of existing members of the Civil Service, whose prospects would be injured by reducing the number of appointments which they could fill.

The scheme finally proposed by Lord Lytton's Government in 1878 was the creation of a close Civil Service for Indians to which would be assigned 15 per cent of the appointments of the Covenanted, and 20 per cent of those of the Uncovenanted

Service. Members of the new Service were to be nominated by local Governments and appointed on probation by the Government of India. Its status was to be the same as that of the Covenanted Service, of which it was to be considered a branch, but the pay was to be less. The Secretary of State (Lord Cranbrook) was averse from the legislation involved by this scheme, and in 1879 a new scheme was sanctioned creating what was known as the Statutory Civil Service. Rules were issued providing that a proportion not exceeding one-fifth of the persons appointed by the Secretary of State to the Indian Civil Service each year should be Indians, nominated by local Governments in India, who were to be on probation for one year. The appointment of persons already in Government service was to be exceptional, and as a general rule young men who combined good family and social position with fair abilities and education should be selected for appointment.[1] To give effect to this scheme, the number of appointments in the Indian Civil Service made on the results of the competitive examination was reduced by one-sixth in 1880, and altogether sixty-nine "Statutory Civilians" were nominated before the system was abolished. The first to be appointed was Kumar Rameshwar Singh, afterwards Maharajadhiraja of Darbhanga, who resigned after a few years.

The creation of the Statutory Civil Service was not the only measure taken by Lord Lytton in the interests of Indians. In the same year that it was created orders were issued ensuring a monopoly of the Uncovenanted Service to "natives of India,"

[1] Lady Betty Balfour, *Lord Lytton's Indian Administration* (1899), pp. 524–35.

i.e., Indians and members of the domiciled community formerly called Eurasians and now known officially as Anglo-Indians. All appointments in both the executive and judicial services carrying a salary of Rs. 200 a month or more were to be reserved to them, thus giving them a total of nearly 2,600 posts at a time when there were only 940 posts reserved for the Indian Civil Service.

The Statutory Civil Service did not fulfil the hopes which had been entertained of it. It was expected to attract men of good family and fair education—*bene nati et modice docti*—but members of the higher classes showed no eagerness to enter it. The new Service had neither the status nor the prestige of the Covenanted Civil Service: it was regarded as a secondary and lower service. Many of those admitted to it were young men who would otherwise have entered the Uncovenanted Service. Deputy Magistrates belonging to the latter were aggrieved at seeing men with no higher qualifications than their own, but without their administrative experience, appointed to a higher service. The system altogether failed to satisfy the aspirations of educated Indians, who had a further grievance because the maximum age for candidates for the Indian Civil Service had been reduced in 1878 from 21 to 19, at which age their knowledge of English could rarely be sufficient to enable Indians to compete successfully with Englishmen. The reduction of the age-limit, it has been said, created a painful impression throughout India. It was regarded as a deliberate attempt to blast the prospects of Indian candidates for the Indian Civil Service.[1] Educated Hindus conse-

[1] Sir S. N. Banerjea, *A Nation in Making* (1925), p. 44.

quently pressed for a reversion to the higher age limit and for the institution of simultaneous examinations in England and India; a resolution in favour of simultaneous examinations was passed at the first meeting of the Indian National Congress in December, 1885, and was reaffirmed in subsequent years. The Government of India was so far impressed with the need of meeting these demands that in 1884 they recommended raising the limit of age, as well as adding an Oriental language to the subjects which might be taken in the competitive examination. They also suggested the appointment to Indian Civil Service posts of a number of Indians sufficient, with those who were recruited on the results of the examination, to make 18 per cent of the total recruitment to superior posts.[1]

In 1886 the Secretary of State appointed a Public Service Commission with instructions "to devise a scheme which might reasonably be hoped to possess the necessary elements of finality and to do full justice to the claims of natives of India to higher employment in the public service." The Commission consisted of fifteen members, of whom six were Indians, and was presided over by Sir Charles Aitchison, Lieutenant-Governor of the Punjab. It reported at the end of 1887 and strongly advocated the maintenance of the competitive system as it stood, provided that the age limits were changed to suit Indian candidates. The system had produced a succession of officers admirably qualified for the performance of their duties, and the Commission was frankly outspoken as to the danger of

[1] L. Wolf, *Life of the First Marquess of Ripon* (1921), Vol. II, p. 117.

abandoning it. As the Indian Civil Service might be said to represent the only permanent English official element in India, it was impossible to overrate the importance of recruiting for it so as to ensure the maintenance of English principles and methods of government. It had been understood from the first that the examination was to bear a distinctively English character and constitute a test of English qualifications ; and it should therefore be held in England, the centre of the educational system on which it was based. This, it was true, limited the number of Indian candidates, but it did not materially interfere with the supply of such young Indians as it might be desired to attract. The idea of a simultaneous examination in India was open to grave objections. It would involve the substitution of different and less desirable qualifications, as the colleges and schools in India could not as yet provide an education of high and liberal character. Further, it would produce inequality of a marked kind, for it would give undue advantage to some classes which had a facility for examinations and would exclude other important classes altogether. The Commission therefore was altogether opposed to any alteration of conditions merely, as it said, to facilitate the entry of any one qualified class of British subjects more than another. The Statutory Civil Service was adjudged a failure, condemned not only by Indians, but by most officials, both European and Indian, and should be abolished.

The solution of the problem of Indianization which the Commission recommended was to reduce the Indian Civil Service to a *corps d'élite* by limiting its numbers to what was necessary to fill the chief administrative appointments of the Government, and also such a number of the smaller appointments as would ensure a complete course of training for junior Civilians, and by transferring a corresponding number of appointments to a local Service to be separately recruited in each province. The latter Service, which was to be called the Provincial Civil Service, should include 108 posts hitherto reserved for the Indian Civil Service (a number in excess of the one-sixth allocated to the Statutory Civil Service) and also the higher posts held by the old Uncovenanted Service, the lower posts being relegated to a Subordinate Civil Service. This scheme was accepted by the Secretary of State and came into operation in 1892, though not altogether in the form recommended by the Commission. Government did not legislate to amend the schedule of posts reserved for the Indian Civil Service, and so give the Provincial Service vested rights in a certain number of them, but issued lists of posts (consequently called "listed posts") to which officers of that Service in each province could be appointed direct without any of them being transferred to the cadre of the Indian Civil Service.

The Commission may be said to have acted up to its instructions of devising a scheme of some finality, for the division of the general administrative staff into three branches, the Indian Civil, the Provincial Civil,[1] and the Subordinate Civil

[1] The Provincial Civil Service in each province is now called after the province, e.g., Bengal Civil Service, Bombay Civil Service, Madras Civil Service. Members of the Indian Civil Service formerly used these names to indicate the Presidency in which they served.

Services, has been maintained up to the present, with some modifications of detail, but not of substance, made by rules issued in 1910 on the recommendation of the Decentralization Commission. The object aimed at, viz., to fill by promotion from the Provincial Civil Service one-sixth of the posts, judicial and executive, set apart for the Indian Civil Service, was not, however, fully attained. The process had to be a gradual one so as not to impair the vested interests of members of the Indian Civil Service, who had been recruited to fill these as well as other posts reserved by statutory schedule; but even so there were in 1923 only eighty-eight listed posts (out of a total of 700 superior posts) and not the full number of 116 which the Provincial Civil Service would have held if the proportion had been worked up to. The number has since been increased and was 153 on 1 January, 1930.

The effect, then, of the new scheme was to admit to higher appointments selected officers of the Provincial Service with approved service, and these had the advantage of not having to enter at the bottom of a cadre. The channel of entrance into the Indian Civil Service was open, as before, to Indian candidates of a younger age, whose admission to it was facilitated by a change of the age limits. The hope that Indian aspirations would be satisfied was again disappointed. The demand for fuller Indianization and for simultaneous examinations was steadily and persistently pressed, and at length met with recognition in the House of Commons, which in 1893 passed a resolution (moved by Mr. Herbert and supported by Mr. Dadabhai Naoroji) in favour of simultaneous examinations to be held in England and India. To this resolution Government did not consider it either necessary or desirable to give effect. Lord Kimberley, the then Secretary of State, in consulting the Government of India on the subject, pointed out that it was indispensable that an adequate number of the Civil Service should always be Europeans and that no scheme would be admissible which did not fulfil that essential condition. The provincial Governments, on being consulted by the Government of India, were opposed to the idea of simultaneous examinations with the exception of the Government of Madras, which accepted the proposal in a rather lukewarm manner, remarking that Indians admitted to the Service might be found wanting at times of emergency and in outbreaks of disorder, but the mischief could in "present" circumstances be quickly repaired.

Other Governments pointed out that the proposal was open to the gravest objections, e.g., that it was a mistake to think that the principles of law and order had penetrated the minds of the people so deeply that the English element could be safely diminished, that if British administration were to be even temporarily disorganized or British control relaxed, grave disorder might break out, and that though the substitution of Indian for British administrators might be popular among a small section of advanced Indians, the Muhammadans were still strongly opposed to it, and it would be unpopular with the masses. The Government of India for their part held that the British element in the Service was already at its minimum strength, and they could not agree to unrestricted competition in examination, which would reduce it to a dangerous degree and would also practically exclude from it Muhammadans, Sikhs and others, whose strength of character and power of conduct were not equalled by their literary proficiency. They justly observed that for the last twenty years they had assiduously endeavoured to promote the appointment of duly qualified Indians to responsible offices in the public services, and they declared that " the necessities of our position in the country continue to limit the possibilities of such admission." The then Secretary of State (Mr. H. H. Fowler) pursued the matter no further, and it was quietly dropped.

The question of Indianization again came to the front in 1912, when a Public Services Commission was appointed with instructions to report *inter alia* on the limitations on the employment of non-Europeans in the public services. Its Chairman was Lord Islington, then Governor of New Zealand, and among its members were Mr. Ramsay MacDonald (subsequently Prime Minister), Mr. Gokhale, Sir Valentine Chirol, Lord Ronaldshay (now the Marquess of Zetland), and Mr. H. A. L. Fisher (subsequently a member of the Coalition Cabinet during the war). The Islington Commission came to the conclusion that the existing system had failed to admit a sufficient number of Indians into the Service : in 1915 only 63 or 5 per cent were Indians. It rejected the idea of simultaneous examinations, which it pointed out was only a means to an end. In place of a particular form of competition it sought a method not only of admitting more Indians to the higher offices, but also of placing them on equal terms as to conditions of service and prospects with Indian Civil Servants. Its proposal was that provision should be made for a minimum of 25 per cent of statutory natives of India in the higher posts, i.e., that 189 posts out of 755 should be filled by them. Forty District and Sessions Judgeships should be set aside for recruitment from the Bar, and forty-one superior posts (fifteen executive and twenty-six judicial) for officers of the Provincial Civil Services. The balance of 108 were to be filled by direct appointment in India, at the rate of nine a year, two by nomination and seven on the results of a competitive examination to be held in India, the probationers so selected being required to undergo probation for three years in England. Effect was not given to these and other recommendations of the Commission, as it was not considered desirable to make important changes during the war.

The report was signed in August, 1915, and was not published till two years later. By that time the proposed measures of Indianization, instead of being welcomed, were condemned by educated Indians as insufficient. The increasing association of Indians in every branch of the administration was declared to be the policy of the British Government in August, 1917; and next year Mr. Montagu, the Secretary of State for India, and Lord Chelmsford, the Viceroy, in their joint report on constitutional changes, expressed the view that the system of recruitment in England must be supplemented by fixing a definite percentage of recruits to be obtained in India. Changed conditions, in their opinion, justified an increase of the Indian Civil Service posts to be held by Indians. This should be fixed at 33 per cent, with an annual increase of 1½ per cent until the position could be reviewed by the Parliamentary Commission which was to be appointed at the end of ten years. The percentage was accordingly fixed in 1920 at 33 per cent, rising by 1½ per cent annually until 1930, when the proportion of 48 per cent, would be reached. A system of competitive examination in India was set up in 1922, under the supervision of the Civil Service Commissioners, and the Indian candidates selected on its results were required to undergo a probation of two years at an English University. "In order to secure to some extent representation of the various provinces and communities," power was reserved to fill one-third of the appointments reserved for Indians by nomination. Following the recommendation of the Islington Commission orders were also passed in 1920 for the promotion of officers from the Provincial Civil Service and for the appointment to judicial posts of Indians practising in the law courts.

The question of Indianization was again considered by the Royal Commission on the Superior Civil Services in India, under Lord Lee of Fareham, which was appointed in 1923 to examine and advise on their position and organization. By this time there was a serious falling off of British recruits to the Indian Civil Service. The number of British recruits had naturally been reduced during the war; after its termination there was a further reduction owing to the unwillingness of men to enter a Service of which the pay was not altogether adequate and of which the prospects were uncertain owing to the introduction of the Reforms scheme. Consequently, the percentage prescribed for British recruitment was largely in defect: there was a shortage from 1915 to 1923 of 125 British entrants to the Service, while Indians were fifteen in excess of their quota. In 1924 the Lee Commission recommended that of every hundred Indian Civil Service posts forty should be filled by the direct recruitment of Europeans, forty by the direct recruitment of Indians, and twenty (superior posts which would be "listed") by promotion from the Provincial Service, so that in fifteen years' time, i.e., by 1939, half (including the "listed" posts) would be held by Indians and half by Europeans. This proposal was adopted, and the Simon Commission has recently recommended that, in view of the need of a British element in the Service, Indianization should not be accelerated further but maintained at this rate.

Nothing could show more clearly the different light in which the question of Indianization was now viewed than the remark made by the Lee Commission in its report: "In the days of the Islington Commission the question was 'How many Indians should be admitted into the public services?'; it has now become 'What is the minimum number of Englishmen which must be recruited?'"[1] It was formerly considered an administrative necessity that the Indian Civil Service, as the service primarily responsible for the government of the country, should be predominantly British, so that peace and order, efficiency and consequent good government, might be maintained. The Service was to contain only a small proportion of Indians because it was

[1] The same remark was made fifteen years earlier by Lord Curzon (*v. infra*).

frankly held, though not always as frankly expressed, that they had not the same *morale*, power of command, and talent for administration as British officers; more was required than academic learning and intellectual acumen. Few were as candid and outspoken as Lord Curzon, who in his budget speech of 1904 said that appointments to the public services in India must be governed by two principles.

"The first is that the highest ranks of civil employment in India, those in the Imperial Civil Service, though open to such Indians as can proceed to England and pass the requisite tests, must, nevertheless, as a general rule, be held by Englishmen, for the reason that they possess, partly by heredity, partly by upbringing, and partly by education, the knowledge of the principles of government, the habits of mind, and the vigour of character, which are essential for the task, and that, the rule of India being a British rule, and any other rule being in the circumstances of the case impossible, the tone and standard should be set by those who have created and are responsible for it. The second principle is that outside this *corps d'élite* we shall, as far as possible and as the improving standards of education and morals permit, employ the inhabitants of the country, both because our general policy is to restrict rather than to extend European agency, and because it is desirable to enlist the best native intelligence and character in the service of the State." [1]

---

[1] Sir T. Raleigh, *Lord Curzon in India* (1906), p. 60. Lord Curzon also said in a lecture on "The Place of India in the Empire," delivered before the Edinburgh Philosophical Institution in 1909: "No one would impose or defend a merely racial bar. The question at issue is rather not what is the maximum number of offices that can safely be given to Indians, but what is the minimum that must of necessity be reserved for Europeans."

The demand for fuller and quicker Indianization was considered again and again, but it was regarded as the aspiration of only a small section of the community, which was not shared in by the masses and which was inconsistent with the greatest good of he greatest number. The declaration of Queen Victoria that "so far as may be, our subjects of whatever race or creed, be freely admitted to office in our service, the duties of which they may be qualified by their education, ability, and integrity duly to discharge," was not overlooked; but stress was laid on the safeguards of "so far as may be" and "qualified duly to discharge," and the declaration was thought to be fulfilled not only by the admission of Indians to the Civil Service, though in comparatively small numbers, but also by setting aside for them posts which had been reserved for the Service as well as by the increasing employment of Indians in other public services; the great bulk of the revenue and judicial work has long been done, and, when efficiently supervised, done well, by them.

Political considerations have necessitated the abandonment of these principles. It was felt that, though there might be a gain in efficiency by restricting the Indian element in the Civil Service, more was lost politically owing to the discontent engendered among the educated classes. Indianization is now transforming the *personnel* of the Service; there were 367 Indians holding Indian Civil Service posts in January, 1930; and the time is not far distant when it will be half British and half Indian. The change seems bound to cause practical difficulties in times of communal tension if the chief local representative of the Crown is either a Hindu or a Muhammadan, for unfortunately, however honourable and impartial he may be, the people generally are apt to suspect that he will be biased in favour of his co-religionists. However this may be, the Service must inevitably lose its unique character of a small body of British officers entrusted with a large part of the administration of a great country and faithfully discharging its trust, in co-operation, be it added, with other public services—police, educational, engineering, forests, medical, etc. In her famous declaration of 1858 Queen Victoria, announcing her intention to administer the government of India for the benefit of all her subjects resident therein, declared : " In their prosperity will be our strength, in their contentment our security." There is no finer testimony to the work done towards that end by the Indian Civil Service, in common with other public services in India, than the " contentment of the masses " which the Secretary of State for India and the Viceroy found to exist sixty years later.[1]

[1] *Report on Indian Constitutional Reforms*, para. 144.

CHAPTER X

SELECTION AND TRAINING

THE East India Company at first engaged men of mature years to carry on its trade in India, but in 1669 decided to send out only young men or youths to be trained up in its business. Young apprentices were for some time appointed, who were mostly obtained from Christ's Hospital, the well-known blue-coat boys' school, which had the advantage of giving its scholars some commercial training. After 1694, however, the lowest grade in the Company's service was that of Writers. The only qualifications required of Writers were youth and an elementary knowledge of accounts; it was made a rule in 1682 that only those who had learnt the method of keeping merchants' accounts should be admitted to the Service. It was necessary to obtain a nomination from a Director (a provision introduced in 1714 in consequence of the number of applications for appointment), to execute a bond with two securities to the amount of £500, and, on appointment, to sign a covenant for the faithful performance of duties [1]; the India Office still keeps up tomes, called Bond Books and bearing the title "Company's Servants Abroad," in which are entered particulars of men newly appointed to the Indian Civil Service.[2]

[1] M. Monier-Williams, *Memorials of Old Haileybury College* (1894), pp. 4–7; Sir W. Foster, *John Company* (1926), pp. 211–2.
[2] Sir M. C. Seton, *The India Office* (1926), p. 128.

After arrival in India, the young Writer was required to obtain a working knowledge of the vernaculars. Diligence was to be stimulated by rewards and idleness corrected by punishment. At Surat, according to Dr. Fryer's *Travels* (1696), "the Company, to encourage young men in their service, maintain a master to learn them to write and read the language and an annuity to be annexed when they gain a perfection therein, which few attempt and fewer attain." At Madras a Tutor was appointed in 1676 who had to give instruction in the vernacular one hour daily. "If any absent or neglect, to forfeit; if any be not six months end perfect, then three more months allowed; wherein he that speakes not the language shall forfeit for every time that he speakes English."

There does not appear to have been any prescribed limits of age before 1784, when it was laid down that no Cadet or Writer should be sent out to India under 15 or above 18 years of age. The maximum was raised by the Charter Act of 1793, which provided that no person should be appointed or sent out to India whose age was under 15 or exceeded 22 years. The same Act required the Directors to take an oath that they would not accept any fees or pecuniary consideration for nominations or appointments. There had been previously a scandalous profit from patronage, and Writerships commanded high prices: one newspaper noticed in 1772 that Writerships had been sold for £2,000 to £3,000 each, and in 1783 it contained an advertisement offering 1,000 guineas for a Writer's place in Bengal.[1] After 1793 the

[1] J. M. Holzman, *The Nabobs in England* (New York, 1926), p. 22.

actual sale of appointments ceased. Nominations were given as the price of political support or to serve private interests or provide for family connexions or friends. It was in this way that the strong connexion of Scotland with the Indian Civil Service started. Henry Dundas, who was President of the Board of Control from 1793 to 1801, freely exercised his patronage in favour of his compatriots; it was the regular practice of young Scotsmen anxious to better their positions to apply to him for nominations through their Members of Parliament.

Even after the duties of the Company's servants had ceased to be purely commercial, the only educational qualification required for admission to the Service was a rudimentary commercial training: a certificate that the applicant for a nomination had gone through a regular set of merchants' accounts was the only test. The average age at which recruits to the Service arrived in India was 16 to 18 years, an age at which no very high intellectual attainments could be expected; even those who were specially educated with a view to the Civil Service in India received only a commercial education. Lord Wellesley was the first to realize that much more was necessary. He pointed out that the Company's Civil Servants were no longer merely the agents of a commercial concern, but helped to administer an empire. The days in which they were employed solely in the capacity of Factors and Merchants were past. They were called on to administer districts and to fill the important offices of magistrates, ambassadors and provincial governors; and they should be instructed in such branches of knowledge as would qualify them for the discharge of their duties, the foundations of their education being laid in England and completed in India. Accordingly, in 1800, Wellesley informed the Directors that the Governor-General in Council had

> "determined to found an establishment at this Presidency" (i.e., in Calcutta) "of the nature of a collegiate institution for the purpose of enabling the servants of the Company to perfect themselves in those acquirements which form the necessary qualifications for the different lines of the service in which they may choose to engage. It is our intention that the junior servants shall be attached to this institution for a certain period after their arrival instead of being employed in the unprofitable occupation of transcribing papers and abandoned to the dictates of their own discretion both with regard to their morals and acquirements."

An exhaustive course of education was proposed. There was to be a general education embracing the general principles of ethics, civil jurisprudence, international law and general history. There was also to be a specialized education, which was to impart knowledge of the languages and history of India, of the customs and manners of its people, of the Hindu and Muhammadan codes of law and religion, of the principles on which the Regulations and laws of British India were based, and, lastly, of the political and commercial interests and relations of Great Britain in Asia.

Lord Wellesley was so certain of the soundness of his ideas, and so intent on carrying them out, that he did not wait for sanction to his proposals, but issued orders for the immediate foundation of a College at which all Civilians were to be educated for three years after their arrival in India, irrespective of the Presidency, Bengal, Madras or Bombay, in which they were to serve. Those who had already joined the Service but had not yet been in it for three years were also to be attached to the College and remain in it for the same period. Considering that it would be a public monument worthy to commemorate the conquest of Mysore, Wellesley gave to the law authorizing the foundation of the College the date of the first anniversary of the reduction of Seringapatam, viz., 4 May, 1800, and to the College itself he gave the name of the College of Fort William. A strong staff was appointed, including some famous Orientalists. The Provost and Vice-Provost, respectively, were the Rev. David Brown and the Rev. Claudius Buchanan; H. T. Colebrooke gave instruction in Sanskrit and Hindu Law, Francis Gladwin in Persian, Captain Charles Stewart (author of the *History of Bengal*) in Persian and Arabic, and William Carey, the famous missionary, in Bengali.

The Directors refused to sanction Wellesley's scheme. It was held to be grandiose and costly; it would be better to give a course of education in England; there was particular objection to the proposal that every Civilian should enter the College and that the Governor-General should decide to which Presidency each should be posted. Wellesley protested vigorously, but could not shake their decision—a disappointment which rankled so much that he expressed his "unqualified contempt and abhorrence of the proceedings and propensities of the Court of Directors." The Directors, however, agreed to the College being maintained solely for the study of Oriental languages, i.e., it was to be merely a school of languages. The building in which it was housed survives, with a modern front and other additions, in that occupied by the Bengal Secretariat, which is still known as Writers Buildings, a name given to it because the young Writers lived in it for some time while studying languages. From 1801 to 1804 Civilians destined for Bombay and Madras, as well as Bengal, spent a probationary period in it ; after the latter year it was confined to Bengal Civilians. They lived a kind of college life, having rooms assigned to them and being, nominally at least, subject to disciplinary rules. Residence in the College was given up in 1835, when the Civilians were allowed to live elsewhere, but the building was used for their examinations until January, 1854, when the College of Fort William was abolished. Lord Dalhousie then instituted periodical examinations which every Assistant Magistrate was required to pass before he could be promoted to a higher grade.

Under the rules and regulations of the College as laid down in 1841, Writers were not eligible for appointments in the public service till the examiners had reported that they had a competent knowledge of two of the prescribed languages. These were Persian and either Hindi or Bengali (at the option of the student) before 1842, when Persian and Hindi were prescribed for those going to the North-Western Provinces, and Bengali and either Persian or Urdu for those who would serve in Bengal. The Writers were required to qualify within twelve months, for which period they were entitled to the assistance of the College Munshis and Pundits, who taught Arabic, Persian, Sanskrit, Urdu, Hindi and Bengali. In case of failure at the end of twelve months, a report was submitted to Government, and another three months might be allowed; if he was still unable to pass, the Writer's name was to be struck off the rolls of the College and he was to return to England. Progress was tested by periodical examinations once every two months in nominally two languages previous to 1842, when a monthly examination was held, and the student had to show progress in at least one language. Study was encouraged by rewards. Medals of Merit were given for diligence and proficiency; high proficiency was rewarded by a donation of Rs. 800, eminent proficiency by a donation of Rs. 1600 as well as a Degree of Honour. Except with the special sanction of Government, no student might reside so far from the College buildings as to interfere with the proper prosecution of his studies and the exercise of supervision and control. If a student, from expensive habits, from idleness or from other improper indulgence, was likely to incur debt or set a bad example to others, a report was to be made to Government and he was liable to expulsion from the College.

The College of Fort William outlived its usefulness many years before it came to an end. The rules were almost a dead letter, and far too long a time was allowed for passing the examinations. With industry or talent a Civilian could pass out in two months, but this was exceptional, for Calcutta was a pleasant place to live in, and the longer a man delayed passing, the longer could he enjoy its pleasures. A pleasant life was also expensive, and many carried away a heavy burden of debt. The young and foolish boasted of having "turned their lakh," i.e., of having debts of a lakh of rupees (then equal to £10,000), and lived to regret it. One young Civilian who passed out in 1828 within two months of landing found that others had been at the College nine months to two years according to the measure of their stupidity or idleness. Sir George Campbell, who passed out in five months in 1843, said that the time spent at the College varied from two months to three years; extensions beyond the prescribed period were obtained on production of medical certificates. Men made their own arrangements for tuition and lived much as they pleased. They appeared at the monthly examinations if there was no convenient excuse for skirking them; for the first year at least the young Writer was "literally not in any way required to do anything." So far from the College being of use as a school of languages, men left it knowing little more of Indian languages than when they left Haileybury; they could neither converse with Indians nor understand any ordinary paper read out in Court. The name of College was by this time, he declared, a fiction, and the idea that anyone who failed to pass within the allotted time would be sent back to England was regarded as a myth. The rule seems, however, to have been enforced earlier, for in 1836 Henry Torrens wrote in *A Ballad*: "All you've to learn are some few dialects. You'll do it (if you don't, why you're deported) in about a year. That's for you Writers." Also, after a period of obsolescence, the rule was revived and enforced in some cases shortly before the College was abolished.[1]

The representations of Lord Wellesley as to the necessity for higher educational attainments bore fruit some years later. In dealing with his pro-

[1] Sir G. Campbell, *Modern India* (1853), pp. 268–9; *Memoirs of My Indian Career* (1893), p. 13.

posals the Directors had in 1802 declared it their intention to give the requisite educational training in England, but took no steps to that end until in 1804 the factory at Canton suggested that Writers should have a preparatory education for two or three years in England and be sent out at the age of 19. The Committee of Correspondence, which was instructed to report on the system of education to be adopted, recommended that a College should be established in England in which young men intended for the Civil Service in India should receive a general education in the classics, mathematics and arithmetic, the elements of general law, and Oriental learning. The Committee also held that it was inadvisable to send out Writers before the age of 18. The Directors approved the Committee's proposal, and in 1805 purchased the estate of Haileybury in Hertfordshire as a site for a College. As a temporary measure, pending construction of the buildings, Hertford Castle was taken and opened in 1806 as "The East India College, Herts." The College was moved from this temporary home to Haileybury in 1809, by which time the buildings were completed.

The object of the College, as set forth in the prospectus issued in 1806, was "to provide a supply of persons duly qualified to discharge the various and important duties required from the Civil Servants of the Company in administering the government in India." Students were to be admitted at the age of 15, and to remain till they were 18 or till they were sent out to India by the Directors. The curriculum included (1) Oriental literature with (*a*) practical instruction in the rudiments of Oriental languages, especially Arabic and Persian; (2) mathematics and natural philosophy; (3) classical and general literature; and (4) law, history and political economy. The College year was divided into two terms of twenty weeks each; and the fees were fixed at fifty guineas a term.

The reservation of appointments to youths educated at Haileybury received legislative sanction in 1813, when an Act of Parliament prohibited any person being nominated, appointed or sent out to India as a Writer unless he had had four terms at the College. In 1826 the rule had to be modified as they were not enough men to fill vacancies, and an Act was passed giving the Directors discretionary power to appoint to Writerships young men between the ages of 18 and 22 without their having to go to Haileybury but subject to their passing a qualifying examination. This arrangement lasted for five years, the first qualifying examination being held in 1827 and the last in 1832. Altogether eighty-three Writers were appointed in this way, among whom may be mentioned Sir Robert Montgomery, Lieutenant-Governor of the Punjab from 1859 to 1865, and Sir H. M. Elliot, the Indian historian.

The age for admission to Haileybury varied at different times. The Charter Act of 1793 required that no one should be appointed or sent out as a Writer who was under 15 or over 22 years of age, and the original prospectus, as we have seen, contemplated admission to the College at the age of 15. Given two years spent at Haileybury, this meant that a Writer need be only 17 when he commenced his service; apparently as a compensation for study at the College till a later age, an Act of Parliament passed in 1829 declared that time spent there after the age of 17 should be allowed to count as service in India. The age for admission was subsequently raised. The India Act of 1833 provided that no candidate at the entrance examination should be under the age of 17 or above the age of 20 years; but in 1837 another Act laid down 21 as the maximum age for admission to the College, and 23 for appointment as a Writer. The staff of the College had long pressed for the exclusion of mere boys, and in 1843 the Directors adopted 17 as the earliest age at which they would give nominations to Haileybury. After this the limits of age remained at 17 to 21 till the abolition of the College.[1]

The India Act of 1833 introduced the principle of competition by providing that for every vacancy at the College at least four candidates should be nominated and the best of them selected by examination. Macaulay, who conducted the measure through the House of Commons, anticipated the happiest results from the change, but the clause was rendered nugatory by the Directors, who had no desire to lose their valued privilege of patronage.[2]

[1] M. Monier-Williams, *Memorials of Old Haileybury College* (1894), pp. 15–19, 105, 244–5.

[2] There was one case of limited competition outside the provisions of the Act. Mr. Butterworth Bayley, Chairman of the Directors, in 1842 offered a Writership for competition (like a close Scholarship) among the boys at Eton. It was won by Charles Thomas Buckland, who then went to Haileybury: there were only two other competitors, of whom one was Thring, afterwards Head Master of Uppingham. Buckland was afterwards called in jest the first Competition-Wallah. M. Monier-Williams, *Memorials of Old Haileybury College*, p. 126.

The entrance examination for Haileybury continued to be merely qualifying, for the Directors limited their nominations and confined them to boys who were likely to pass it. A few failed to qualify, and a certain number were weeded out at Haileybury. It has been estimated that of the original nominees one-fifth were eliminated as the result of different examinations, viz., the entrance, those held at the end of each term, and the final. Those who failed were usually given cadetships in the Company's cavalry. "It was the fashion to send into the Cavalry a young man too idle or too stupid to go through Haileybury and the Director put another in his place in the Civil Service": incidentally, the Directors were so pestered by applicants for cadetships that the admission of ladies into the India Office had to be prohibited. There were some bad cases of nepotism—one Scotch Director is said to have got appointments under the Company for most of his nineteen children—but on the whole the Directors showed a sense of responsibility in making nominations; they made them individually and not as a Board.[1] They generally reserved them for boys of some promise and would even exclude members of their own families who were not likely to do them credit. The entrance and subsequent examinations also served to maintain a fair standard. The system had another advantage. It led to what may be called family connexions with India and a tradition of service which was handed down from generation to generation: nineteen, for instance, of the Thackeray family, beginning with the grandfather

[1] Sir G. Campbell, *Memoirs of My Indian Career* (1893), Vol. I, pp. 8, 138, 139.

of the novelist and including his father, were members of the Service.[1] There was also a strong *esprit de corps* among the men who came from Haileybury, stronger indeed than was found later among men recruited by competition, who spent an all too short period of probation, not at one institution but at different Universities and Colleges. The Haileybury men took an honourable pride in the Service, and this feeling was shared by the Directors, who took a personal interest in them and treated them more as members of a big official family than as mere employés of the Company. Relations with the India Office were consequently more pleasant and genial than they were later. The education at Haileybury may not have reached a high level, but men soon learnt in the practical school of experience, more especially as they went out to India at an age when their minds were still plastic; they were thus able to acquire familiarity with Indian tongues and to adapt themselves to Indian conditions more easily than older men.

Whatever may have been its theoretical defects, the system was justified by its results. The Directors were for the most part men who had long experience of India and a just appreciation of Oriental conditions. They knew that the people of India were accustomed to having authority exercised by a governing class and were keenly alive to the character of its personnel. They accordingly gave their nominations to youths of a class which might be expected to command respect in India. They realized that this was not enough and that special training was essential for administrative work, and this they provided in a college founded for the

[1] Sir W. W. Hunter, *The Thackerays in India* (1897), p. 65.

purpose, which soon acquired the tradition of service to India.

Appointments in the Indian Civil Service were thrown open to competition by Act of Parliament in 1853, when the Company's Charter was renewed for the last time. All British subjects were eligible, without distinction of race. It was not till many years later that the competitive system was adopted for the English Civil Service.[1] The right of the Directors to make nominations for admission to Haileybury and for appointments in India was allowed to continue only till the end of April, 1854. A Committee was appointed in 1854 to advise on the measures to be taken to give effect to the Act. Its Chairman was Lord Macaulay, who had long advocated the competitive system on the ground that it raised the standard, whereas a system of pass examinations, such as the Haileybury entrance examination, tended to lower it. The other members of the Committee were Lord Ashburton, Rev. Henry Melvill (Principal of Haileybury College), Rev. Benjamin Jowett (afterwards Master of Balliol College), and Mr. (afterwards Sir) John Lefevre. The Committee recommended the selection of candidates on the results of a competitive examination, the requirement of a period of probation before they were finally appointed, and the abolition of the College at Haileybury.

These recommendations having been accepted

[1] Government was ready to deprive the Directors of patronage, but not to give up its own. A Civil Service Commission was appointed in 1853 which recommended the filling of posts by competitive examination. All that was done was to require a qualifying examination until 1870, when competitive examinations were introduced for appointments in all Government offices except the Foreign Office.

by Government, an Act was passed in 1855 directing that the College should be closed not later than the end of January, 1858: time had to be allowed for students to complete their course, and it was actually closed in December, 1857.[1] Other recommendations were embodied in regulations issued in 1855, some of which however were only of temporary duration. What was of more permanent value was the principle which the Committee laid down that a high standard was to be set and maintained and that the examination should be so conducted as to ensure the selection of candidates with thorough and not merely superficial knowledge. To know one subject thoroughly was to be of more account than a smattering of several: knowledge of wide surface but small depth was to be discounted. The new recruits to the Service were given the hybrid and somewhat derisory name of Competition Wallah—a sobriquet which has survived chiefly because of the charming book, *Letters from a Competition Wallah*, published by Sir George Trevelyan in 1864.

Since the competitive system was introduced there have been many changes in the limits of age prescribed for candidates, as shown in the marginal table, from which it will be seen that the age for admission to the examination has never been lower than 17 or higher than 24.

1855–9	18–23
1860–4	18–22
1865	17–22
1866–78	17–21
1879–91	17–19
1892–1905	21–23
1906–20	22–24
1921–30	21–24

[1] The last of the Civil Servants who went to India from Haileybury died in 1930—Mr. William McQuhae, who served in Madras and retired in 1879.

Lord Macaulay's Committee recommended that the minimum age should be 18, and the maximum 23, on the ground that though it was desirable that Civil Servants should enter on their duties while young, it was also desirable that they should have received the best, the most liberal, and the most finished education that Great Britain afforded. An excellent general education, such as would enlarge their understanding, should precede the special education which would quality them for their duties in India. It was further desirable in their opinion that a considerable number should be men who had taken the first degree in Arts, i.e., the B.A., at Oxford or Cambridge ; the admission of boys of 18 was to be exceptional, and 25 was the latest age at which Writers should be permitted to go out to India.

Regulations issued in 1855 laid down that candidates should be above 18 and under 23 years of age, and that those who obtained the highest marks at the competitive examination were to be "selected candidates" for vacancies, to which they would be appointed if they passed a subsequent examination. During the period between the two examinations the selected candidates were to be on probation undergoing a course of special training. After the first year of probation there was to be an examination in law, the history of India, political economy, and Indian languages, which should be followed a year later by a second examination in the same subjects. Those who passed these examinations should be entitled to be appointed to the Civil Service.

The arrangements prescribed by these regulations were not adhered to. From 1855 to 1859 candidates passed only the open competitive examination and had no subsequent examination in specialized Indian subjects. From 1860 to 1865 they spent one year of probation in England, at the end of which their knowledge of those subjects was tested by examination. The maximum age for admission to the competitive examination was also reduced in 1859 from 23 to 22, in order that service might be begun at an age not later than 23 and that the reduced age might not preclude the candidature of men who had taken the degree of B.A. On arrival in India the entrants to the Service were kept at the Presidency towns (Calcutta, Madras and Bombay) until they had passed examinations in the languages of the provinces to which they had been appointed. Good men took five or six months, the idle fourteen or fifteen months, to pass; as before, many wasted their time and ran into debt. From 1866 to 1879 the period of probation was two years; there were three periodical test examinations at half-yearly intervals and a final examination at the end of the two years,[1] on the result of which seniority depended. In 1865 the maximum age of admission to the competitive examination was reduced from 22 to 21, and next year the minimum was lowered from 18 to 17, the object being explicitly to attract "from the principal public schools many distinguished youths who have not yet taken the first step towards a University or professional career at home." The result was to substitute the school-leaving age for the University age.

The working of the system was reviewed in 1874

[1] A. Cotterell Tupp, *The Indian Civil Service and the Competitive System* (1876), p. 77.

by Lord Salisbury, then Secretary of State for India, in a letter addressed to the Civil Service Commissioners. Doubts as to its merits were being felt : it was thought that the competitive examination was putting a premium on cramming ; the age of candidates (17 to 21) had the disadvantage of preventing them from going to a University during the probationary period. The knowledge of selected candidates was carefully tested by periodical examinations, but otherwise they were left much to themselves. It had been proposed, therefore, that candidates should be required to pass the competitive examination at or about the age of 18, on the grounds that competitive tests were better adapted to a younger age and that the age at which Civilians commenced their service to India was too advanced.[1] A Committee which met at Oxford, under the chairmanship of Dean Liddell, of Christ Church, recommended that 18 or 19 should be adopted as the age for candidates so as to enable those who were successful to go to a University and take a degree. Lord Salisbury so far accepted this view that the maximum age was fixed at 19 for the examinations held in 1879 and subsequent years, the minimum of 17 being retained. The probationary period remained the same, and there was the same system of periodical and final examinations ; but to encourage probationers to go to the University, an allowance of £300 was given to those who spent their two years of probation there and passed the final examination. The object of the change, as officially explained, was to bring the selected candidates to their work in India at

[1] Report on the Selection and Training of Candidates for the Indian Civil Service, 1876.

an earlier age than heretofore and to secure for them, as far as was possible, the moral supervision of some academical body during their period of probation. The general result was that boys took the examination at the school-leaving age, spent two years at a University but without taking a degree, and arrived in India at the average age of 20. Objections were raised to the change on the ground that the candidates were immature in character and defective in general culture and experience.

Hitherto the question of the age of candidates had been considered chiefly with an eye to English conditions. Another interest now came to the front, viz., that of educated Indians, who complained that their circumstances had not been taken into account and that they were placed at a disadvantage by the low age limits. They had to have a thorough knowledge of English if they were to compete, and it was difficult for them to complete their English education without becoming over age, while parents objected to sending their sons to England while they were of tender years. Nor was criticism wanting in England, where exception was taken to the low maximum age of 19 on the ground that it encouraged cramming. The Scottish Universities memorialized the Secretary of State for India, urging a reversion to the former age limit of 22, and Dr. Jowett, of Balliol College, which more than half the probationers joined, also addressed him in 1882, pointing out that they were immature youths and that the result of lowering the age limits had been to reduce the number of candidates from 350 to under 150. He urged that 18 to 20 should be prescribed as the age limits, and that the period of probation should be extended to three years, so that probation in England might begin at the average age of 19 and service in India at 22; young men of 22 or 23 were, he contended, superior to those of 20 or 21, not only in acquired learning but also in knowledge of the world, good sense and good manners.[1]

The vexed question of the age limits was reviewed with reference to the conditions suitable to Indian candidates by the Public Service Commission (1886–7) under Sir Charles Aitchison: by the terms of reference the question as affecting English candidates was excluded from its inquiry. The conclusion it reached was that the minimum and maximum ages for Indian candidates should be 19 and 23 years respectively, so that selected candidates might enter on their special training at an age at which their general education was complete. It was thought that the longer and more complete their English training was, the greater would be their grasp of the economic and political principles of administration; while the higher age limit had also the merit of widening the field of choice and securing the best-qualified candidates.

As a result of the recommendations made both by the Commission and by English educational experts, the minimum age limit was raised, with effect from 1892, to 21 and the maximum to 23. This meant that the University age was substituted for the school-leaving age and that men who had already passed the examinations for the B.A. degree at an English university could compete. At the same time, as 24 was thought to be the latest age

[1] E. Abbott and L. Campbell, *Life and Letters of Benjamin Jowett* (1897), Vol. I, pp. 138–9, Vol. II, p. 348.

at which men should begin their service, the period of special training was reduced to one year. The periodical examinations of candidates were discontinued, and there was only one examination held at the end of the year's probation in the law, languages and history of India as well as in riding. Previously probationers had been required not merely to study codes and books of law but also to attend the police courts for criminal law, county courts for civil law, and the higher courts for both, and to report on the cases they heard, with notes both on the principles and procedure which they illustrated. In this way they learnt something of the practical administration of justice, and the abandonment of this part of the course was regretted by many who regarded it as one of the most valuable parts of the training. For the year of probation a meagre allowance of £100 only was given, provided that it was spent at a university. After appointment to the Service men had to pay for their passages to India with their own or borrowed money. Seniority depended on the combined marks of the competitive and final examinations. The adoption of these higher age limits has been adversely criticized. While it is admitted that the new entrants to the Service had a fuller education and more developed powers of judgement, their maturity has been thought to have its drawbacks, because they are less adaptable to Indian conditions and slower to learn the vernacular languages, a knowledge of which is essential to a knowledge of the people.

The age limits remained at 21 to 23 till 1906, when they were made 22 to 24, so that, allowing for a year's probation, it was possible for actual service in India to begin as late as the age of 25. A reversion to the ages of 17 and 19 was recommended by the Royal Commission on the Public Services in India, presided over by Lord Islington, which was appointed in 1912 and submitted its report in 1915. The recommendation that there should be a reversion to the low age limits of nearly half a century earlier seems at first sight a complete *volte face*, as those limits had been condemned on the ground that they handicapped Indian candidates and resulted in the appointment of men who were too young to have the maturity of judgement and character necessary for the duties devolving upon them. It was admitted that the higher age limit was more favourable to the chances of Indian candidates, as indeed appeared from the statistics: Indian candidates secured only 2½ per cent of the vacancies between 1878 and 1891, when the limits were 17 and 19, and 5·6 per cent between 1892 and 1912, when they were either 21 and 23 or 22 and 24. On the other hand, from the administrative point of view, there were many cogent arguments in favour of a change. Men who began their service at the age of 25 were less easy to train in the detailed drudgery of administrative work; their minds were more set and their ideas cast in a mould by no means Indian; efficiency was apt to be impaired by their not attaining responsible office till a comparatively late age and by retirement being deferred to a time when they had lost their pristine vigour. The consideration, however, which had most influence with the Commission was that the existing limits admitted of only a single year's probation, which was far too short a time for specialized training in the law, languages, history and customs of India. The legal knowledge with which the young Civilian was equipped when he came out to India was particularly defective, and it was essential that he should have a fuller legal training. The Commission therefore proposed that the period of probation should be extended to three years. The best age for arriving in India from a medical point of view, and for commencing service from an administrative point of view, was 22 or 23. The age limit for the open competitive examination should consequently be fixed at 17 to 19, so as to admit of a longer preliminary training and not postpone unduly the commencement of service. These recommendations were not adopted. All that was done was to reduce (in 1921) the minimum age to 21 (the upper age limit of 24 being retained) and to authorize, but not to prescribe, an extension of the probationary course to two years.

Views diametrically opposed to those of the Islington Commission were subsequently expressed by the Lee Commission, i.e., the Royal Commission on the Superior Civil Services in India under the Chairmanship of Lord Lee of Fareham, which published its report in 1924. Briefly, it held that the age limits for candidates for the competitive examination in England should be kept at 21 to 24, and consequently the period of probation at one year, as it was undesirable for recruits to begin their work in India above the age of 25.

The war completely upset the arrangements for making appointments to the Civil Service. The competitive examination, which is a statutory obligation, continued to be held, but the number of appointments was limited. From 1915 to 1918 only twenty-nine new men (seventeen British and twelve Indian) were admitted to the Service; in the first three years after the war (1919–21) no less than 206 had to be admitted to make up the shortage. Special measures were introduced to cope with the situation. In order that men who fought for their country might not be penalized for patriotism, and also in order to maintain the British element in the Service, an Act was passed in 1915 allowing ex-Service men to be appointed, not by a competitive examination, but by selection, subject to their satisfying a qualifying educational test. Men who had served in the combatant forces and had consequently been unable to compete were also allowed an age deduction on account of the period of their military or naval service. Another war measure was the provision, introduced in 1917, that the competitive examination was barred to men who had applied for exemption on the ground of conscientious objection to combatant service. Apart from any other principle, pacifists are not suitable for service in a country like India, where a Magistrate may find it necessary to use armed force to put down disorder: they would be quite out of place in the North-West Frontier Province, where the officer in charge of a district may be out three nights a week after gangs of raiders from tribal territory, whose incursions year by year result in the killing, wounding and kidnapping of hundreds of British subjects. In order also to exclude aliens, it was made a rule that if a candidate was not born within His Majesty's dominions or allegiance, his father must have been at the time of his birth, and must have continued till death, to be a British subject or the subject of a State in India.

After the introduction of the Reforms scheme an

entirely new situation arose. Special measures, which have been mentioned in the last chapter, were taken for the recruitment of Indians; and after 1922 competitive examinations were started in India as well as England. The period of probation for Indian candidates selected in India was fixed at two years under the discretionary power already referred to, but remained one year for those selected in England: the former were required to pass an intermediate examination at the end of the first year and the final examination at the end of the second. The difference in the period of probation may be justified on the ground that Indians who have been educated in India have had a somewhat narrower life and a more limited horizon than those educated in Great Britain, and that two years are none too long a time for them to become acquainted with the working of British institutions. The allowance was at the same time raised to £300 a year, and in the case of selected candidates possessing an Indian domicile, to £350 a year, besides which the India Office engaged first-class passages to India after the final examination was passed. Owing to the measures taken for admission of Indians, there are now three methods of recruiting for the Service. Candidates are selected on the results of annual competitive examinations in England, and on the results of similar examinations held in India for selected Indian nominees, and some direct appointments of Indians are made by nomination in India.

As regards British candidates, the pressing question after the inauguration of the Reforms scheme was not of any particular system of selection, but of how candidates were to be attracted at all. By

1922 the flow of British candidates seemed to be almost about to stop, not only for the Indian Civil, but also for other public services in India. A Committee was specially appointed that year, under the chairmanship of Lord MacDonnell, to suggest means of stimulating recruitment, but the political situation was beyond its control and it could devise no effective way of restoring the popularity of the Service. The loss of its popularity was due primarily to the uncertainty of its prospects. Provisions intended to safeguard its members had been inserted in the Government of India Act, but these were not thought sufficient to guarantee the security of the Service against possible changes, and in the meantime work had to be carried on under disheartening conditions. In addition to this, the financial prospects of entrants to the Service were not attractive, as pay had not been raised proportionately to the rise in the actual cost of living.

As long ago as 1913 representations had been made that salaries remained the same and that no account had been taken of higher prices. This matter was inquired into, *inter alia*, by the Islington Commission (1912–15), but its report was not published till 1917, as it was considered inadvisable during the war to give an opportunity for controversy regarding the many vexed questions with which it dealt. Following its recommendations, a time scale with overseas allowances was substituted in 1920 for the existing grade system. It was estimated that this would give a rise of pay averaging 15 per cent, but the actual increase amounted only to 8 per cent, owing largely to a fall of the exchange value of the rupee. This small increase did not correspond to the rise in the cost of living for a European living in India, which between 1914 and 1923 was no less than 60 per cent. Commercial firms, recognizing the change of economic conditions, had given their European staff in India increases of pay amounting to 50 or even 75 per cent besides other concessions, compared with the 8 per cent increase allowed to Civil Servants.

The Lee Commission of 1923–4 found that the disparity of remuneration between a commercial and an official career had become so great that something had to be done without delay to restore contentment, "bearing in mind however the need for economy in Indian administration." Even with this caution, the concessions made on its recommendations were substantial enough to remove the financial difficulties of men already in the Service, more especially the grant of a certain number of passages to and from England at fixed periods of years, for which their pay was hitherto inadequate. Another concession made a few years earlier, which should have proved an attraction to new entrants to the Service, was the assumption by Government of the full charge of pensions. Hitherto members of the Service had themselves paid part of their pensions by monthly contributions of 4 per cent of their pay; the capital value of their contributions has been calculated (by the Lee Commission in 1924) to be £250 a year or a quarter of the total pension. The deduction of 4 per cent was still made, but it was paid into a provident fund for their benefit on retirement: the effect of the change is practically to raise pensions for new entrants from £1,000 to £1,250 a year.

In spite of all this the distrust of the Service still

lingered in Great Britain, men, for instance, being apprehensive that political changes might cut short their careers and prevent their service being long enough to earn the full pension; but it was gradually dissipated by an improvement in political conditions in India and by propaganda at the Universities, where meetings were held at which reassuring statements were made, among others by the Secretary of State for India himself (Lord Birkenhead), as to the prospects and attractions of work in India.

Owing to the short duration of the period of specialized training, and to its having to be spent in the British Isles, a young Civilian arrives in India somewhat poorly equipped for his work. He has a highly trained intelligence and a grasp of general principles, but the special training which should form a bridge between his general education and practical work is only fragmentary. He has a rather meagre acquaintance with the language of his province, which is chiefly useful for the grounding in grammar which he has received, and he has studied the Indian Penal Code, the Code of Criminal Procedure, and the Law of Evidence, but he has only book learning, for he has never seen a trial conducted in accordance with them.

The real training of a young Civilian begins in India with practical work in different branches of the administration. On arrival he is made an Assistant Magistrate with powers of the lowest class and is posted to the headquarters of a district to learn his work under the supervision of a Collector. Mr. Cotterell Tupp stated in 1876 that the Assistant Magistrate became an actual official by being sworn in on reaching the station to which he was posted. The ceremony, if such it may be called, was performed before the District Magistrate, or if he was absent from headquarters, before the Joint Magistrate, the officer next to him in status. It consisted of the young Civilian swearing allegiance to the Government and affirming solemnly his intention to administer justice honestly and uprightly.[1] This was probably only a provincial or local custom: no such ceremony now takes place.

A further course of examinations still awaits the young Civilian (except in the United Provinces) before he can be given higher magisterial powers. He is required to pass what are called departmental examinations, first by a lower and next by a higher standard, in the language of his province, in criminal law and in revenue law. In the meantime, however, he gains experience and knowledge by the trial of petty cases in Court, work in different departments, and local inquiries. More is learnt by the exercise of responsibility than in the grove of Academe, and latent powers are called out when men are thrown on their own resources in early manhood. Charles Metcalfe, for example, was 24 years old in 1809 when he negotiated a treaty with Ranjit Singh which held good for nearly forty years, and only 26 when he became Resident at Delhi. As pointed out long ago in *Letters from a Competition Wallah*, the real education of an Indian Civil Servant

"consists in the responsibility that devolves upon him at an early age, which brings out whatever good there

[1] *The Indian Civil Service and the Competitive System* (1876), p. 83.

is in a man; the obligation to do nothing can reflect dishonour on the Service; the varied and attractive character of his duties; and the example and precept of his superiors, who regard him rather as a younger brother than as a subordinate official."

CHAPTER XI

OTHER SPHERES OF ACTIVITY

NEARLY a century ago the Indian Law Commission under Macaulay remarked that members of the Civil Service in India passed their lives in acquiring information and experience which in any other pursuit would be of little or no service to them.

> "They are transferred when just entering on manhood to the country which they are to govern. They pass the best years of their lives in acquiring knowledge which is most important to men who are to fill high situations in India, but which in any other walk of life would bring little profit and little distinction, in mastering languages which, when they quit this country, are useless to them, in studying a vast and complicated system of revenue which is altogether peculiar to the East, in becoming intimately acquainted with the interests, the resources, and the projects of potentates whose very existence is unknown even to educated men in Europe."[1]

The general truth of these remarks, even at the present day, may be admitted; but on the other hand they do not refer to the fact that work in the Indian Civil Service calls forth inherent qualities or produces certain habits which make for success in any calling, such as business-like methods, organizing capacity, adaptability to different conditions and readiness to take responsibility; and a

[1] Introductory Report upon the Indian Penal Code, *Life and Works of Lord Macaulay* (1897), Vol. VII, p. 470.

survey of the work which has been undertaken out of India by men who have had their training in that country indicates that these qualities and habits have had their value in countries other than India and in pursuits other than that of Indian administration.

It was at one time not an uncommon experience for ex-members of the Indian Civil Service to be appointed to Colonial Governorships. Lord Metcalfe, as recorded in his epitaph, which was written by Macaulay, had the three greatest Dependencies of the British Crown successively entrusted to his care. He acted as Governor-General of India in 1835–6, and after his retirement was Governor of Jamaica from 1839 to 1842, and Governor-General of Canada from 1843 to 1845. Sir George Anderson, who left Bombay in 1844, was appointed Governor of the Mauritius in 1849 and then became Governor of Ceylon. Jamaica also had as Governors two other retired members of the Service. The first was Sir John Peter Grant, who had been Lieutenant-Governor of Bengal from 1859 to 1862. He was appointed Governor of Jamaica in 1866 after Mr. Eyre had been superseded in connexion with the suppression of a negro rebellion. To Grant was entrusted the task of introducing a new constitution into Jamaica, which had previously had a form of representative government, and of virtually converting it into a Crown Colony. This task he successfully accomplished ; he reformed the administration of the island and restored its finances within two years, converting a deficit of £80,000 into a surplus in spite of the expenditure entailed by the reforms. It is said of him that he hated any form of exercise but was never idle : " indolent by nature, he would get through volumes of work lying on a sofa or even in his bath."[1] He held office in Jamaica for seven years, and his successor there (1874–7) was Sir William Grey, who had also been Lieutenant-Governor of Bengal (1867–71).

One of the ablest of the Indian administrators who became a Colonial Governor was Sir Bartle Frere. He was a member of the Indian Civil Service for thirty-three years, for the last five of which (1862–7) he was Governor of Bombay. He then retired and in 1872 was sent on a mission to the Sultan of Zanzibar, to negotiate for the suppression of the slave trade, which he successfully accomplished. In 1877 he was appointed Governor of Cape Colony and first Commissioner of South Africa, with instructions to ensure peace and effect federation: so little was the hopelessness of the task at that time realized that it was even thought that he might be the first Governor-General of the South African Dominion. So far from being peaceful, his short administration is memorable for the Kaffir War of 1878 and the Zulu War of 1879, and he was recalled in 1880. But, as Sir Charles Lucas has pointed out,

> "if he had lost the confidence of Secretaries of State, he had won that of the colonists in South Africa." "His policy was that of the coming time; he sketched out in advance the South Africa that should be; and his whole life was one long tribute to the honour of the British name."[2]

The number of Colonial Governors appointed

[1] A. Chichele Plowden, *Grain or Chaff?* (1903), pp. 68–72.

[2] Sir C. P. Lucas, *History of South Africa to the Jameson Raid* (1900), pp. 266, 281, 300.

from among ex-members of the Service might have been greater if offers of Governorships had been accepted. Sir Alfred Lyall was offered the Governorship of the Cape in 1889 and that of New Zealand four years later, but declined both. He had a connexion of forty-eight years with India, for he entered the Civil Service in 1855, and, after being Lieutenant-Governor of the North-West Provinces (1882–7), was for fifteen years (1888–1903) a member of the India Council, where he was the right-hand man of the Secretary of State for India. Sir George Clerk also refused the Governorship of the Cape about forty years earlier. He had been Lieutenant of the North-West Provinces in 1843 and Governor of Bombay in 1847–8 ; and after declining the Governorship of the Cape, went there in 1853 to delimit its boundary, the British Government having decided to have no responsibilities beyond the Orange River ; it was he who handed over the government of the Orange Free State to the Boers. On returning to England he worked both as permanent Under-Secretary and as Secretary to the India Board (1856–7), and he was the first permanent Under-Secretary of State for India (1858–60). He was then again made Governor of Bombay, but his second term of office lasted only two years, for ill health forced him to resign.

Several other members of the Service have had African as well as Indian administrative experience. Sir Auckland Colvin was one of a line of distinguished administrators who rescued the finances of Egypt from chaos and introduced reforms which led to a regeneration of the country. After twenty years in India, his services were lent to Egypt, where in 1878 he was placed in charge of the cadastral survey, work for which his experience as Settlement Officer had qualified him. Next year he became Commissioner of the Debt (Caisse de la Dette Publique) in succession to Lord Cromer. In 1880, when the latter went to India as Finance Member of the Governor-General's Council, Sir Auckland again took his place as the English Controller-General under the dual system then in force. When the Egyptian Army mutinied under Arabi in September, 1881, he proved himself a tower of strength; in the account of his conduct which is given in *Modern Egypt* (1908), Lord Cromer says that in the hour of trial he did not fall short of Warren Hastings's motto, *Mens æqua in arduis*, "which might fitly apply to the whole of that splendid body of Englishmen who compose the Indian Civil Service." The insurrection was only deferred and was followed by the British occupation, with Sir Auckland Colvin occupying the post of Financial Adviser to the Khedive, which has been described by Lord Milner as the corner-stone of English influence in the Egyptian administration. Sir Auckland returned to India in 1883 to succeed, for a third time, Lord Cromer as Finance Member, and four years later he became Lieutenant-Governor of the North-West Provinces, an appointment which his father, John Russell Colvin, had held at the time of the Mutiny.

Three other heads of provinces have been connected with the administration of different parts of Africa, viz., Lord Meston of Agra and Dunottar, Sir William Marris and Sir John Maffey. Lord Meston, who was Lieutenant-Governor of the United Provinces from 1912 to 1917, has had a varied record of service overseas. As Mr.

James S. Meston he was Adviser to the Governments of the Cape Province and the Transvaal from 1904 to 1906; as Sir James Meston he was a member of the Imperial War Cabinet in 1917. On his retirement from the Indian Civil Service in 1919 he was created a Baron, and as Lord Meston he is now Vice-Chairman of the Supervisory Commission of the League of Nations. Only three other Indian Civilians have been raised to the peerage—Lord Teignmouth (Sir John Shore), Lord Lawrence, and Lord MacDonnell. Sir William Marris, whose services were lent to the Transvaal Government from 1906 to 1908, assisted in the organization of administration there and was Deputy Chairman of a committee which inquired into the question of railways in Central South Africa. He subsequently helped Mr. Montagu and Lord Chelmsford materially in the drafting of the famous report on constitutional reforms in India which bears their names, was Governor of Assam from 1921 to 1923 and of the United Provinces from 1923 to 1928, and after retirement became Principal of the Armstrong College at Newcastle-on-Tyne. Sir John Maffey was Chief Commissioner of the North-West Frontier Province from 1921 to 1924 and has been Governor of the Sudan since 1926.

These do not complete the list of those who have served in Africa as well as in British India. Sir Raymond West, a Judge of the High Court in Bombay, was deputed to Egypt in 1885 to assist in the reform of its judicial administration. In more recent times Sir Bampfylde Fuller, who was Chief Commissioner of Assam from 1902 to 1905 and then Lieutenant-Governor of Eastern Bengal and Assam (1905–6), earlier in his service spent a year (1896–7) as Agricultural Adviser to the Egyptian Government, using part of his furlough for the purpose. Sir Edward Henry, of Bengal, was deputed in 1900 to organize the civil police in Johannesburg and Pretoria after their occupation during the Boer war. Mr. C. C. Lowis, who conducted the census of Burma in 1901, was Census Commissioner in Egypt from 1906 to 1908. Mr. G. C. Leftwich, C.B.E., of the Central Provinces, was Indian Trade Commissioner in East Africa from 1921 to 1923, an office which was created at his suggestion. Mr. Leftwich, when on furlough, had visited Africa and was impressed with the need of an agency to protect Indian interests. He offered to resign the Indian Civil Service and organize an agency, and his offer was accepted. Another Indian Civilian has been connected with the Consular Service since retirement, viz., Mr. C. A. Kincaid, C.V.O., of the Bombay Presidency, who had thirty-five years' service in India and has been Vice-Consul at Cherbourg since 1927; he was appointed Officier d'Instruction Publique in 1928.

Sir Mortimer Durand added wide diplomatic experience in Europe, America and other parts of Asia to that which he acquired in India. When he had only six years' service, he was Political Secretary to Lord Roberts in the Kabul campaign, and he was subsequently Foreign Secretary to the Government of India for ten years (1884–94). During this period he was able to conclude two agreements with Abdur Rahman, the Amir of Afghanistan, the first in 1888 and the second in 1893. The latter is known after him as the Durand agreement, while the outer line which he settled as the boundary between the Indian Empire and Afghanistan is commonly called the Durand line. Another achievement of his is less well known. The present popularity of football in India is largely due to him, for he started Association tournament play at Simla; the Durand Cup Tournament is still an important event in the Indian football year. Sir Mortimer left India in 1894 and for the next twelve years was in the diplomatic service, as Minister of Teheran (1894–1900), as Ambassador at Madrid (1900–3) and as Ambassador at Washington (1903–6).

Sir Richard Dane, of the Punjab, who had had long experience of the administration of the Salt Department in India, was Foreign Chief Inspector of Salt Revenue in China from 1913 to 1918; his services to China were recognized by the bestowal of the First Class Order of the Excellent Crop and the First Class Order of the Tiger. After him Sir Reginald Gamble, who served first in Bombay and then in the Punjab, held the same office from 1918 to 1922.

Mr. E. V. Gabriel, C.S.I., C.M.G., C.V.O., C.B.E., of Bengal, was Financial Adviser and Assistant Administrator in Palestine in 1918–19; and during recent years, owing to the acceptance by Great Britain of the mandate for that country, the services of Indian Civilians have been utilized in connexion with its economic development and administration. In 1930 Sir John Hope Simpson, formerly of the United Provinces, was sent by the British Government to Palestine to confer with the High Commissioner and report on questions of land settlement, immigration and development; as is well known, his report is a State document of the first importance, for on it has been based the statement of policy with regard to the position of the Jewish and Arabian populations of Palestine which has been issued by the British Government. In the same year also Mr. C. F. Strickland, who has been Registrar of Co-operative Societies in the Punjab and is still a member of the Service, was deputed to Palestine to inquire into the economic position of the fellaheen, and, in order to relieve them of the burdens imposed by usury, to instruct them, as well as the officers of the local administration, in the objects and methods of co-operative credit societies. In 1931 Sir Samuel O'Donnell, of the United Provinces, was made Chairman of a Commission which was appointed to inquire into the revenue, expenditure, and general organization of the Administration in Palestine, and also to examine the need of the grant-in-aid of the Administration in Transjordan. A few days later the Secretary of State for the Colonies appointed another Commission, consisting of Mr. W. Gaskell, C.I.E., of the same province, and one other member, to examine and report on the financial position of British Guiana and to advise on measures for reducing expenditure and increasing revenue.

Sir John Hope Simpson, who was Acting Chief Commissioner of the Andaman and Nicobar Islands for two years before his retirement in 1916, was a Member of Parliament from 1922 to 1924, when he was appointed Chairman of the India Colonies Committee, and from 1926 to 1930 was Vice-Chairman of the Refugee Settlement Commission at Athens, an organization working under the auspices of the League of Nations, which had to deal with an influx of over a million Greek refugees from Asia Minor and arrange for finding them employment and homes. When its work was transferred to the Greek Government at the end of 1930, Sir John Hope Simpson was decorated with the Grand Cross of the Order of the Phœnix and thanked by the President of Greece for the service he had done that country. Sir John Campbell was a colleague of his both in the United Provinces and in work for the Greek refugees. His career since retirement has been one of remarkable versatility, for he was Financial Officer of the University of London in 1922, was Vice-Chairman of the Greek Refugee Settlement Commission from 1923 to 1926, has been Economic and Financial Adviser to the Colonial Office in London since 1929, and is a representative of India on the Opium Advisory Committee of the League of Nations.

Sir William Vincent, of Bihar and Orissa, was President of a Commission which inquired in 1916 into the medical arrangements for the campaign in Mesopotamia ; and Sir John Hewett, Lieutenant-Governor of the United Provinces from 1907 to 1912, went there in 1918 to inquire for the Army Council into the administration and finance of schemes for the development of irrigation and agriculture. A number of other members of the Service were associated with the administration of Mesopotamia both during the period of occupation and afterwards when it came under the mandate system and was known as Iraq. During the war regular government disappeared with the disappearance of the Turkish officials, who went away with their army. The machinery of administration had to be re-created by the Civil Commissioner and a staff of Political Officers and Assistant

Political Officers drawn from the Army, the Indian Political Department and the Indian Civil Service; and when the government of occupation was replaced by a national government with a Council of Arab Ministers, some continued to serve there in an advisory capacity. One of those who helped to build up the civil organization behind the fighting line was Mr. (afterwards Sir Henry) Dobbs, who during 1915 and 1916 was in charge of the revenue administration and of several other departments, such as excise and education. "To him," writes Sir Arnold Wilson in *Loyalties: Mesopotamia, 1914–17*, "is due the credit for laying the sound foundations in all these departments on which all subsequent developments were based, and it was with peculiar satisfaction that those officers who had worked with and under him welcomed his appointment, in 1923, as High Commissioner of Iraq and British Consul-General in succession to Sir Percy Cox." These offices Sir Henry Dobbs held till 1929.

After him, three Indian Civilians, Mr. Philby, Mr. Garbett and Mr. Howell, were in charge of the Revenue Department in Mesopotamia. Mr. Evelyn B. Howell, C.S.I., C.I.E., of the Punjab, was Deputy Civil Commissioner in the Basra Wilayat in 1916–17, acted for a time as Military Governor at Baghdad—he had the rank of Lieut.-Colonel—and was Revenue Commissioner from 1918 to 1922. Mr. Colin Garbett, C.M.G., C.I.E., of the same province, was Revenue Commissioner in 1917, when he also held the special office of Administrator in charge of Agricultural Development. Mesopotamia was at that time threatened with a famine, and Mr. Garbett initiated and administered a scheme of agricultural development by means of which not only was famine averted and the army provided with supplies, but 50,000 Armenians and Assyrians, who had been driven out of their own country, were saved from starvation. "For the first time in history," wrote Sir John Hewett, who saw the scheme in working, "the Arab has seen an administration devoting every effort to promoting his material benefit and the regeneration of the country. . . . Wherever one goes one sees evidence all round of the beneficial results of the agricultural development scheme."[1] The health of Mr. Garbett broke down under the strain and he was forced to take leave, but he came back in 1920 as Secretary to the High Commissioner for Iraq, a post which he held until 1922. He then returned to India, as also did Mr. Howell, who has since become Foreign Secretary to the Government of India.

Two others, viz., Mr. Bourdillon and Mr. Philby, did not resume work in India. Mr. B. H. Bourdillon, C.M.G., C.I.E., of the United Provinces, served in Mesopotamia during the war, was appointed Judicial Assistant in the Persian Gulf in 1918 and Land Acquisition Officer at Baghdad next year, and since then has filled different high offices, such as those of Secretary, and of Councillor, to the High Commissioner of Iraq. Since 1929 he has been Colonial Secretary in Ceylon.

Mr. H. St. J. Philby, C.I.E., of the Punjab, was placed on special duty in the Persian Gulf in 1915, served as Political Officer in Mesopotamia, and succeeded Sir Henry Dobbs as Revenue Commissioner in 1916. On the occupation of Baghdad

[1] *Report for the Army Council on Mesopotamia* (1919), p. 9.

he was placed on special duty there, and among other duties was official editor of a newspaper published in Arabic; he had obtained the Degree of Honour in that language while in India. In October, 1917, he was sent on a political mission to Riadh, the headquarters of the Wahabis under Ibn Saud in Central Arabia. He was the sole British representative in Arabia for a year, crossed Arabia to Jidda, and was the first European to visit the southern provinces of Najd: his fine work as an explorer was recognized by the award to him of the Founder's Medal of the Royal Geographical Society in 1920. He became Adviser to the Ministry of the Interior in Mesopotamia when a provisional Government with a Council of Ministers was established towards the end of 1920, was Chief British Representative in Transjordania from 1921 to 1924, and retired from the Indian Civil Service in 1925.

Mr. Philby is not the only explorer who has come from the ranks of the Indian Civil Service. One of the great African travellers was William Cotton Oswell, who was also a famous hunter. He was known as "the Nimrod of South Africa," and according to Livingstone had more hairbreadth escapes than any man living. Oswell was in the Civil Service in Madras for ten years, and having been ordered to go to South Africa for his health, spent two years there, hunting in country which had hitherto not been visited by white men. From 1849 to 1851 he was associated with Livingstone in his exploration, accompanying him when he discovered Lake Ngami in 1849 and when he came upon the Zambesi in 1851. Dr. Campbell says in his recent work on Livingstone that Livingstone could not have accomplished what he did during these two years without Oswell.

> "To his generosity the initial success of the expedition was due. He furnished the guides at his own expense and much of the supplies also. At a subsequent stage of the adventure, taught by experience, he did more. Livingstone's gratitude to and affection for this noble-hearted associate never underwent any diminution." [1]

Livingstone named a son, born soon after the discovery of the Zambesi, William Oswell, after him; and it was fitting that Oswell should be one of the pall-bearers, with Stanley, Kirk and others, at the interment of Livingstone's remains in Westminster Abbey. After leaving South Africa, Oswell volunteered for service during the Crimean War, and did good work both in the trenches and in the hospitals.

After this sketch of the work done by Civilians overseas, we may mention the names of some of those who have rendered public service in the British Isles. Since India passed under the Crown, a number of distinguished Civilians have been able as members of the Council of India to give the benefit of their knowledge and experience to the control of Indian administration, and three have been Permanent Under-Secretaries of State for India, viz., Sir George Clerk (1858–60), Sir Thomas Holderness (1912–20) and Sir William Duke (1920–24). Since 1924, also, Sir Louis Kershaw, of Bengal and Bihar and Orissa, has been first Assistant Under-Secretary of State for India. Prior to the present limitations of the term of office, some of the members of Council had an extraordinarily long

[1] Dr. R. J. Campbell, *Livingstone* (1929), p. 119.

service. Sir Frederick Halliday, who first went out to India in 1825, and was Lieutenant-Governor of Bengal during the Mutiny, served on the Council from 1868 to 1886, and was thus connected with the government of India for sixty-one years; and Sir Philip Hutchins, of Madras, retired from the Council in 1908, fifty years after he first joined the Civil Service.

Sir Charles Trevelyan, who married a sister of Lord Macaulay and was the father of Sir George Trevelyan, had the singular experience of being in both the Indian and the Home Civil Service and of coming back to India twice, first as a Governor and next as a member of the Viceroy's Council. He resigned the Indian Civil Service in 1838, after being in it for twelve years, his last appointment being that of Secretary to the Board of Revenue. Two years later he was appointed Assistant Secretary to the Treasury, an office which he held for nineteen years. He was in charge of the administration of relief works during the Irish famine (1845–7) and, with Sir Stafford Northcote, was selected by Mr. Gladstone in 1853 to inquire into the methods of recruitment for the English Civil Service. They recommended its being thrown open to competition: hence, Trevelyan was the original of Sir Gregory Hardlines in *The Three Clerks* of Anthony Trollope, who said that "he intended to lean very heavily on that much-loathed scheme of competitive examination of which at that time Sir Charles Trevelyan was the chief apostle." The only immediate result of the report was the appointment in 1855 of Civil Service Commissioners, who required nominees for posts in the Home Civil Service to undergo a qualifying examination: the system of entrance by means of competitive examinations was not introduced till 1870. In 1859 Trevelyan was appointed Governor of Madras, but held office for little over a year. He was strongly opposed to proposals made by Mr. Wilson, Financial Member of the Government of India, for the imposition of three new taxes, viz., the income tax, a licence tax on traders, and a tax on home-grown tobacco. In order to make his opposition effectual, he gave publicity to a minute of dissent recorded by his Council and himself, and was thereupon recalled. This did not stand in the way of his appointment in 1863 as Financial Member of the Government of India. The only other instances, so far as the writer is aware, of men being transferred from the Indian to the English Civil Service, are those of Mr. A. W. Watson and Mr. Vernon Dawson, both of Bengal. The former, having worked in the Ministry of Munitions during the war, was appointed Assistant Secretary in the Ministry of Labour on its close and had his services permanently transferred to it. The latter, after twelve years' service in India, was temporarily in the India Office from 1918 to 1921, when he retired from the Indian Civil Service on a medical certificate and was appointed permanently to the India Office, where he is now a Principal.

Two retired Civilians, each of whom had been Inspector-General of Police in Bengal, have been Commissioners of the Metropolitan Police. The first was Mr. James Monro, who, as Assistant Commissioner in charge of the C.I.D. from 1884 to 1888, had to deal with the dynamite outrages in London. He was appointed Commissioner of Police at the end of 1888 and was known as a sound and level-headed administrator till he came to loggerheads with the Home Secretary, over the question of adequate pensions for the men in his force, and so far forgot one of the primary principles of the Civil Service as to enlist the help of the Press and supply it with material for opposition to the Home Secretary. He resigned his post in 1890,[1] and three years later returned to India, where he founded a medical mission at Ranaghat, in his old province, and devoted twelve years to its management. The second ex-Civilian to serve as Commissioner of Police in the Metropolis was Mr. (afterwards Sir) Edward Henry, who as Inspector-General of Police in Bengal (1891–1900) had introduced the finger-print system for the identification of criminals in that province. On his retirement in 1901 he was appointed Assistant Commissioner of the Metropolitan Police in order that he might introduce the system at Scotland Yard, and two years later he became Commissioner of Police, a post which he resigned in 1918 after bringing the Metropolitan Police to a high standard of efficiency.

The Indian Civil Service may be said to have a close connexion with the science of dactylography, for one of its pioneers was a Civilian, Sir William J. Herschel, a son of the great astronomer, Sir John Herschel. From about 1859 Herschel tested the individuality and persistence of finger-prints, discovering the value of the papillary ridges for purposes of identification, and started the practice of requiring finger-prints to be affixed to deeds of

[1] Sir Edward Troup, *The Home Office* (1925), p. 106; F. J. Moylan, *Scotland Yard and the Metropolitan Police* (1929), pp. 49–50.

contract written in Bengali. He did not publish anything on the subject, and when in 1880 Dr. Faulds, an English doctor at Tokio, wrote to *Nature*, describing the results of his own researches and suggesting the value of finger-prints for identifying criminals, Herschel was content to write to the same journal, mentioning the work he had done for the previous twenty years, without laying any claim to priority. He did, however, urge Government to make it obligatory for finger-prints to be affixed to certain classes of deeds, such as transfers of property, as a safeguard against fraud. The practice was not finally adopted by the Government of Bengal for police purposes and the registration of deeds till 1892, and in the meantime Sir Francis Galton had reduced this method of identification to a science, and Sir Edward Henry had worked out a sound and practical system of classification for police purposes, which has since been adopted throughout the world.

During the present century three Irish members of the Civil Service have held high office in their home country. The vast knowledge of land systems and the experience of the settlement of vexed questions of land tenures which he had gained in India led to the appointment as Under-Secretary to the Lord-Lieutenant in Ireland of Lord MacDonnell, who was Lieutenant-Governor of the North-West Provinces from 1895 to 1901. With Mr. George Wyndham, the Chief Secretary, who described him as a colleague rather than a subordinate, he was responsible for the Land Purchase Act of 1903. He was raised to the peerage in 1908, and was a member of the Irish Convention of 1917–18. Another authority on Indian land revenue, Mr. Michael Finucane, of Bengal, was appointed Estates Commissioner in Ireland in 1903 and was made a member of the Privy Council, an honour rarely conferred on Indian Civil Servants.[1] Mr. James McNeill, after a service of twenty-five years in Bombay, in the course of which he went to the West Indies on a commission of inquiry into Indian immigration, devoted himself to public causes in Ireland, and became Chairman of the Dublin County Council in 1922, and a member of the Committee appointed that year by the Provisional Government to draft a constitution. He was also Chairman of an Agricultural Commission appointed by the Government of the Free State and spent four years in London as the first High Commissioner of the Free State. He was appointed Governor-General of the Free State at the end of 1927 and enhanced his popularity by declining a ceremonial reception in Dublin, saying that he was merely an Irishman returning home.

Ever since the creation of the Indian Civil Service, some of its members have, after retirement, sought and obtained election to the House of Commons, though there has been no general inclination to political life in England. Some have proved themselves able speakers and fluent debaters in the course of their Indian careers, but others have felt that they could write, and also act, better than they could speak. One such was Lord Teignmouth, who wrote:

"A man may make a tolerably good Governor-General and an inefficient Member of Parliament. Our habits

[1] Other Privy Councillors have been Lord Lawrence, Sir Henry Montgomery (of Madras), Sir Alfred Lyall, Sir Mortimer Durand and Lord MacDonnell.

are deliberative, not oratorical, and although I might vote with common sense and conscience, I could never speak with grace. In truth, unless I am irritated, I doubt if I could make a speech of a quarter of an hour on any subject before the people ; I write, as you would perceive, *currente calamo*."

One of his contemporaries in the Civil Service, Nathaniel Halhed, who was a distinguished Oriental scholar, was not so aware of his oratorical limitations or was more determined to overcome them. When at length he had succeeded in making a speech in the House of Commons, he rushed out of the House exclaiming "*Liberavi animam meam.*"

Of those ex-Civilians who have been Members of Parliament, three had been heads of provinces: Sir George Campbell, Sir Richard Temple, and Sir Henry Cotton. Sir Richard Temple, who was a M.P. from 1885 to 1895, was a well-known Parliamentary figure. He was one of the most popular men in the House ; he was a favourite of *Punch*, which delighted in caricaturing his rugged features ; and he established a record for regular attendance, taking part in 2,072 out of 2,118 possible divisions in six years. He was equally assiduous as a diary-writer, for he kept a parliamentary journal running to four pages a day, which was the basis of a book, *Life in Parliament*, which he published in 1893. Sir Henry Cotton, who represented East Nottingham from 1906 to 1910, was at the head of a group of Members known as the Indian group, for they had all been in the Indian Civil Service, viz., Sir John Jardine and Mr. T. Hart-Davies of Bombay, Mr. Donald Smeaton of Burma, and Mr. C. J. O'Donnell of Bengal.

Over twenty years before this, another retired Civilian, Sir William Wedderburn, had headed in the House of Commons what was called the Indian Parliamentary Committee. This was a body or group of Members, including John Bright, interested in Indian affairs, which endeavoured to secure combined parliamentary action when they were debated. Sir William Wedderburn, who had held high office, both executive and judicial, in Bombay, acting not only as Chief Secretary (1885) but also as a High Court Judge (1887), was an ardent supporter of the Indian National Congress.

That body owed its institution largely to the initiative and organizing ability of another Civilian, Allan Octavian Hume, who is consequently called "the father of the Indian National Congress." Hume had a distinguished career in the Indian Civil Service. He first became a marked man during the Mutiny, when he did excellent work as District Magistrate of Etawah. He was engaged in several pitched battles and skirmishes against the mutineers, was mentioned in dispatches for gallantry in one action, and was extolled in Kaye's *History of the Mutiny* for heroism in another. In pacifying his district he combined both justice and mercy, keeping down the number of executions and devising a patent drop for those whom he hanged: men, it is said, prayed that they might be tried by Hume and that, if found guilty, they might be hanged by him.[1] After the Mutiny he was made a C.B., was appointed Secretary to the Govern-

[1] G. O. Trevelyan, *Letters from a Competition Wallah* (1907), p. 246.

ment of India in the Department of Revenue and Agriculture (from its creation in 1871 until 1879), and eventually became Member of the Board of Revenue in the North-West Provinces. On his retirement in 1882, after thirty-three years' service, he championed the claims of Indians to a fuller share in the government of their country and drew up the prospectus of the Indian National Congress, which, in outlining its objects, declared that indirectly it would form the germ of a native Parliament. Hume was apprehensive of economic stress and political unrest producing a revolutionary movement among the men of the younger generation, in whom the ferment of Western political ideas was at work. He had, indeed, obtained information from Hindu religious leaders, with whom he was in touch, of widespread unrest which was expected to lead to an outbreak, sudden and violent, of crimes, murders, robbery of bankers and looting of bazaars. It was anticipated that there would be a general development of lawlessness, paralysing the authorities, and that when it was sufficiently formidable, a certain number of the educated classes should join the movement, give it cohesion and direct it as a national revolt. In view of this information, which he verified from his personal knowledge of some parts of the country, Hume was convinced that it was essential to give the forces at work an overt and constitutional channel for discharge instead of leaving them to work underground, as they had already begun to do.[1]

Hume was Secretary or Joint General Secretary

[1] Sir William Wedderburn, *Allan Octavian Hume* (1913), pp. 77–85.

to nineteen out of the first twenty-two National Congresses, and the lead which he gave was followed by Sir William Wedderburn, who presided over the fourth meeting of the Congress in 1889, became the head of the Indian party in England as Chairman of the British Committee of the National Congress, which was formed that year, and remained Chairman until his death in 1918. Sir Henry Cotton, also, after retiring as Chief Commissioner of Assam, returned to India to preside over the Congress when it met at Bombay in 1904, by which time it had become a force in the land. Sir Surendra Nath Banerjea, who was one of the early leaders of the Congress movement, writes: "It is worthy of note that among Englishmen the staunchest friends of the Congress movement in its early days were all members of the Indian Civil Service who had risen to distinction in that service"[1]; while Sir Bampfylde Fuller remarks in *Some Personal Reminiscences* (1930) that "it is not too much to say that the idea of Indian nationality was named and baptized under the sponsorship of the Indian Civil Service."

Of Civilians who have distinguished themselves in the world of finance the greatest was Sir David Barbour, who was one of the authorities of his day on questions of currency and finance. A mere recitation of the Commissions on which he served will suffice to show the place he held among financial experts, such as the Royal Commission on Gold and Silver (1886), the Royal Commission on the Sugar-Growing Colonies of the West Indies (1897), the Indian Currency Committee (1898), a Committee on the Currency of the West African

[1] *A Nation in Making* (1925), p. 273.

Colonies (1899), a Committee on the Currency of the Straits Settlements (1902), and the Royal Commission on Shipping Rings (1907). He was also deputed as Special Commissioner to inquire into the finances of Jamaica and (in 1900) of the Orange River Colony and the Transvaal, and he was Chairman of the Royal Commission on London Traffic in 1903. Another financial expert, Sir Edward Cook, of the United Provinces, who was Secretary to the Government of India in the Finance Department, has been Financial Adviser to the Government of Siam, completing his term of office in 1930; and as stated above, Sir John Campbell is Financial Adviser to the Colonial Office.

Among others who have held high office in the Government of India may be mentioned Sir Edward Buck, who was a Secretary for no less than fifteen years (1882–97), and whom Lord Dufferin described as "the great genius of his administration"; he represented the Government of India at the Colonial Exhibition held in London in 1886, and after retirement identified himself with the work of the International Institute of Agriculture, whose headquarters are at Rome. Sir Claude Hill, who was a Member of the Governor-General's Council from 1915 to 1920, has been closely connected with the direction and organization of Red Cross work for many years. He was Director-General of the League of Red Cross Societies from 1921 to 1926, and since the latter year has been Lieutenant-Governor of the Isle of Man. Sir David Chadwick, of Madras, formerly Secretary to the Government of India, has been Secretary to the Imperial Economic Committee since 1926. Mr.

P. W. Monie, C.S.I., also of Bombay, is Honorary Administrator of Toc H.

Sir George Boughey, Bart., after service in the United Provinces, was for eight years (1921–9) Secretary of the Royal Colonial Institute (now styled the Royal Empire Society). Mr. William Perry, of Bombay, became Assistant Secretary to the Royal Society of Arts in London. Mr. Percy Lyon, C.S.I., formerly a Member of the Executive Council in Bengal, was for some years Treasurer of Oriel College, Oxford; and Sir Henry Howard, also of Bengal, who was long associated with the direction of Indian finance, both in the Finance Department of the Government of India and as Controller of Finance at the India Office, has for some years past been Senior Bursar at St. John's College at Cambridge, where he is also well-known on the towpath as a rowing coach. Three other retired members of the Service are holding office under academic bodies associated with the University of London: Mr. Maurice Webb, of Bombay, as Secretary to the Senate; Mr. J. H. Lindsay, of Bengal, as Secretary to the School of Oriental Studies; and Mr. E. L. Tanner, of Bihar and Orissa, as Treasurer, University College.

Not a few retired Civilians have come to the front in the business world. Among such may be mentioned Lord Meston, who holds the Chairmanship of the Calcutta Electric Supply Association, Ltd., and of the Sudan Light and Power Company, Ltd., and other offices of commercial responsibility; and Sir Geoffrey Clarke, of the United Provinces, formerly Director-General of Posts and Telegraphs in India, who is Joint Managing Director of the Telegraph Construction and Maintenance Company, Ltd., and holds the office of Deputy Chairman of the London Chamber of Commerce. Mr. M. M. S. Gubbay, formerly Secretary to the Government of India in the Finance Department, became General Manager of the P. and O. Banking Corporation on retirement in 1921. The late Mr. G. G. Sim, C.S.I., C.I.E., who as Financial Commissioner of Indian Railways had a large part in working out the scheme for separating railway finances from the general finances of India, also entered business on retirement and became Deputy Chairman of Vickers-Armstrong, Ltd., and of Vickers, Ltd.—an unusual achievement for an Indian Civilian. Even more varied has been the career of Sir Walter Lawrence. On retiring from the Indian Civil Service he was for three years Agent to the Duke of Bedford, and then returned to India as Private Secretary to Lord Curzon (1899–1903). In 1904 he was engaged in writing articles on Indian affairs for *The Times*, and next year he again returned to India as Chief of the Staff of the Prince of Wales during his Indian tour : his subsequent services during the war have already been referred to in Chapter V. Few have taken to business life in India. On retirement, a Punjab Civilian, Mr. E. A. A. Joseph, C.I.E., was for five years Agent and General Manager of the Assam Railways and General Trading Company. Ltd. ; Mr. J. C. K. Peterson, C.I.E., of Bengal, became Secretary to the Tata Iron and Steel Company; and Mr. W. J. Thompson, after conducting the census of Bengal in 1921, became Secretary to the Bengal Telephone Company at Calcutta.

Many Civilians in the judicial branch of the Service have been called to the Bar, but few have practised. One who has done so is Mr. E. M. Konstam, C.B.E., who, after 12 years' service in Bengal, retired on account of ill-health, and is now a K.C. and an authority on the law of rating. A certain number have taken orders in the Church of England after retirement. One of the earliest, if not the earliest to do so, was Henry George Keene, who may well be said to have played many parts in his time, for he was first in the Army and took part in the siege of Seringapatam in 1799. He was then transferred to the Company's Civil Service, which he resigned in 1817, when he was ordained. He did not altogether lose his connexion with India, for he became Professor of Arabic and Persian at Haileybury College. His son, of the same name, who was a writer on Indian historical subjects and editor of the *Oriental Biographical Dictionary*, was also a member of the Service. Sir William Herschel, to whom reference has already been made in another connexion, took orders in the Church of England, twenty-eight years after leaving the service, at the age of 73. Others who have been ordained after retirement have been the Rev. Sir Nicholas Beatson-Bell, after his retirement in 1922 from the Governorship of Assam; the Rev. E. H. Moscardi, who served in Bombay from 1876 to 1902, and was ordained in the latter year; and the Rev. E. J. Bolus and the Rev. H. G. Blomfield, who were ordained in 1926, the former after twenty-one years' service in Bombay, and the latter after fifteen years' service in Bengal. The Rev. William R. G. Moir, a Judge of the United Provinces, passed through the Divinity Hall, Edinburgh, on his retirement, and in 1923 was licensed by the Presbytery to preach.

Mention should also be made in this connexion of one who, after a few years in the Indian Civil Service, devoted his life to the evangelization of India, Commissioner Booth-Tucker, of the Salvation Army. Frederick St. George Lautour Tucker, to give him his original name—he changed it to Booth-Tucker after his marriage to a daughter of General Booth—was born in India and belonged to an old Anglo-Indian family. He was the son of a Bengal Judge and the grandson of a Director of the East India Company who was twice its Chairman, and he had many relatives in the Service. He joined the Service in 1876, spent five years in the Punjab, and then resigned in order to join the Salvation Army. He returned to India, adopted the Indian name of Fakir Singh and preached Christian doctrines from 1881 to 1896, living up to the name of *fakir*, for he wore Indian dress, went about the country barefooted, and begged his food. He returned again to India in 1907, and for the next twelve years was in charge of the operations of the Salvation Army in that country and Ceylon. He will perhaps be remembered longest for the admirable social service he rendered to India by means of weaving schools and agricultural settlements, especially the settlements which he started for the reclamation of criminal tribes. The value of his work in this last direction was so fully appreciated by provincial Governments that several made over to him the charge of reformatory work among those criminal tribes.

CHAPTER XII

CIVILIANS AND LITERATURE

IN a chapter on "Literary Civil Servants on the Company's Bengal Establishment" in *Bygone Days in India* (1922) Mr. Douglas Dewar points out that a survey of the Bengal Civil Establishment, to which the majority of the Company's servants belonged, shows that, apart from those whose literary efforts were confined to official reports, barely a couple of dozen left books behind them. The reasons for the paucity of men with literary gifts are, he believes, partly that the Company's servants were very hard-worked men, but chiefly that "in the days of patronage comparatively few 'brainy' men entered the Company's civil service." It must be conceded that until 1856, when the "Competition Wallahs" first joined the Service, the number of men who attained literary eminence was comparatively small, but on the other hand there were some great names among them, and much of the work produced was of a high quality. Three wrote historical works of the first class, beginning with Orme, who in 1778 published *A History of the Military Transactions of the British Nation in Indostan from the year 1745*, which readers of *The Newcomes* will remember was the favourite book of Colonel Newcome. Mountstuart Elphinstone's *History of India*, which was published in 1841, earned for him the name of the Tacitus of modern historians, and though it has been largely superseded as the result of later researches, Mr. Vincent Smith describes it as a work of permanent value and justly famous. The third of the great Indian historians of this period was Sir Henry Elliot, who died in 1853, leaving materials for a history of India during the Muhammadan period which Professor Dowson published under the title of *The History of India as told by its own Historians* (1867–1877). Henry Thoby Prinsep wrote much, but is best remembered by his *History of the Political and Military Transactions in India during the Administration of the Marquess of Hastings, 1813–23*, published in 1825. A number of Civil Servants also left accounts of the Mutiny, in which they had been actors, such as Martin Gubbins, William Edwards, Charles Raikes, and Mark Bensley Thornhill, the last of whom is better known by his *Haunts and Hobbies of an Indian Official* (1899).

The Company's Civil Service can claim one recognized but now little known poet, John Leyden, a friend of Sir Walter Scott, with whom he collaborated in *The Minstrelsy of the Scottish Border*. Born in a shepherd's cottage, Leyden was a natural genius. He was entirely self-taught, but soon acquired fame for the width and depth of his learning. He was offered the humble post of Assistant Surgeon in the Company's service on condition that he qualified for it, and this only took him a few months. In India he was admitted to the Civil Service and found more congenial occupation, being appointed to the varied posts of Professor in the College of Fort William, Judge of a Bengal district, and Assay Master. In 1811 he accompanied Lord Minto's expedition to Java as Malay interpreter, and on its landing, dashed into the surf in order to be the first Briton to set foot on the island. He died there of fever, mourned by Sir Walter Scott, who wrote a biography of him and deplored his loss in *The Lord of the Isles* in the words:

> His bright and brief career is o'er,
>   And mute his tuneful strains;
> Quenched is his lamp of varied lore,
> That loved the light of song to pour:
> A distant and a deadly shore
>   Has Leyden's cold remains.

His poems, which were published posthumously in *Poetical Remains*, are said to have the fire and vigour of the Scottish border.

Leyden was one of a small group of Oriental scholars, of whom the greatest was Henry Thomas Colebrooke, who retired in 1815. Max Muller describes him as *facile princeps* among Sanskrit scholars and the founder of Sanskrit scholarship in Europe. Sir William Muir, on the other hand, was attracted by the study of Islamic history, and his *Life of Mahomet* (1878) and *The Caliphate, Its Rise, Decline and Fall* (1891), still hold their place in the literature of the subject. Sir William Muir was Lieutenant-Governor of the North-West Provinces from 1868 to 1874, retired after forty years' service and, after serving ten more years on the India Council, was Principal and Vice-Chancellor of Edinburgh University from 1885 to 1902.

Another Civilian of a later generation who had the true poetic afflatus was Sir Alfred Lyall, one of the last of the Haileybury men, who joined the Service in 1855. His poems are contained in one small volume and are under thirty in number, but they include such gems as *The Old Pindaree*. Sir Alfred Lyall was not a prolific, but he was an extraordinarily versatile, writer ; and though his writings are few, they have a rare quality. His *Rise and Expansion of the British Dominion in India* (1893) is a scholarly historical study, while his *Asiatic Studies* (1st series, 1884 ; 2nd series, 1899) show the wide range of his knowledge of Indian religious beliefs.

Sir Alfred Lyall dealt with the religions of the peoples in the plains. Our knowledge of the religious beliefs of the Himalayan races is largely due to Brian Houghton Hodgson, who also made extensive researches into the philology, ethnology and zoology of that region, the results of which were published between 1830 and 1882. Hodgson first commenced the study of the men, the beasts and the birds of the Himalayas when he was in Nepal, where he spent over twenty years, first as Assistant Resident and then as Resident. He had a high reputation for saintliness among the Nepalese on account of his abstemious, almost ascetic life ; he became a vegetarian after an illness in 1837, and was known as "the Hermit of the Himalayas." In spite of his great influence and the services which he had rendered, notably in inducing Nepal to remain neutral during the Afghan War, a difference over the policy to be adopted towards the Government of Nepal led to his removal from the office of Resident in 1843 by Lord Ellenborough, who appointed Sir Henry Lawrence in his place and added insult to injury by gazetting Hodgson as Sub-Assistant Commissioner at Simla, a post which would have been suitable for a newly-joined officer. Hodgson resigned in disgust but did not sever his connexion with India. He pursued his researches with unabated zeal and for thirteen years (1843–58) lived the life of a scholar-recluse in Darjeeling. He did not, however, lose touch with affairs, and used his influence to persuade the Government of Nepal to allow Gurkhas to be recruited for the Indian Army and also to support the British during the Mutiny.

Hodgson, in the words of Sir Joseph Hooker, "unveiled the mysteries of the Buddhist religion, chronicled the affinities, languages, customs and faiths of the Himalayan tribes, and completed a natural history of the animals and birds of those regions." His labours earned him an international reputation. France, ever quick to recognize learning, gave him a seat in the Institute of France and the Cross of the Legion of Honour. M. Eugène Burnouf, in dedicating to him *Le Lotus de la Bonne Loi* (1852), described him as "the founder of the true study of Buddhism on the basis of the texts and original remains." Bunsen in 1854 declared him to be "our highest living authority and best informant on the ethnology of the native races of India." Sir Harry Johnston, after saying that for the political services which he rendered after retirement he deserved a peerage and a splendid pension, states: "Brian Houghton Hodgson was one of the greatest in achievements among European pioneers in India and should have his statue set up in some prominent city of our Indian Empire and his bust in Westminster Abbey." [1]

Reference may fittingly be made here to the ornithological work of Allan Octavian Hume, the

[1] *Pioneers in India*, p. 286.

author of *The Game Birds of India* (published in 1879 and illustrated by Colonel Marshall). Hume was such an acknowledged authority on the subject that he was known as "the Pope of ornithology." He employed agents and collectors in different countries of Asia, spent about £20,000 in making an ornithological museum and library (the largest in the world as regards Asiatic birds), and in 1885 gave a collection of 82,000 birds and eggs to the Natural History Museum in Kensington.

There has been no lack of literary talent among the men who joined the Service under the competitive system, and the quantity and quality of their productions have been somewhat remarkable if allowance is made for the increasing pressure of official duties and the degree to which the writing of official reports is apt to impair both the power and the style of expression. Sir Charles Elliott, Lieutenant-Governor of Bengal (1890–5), once remarked:

> "There is no leisured class amongst us who have time to look around, collect and digest information, and give it out in a literary form. We are all slaves of the desk. . . . We most of us work more incessantly than almost any class in any other country."

Notwithstanding the preoccupation of work, many men have found it possible to engage in literary pursuits or to combine with their official duties scholarly researches into Indian history, philology, religions, ethnology, numismatics, ornithology, economics, etc. Some have specialized on a particular subject, but others have had a large circle of interests, such as Sir William Hunter, whose writings are distinguished by their variety and literary grace. In 1863, when he had been in India only a year, he formed the idea of writing a history of India that would do justice to its people and vindicate the conduct of England in her dealings with them. His first book, *The Annals of Rural Bengal*, published five years later, was a brilliant success, which was greeted by Meredith Townsend, then editor of *The Spectator*, with the remark that Hunter wrote Indian history with the insight of Colonel Tod and the research of Grant-Duff in prose almost as good as that of Froude. This literary triumph was followed by others, such as *The Old Missionary*, which has been called a poem in prose, *The Thackerays in India*, etc. Sir William Hunter did much to make England's work in India and Indian needs and aspirations known to England in essays which were reprinted in 1903 under the title *The India of the Queen*. His great *History of the British in India*, however, was never completed, only two volumes (for the period 1600–1708) being published just before his death in 1900.

The historical work done by Sir William Hunter has been carried on and supplemented by others of his Service; it is significant that all but two of the chapters of the historical volume of the *Imperial Gazetteer of India* were written by Indian Civilians. Pre-eminent among them is Mr. Vincent Smith, who, after being Chief Secretary in the United Provinces, devoted his abilities to Indian historical research. The fruits of his labours are seen in his *Early History of India* (1904), which was the first general history of the pre-Muhammadan period, in such works as *Asoka* (1909) and *Akbar, the Great Mogul* (1919), and in the *Oxford History of India* (1919). The last was the outcome of nearly half a century's study of Indian history, and is a specially fine piece of work considering the mass of material compressed within a single volume, the lucidity with which the subject is dealt with, and the way in which interest in it is sustained.

Other Civilian writers have written on special periods or special aspects of Indian history. Mr. R. Sewell has told the story of Vijayanagar in *A Forgotten Empire* (1900), Mr. W. Irvine has added to our knowledge of the Mughal period by his translation of Manucci's *Storia do Mogor* (1907 and 1908), Mr. Henry Beveridge by his translations of the *Akbarnama* (Calcutta, 1907 and 1912) and *The Memoirs of Jahangir* (Calcutta, 1909 and 1914), and Mr. S. M. Edwardes by *Mughal Rule in India* (1930), which he wrote jointly with Mr. H. L. O. Garrett; Sir Edward Gait has written the *History of Assam* (Calcutta, 1906), Mr. S. S. Thorburn *The Punjab in Peace and War* (1904), Mr. G. E. Harvey the *History of Burma* (1925), and Mr. C. A. Kincaid, in collaboration with Rao Bahadur D. B. Parsnis, the *History of the Maratha People* (in three volumes, published in 1918, 1922 and 1925). Others have specialized in modern history, e.g., Sir Verney Lovett has written *The History of the Indian Nationalist Movement* (1920) as well as a general history, *India* (1923, in the Nations of the World series); Mr. R. C. Dutt *India in the Victorian Age* (1904) besides a *History of Civilization in Ancient India* (1889); while Sir Charles Crosthwaite has described the events in which he himself took so large a part in *The Pacification of Burma* (1912). Reference should also be made in this connexion to Mr.

C. E. Buckland's *Bengal under the Lieutenant-Governors* (Calcutta, 1901), as well as to his *Dictionary of Indian Biography* (1906), which is the only biographical work dealing exclusively with India.

Mr. W. H. Moreland has illuminated the economic history of the Mughal Empire, and in particular the condition of the peasantry, by scholarly studies based on Dutch and other original authorities, such as *India at the Death of Akbar* (1920), *From Akbar to Aurangzeb* (1923) and *The Agrarian System of Moslem India* (1929). Mr. H. K. Trevaskis has given an economic history of the Punjab from the earliest times down to 1890 in *The Land of the Five Rivers* (1928), while modern economic conditions in India are described with insight and knowledge in Mr. J. C. Jack's *The Economic Life of a Bengal District*, Mr. Yusuf Ali's *Life and Labour in Northern India* (1907), and Mr. M. L. Darling's *The Punjab Peasant in Prosperity and Debt* (1925), and *Rusticus Loquitur* (1930). Mr. Jack's book was a wonderful *tour de force*, for he wrote it, and incidentally reduced to order the mass of statistics necessary for its preparation, in five days before leaving for the front in France. In spite of the rapidity with which the book was written, it has, as his friend and fellow-Civilian, Mr. Ascoli, says in a foreword to the latest edition, an extraordinary completeness of economic information, and—what commends it more to the general reader—the dry figures of statistics have been transformed into a living picture of Bengali life.

Ethnology is another branch of knowledge in which Civilians have had an acknowledged preeminence owing to the unique opportunities afforded by the census operations for making inquiries into the constitution and customs of the tribes and castes of India. It was in the census of 1881 that Sir Denzil Ibbetson first made his mark as an ethnologist, and this was the beginning of a distinguished career, which culminated with his appointment as Lieutenant-Governor of the Punjab: an inscription in the church at Simla worthily commemorates his combination of qualities—"untiring in administration, fearless in doing right, a scholar and a man of affairs, loyal in co-operation, devoted in friendship, he gave to India his love and life." The line of ethnologists has been continued by Sir Herbert Risley, Sir Edward Gait, Mr. William Crooke, and Mr. R. V. Russell. Mr. Crooke wrote not only on the tribes and castes of northern India, but also, among other subjects, on their religion and folklore, while Mr. Macauliffe dealt exhaustively with the faith and scriptures of the Sikhs in *The Sikh Religion* (1912), a monumental book of six volumes. Even more monumental is the work of Sir George Grierson, who in 1929, at the age of 78, completed his great *Linguistic Survey of India*. He brought to this vast undertaking a knowledge of 180 Indian languages and 480 dialects; and the value of the work which he did for the advancement of learning was recognized by the bestowal on him of the Order of Merit, an honour never before conferred for services in connexion with India.

The limitations of space preclude all but a passing reference to the achievements of other Civilians in special erudite studies, such as Dr. Fleet in epigraphy and Mr. Edward Thomas and Mr. H. Nelson Wright in numismatics; but it may be mentioned that in the field of ornithology a successor to Mr. A. O. Hume has been found in Mr. Douglas Dewar, the author of *Indian Birds*, *Birds of the Plains*, *Bombay Ducks* and other books on Indian Natural History. Only a brief reference also can be made to many memoirs and reminiscences, which, with their accounts of arduous days well spent, are not only good reading but an instructive record of the work and responsibilities of the Civil Service in India. Some have been written by men whose service began before the Mutiny and are self-revelations of strong personalities, such as *Thirty-eight Years in India* (1881), by William Tayler, *Memoirs of my Indian Career* (1893), by Sir George Campbell, and *Men and Events of my Time in India* (1882) and *Story of my Life* (1896), by Sir Richard Temple. Others are of more recent date and are fairly well distributed among the different provinces. Sir Henry Cotton, a Bengal Civilian, wrote *Indian and Home Memories* (1911); Sir Andrew Fraser, of the Central Provinces, who became Lieutenant-Governor of Bengal, *Among Indian Rajahs and Ryots* (1912); Sir Evan Maconochie, of Bombay, *Life in the Indian Civil Service* (1926); Sir Claude Hill, of the same Presidency, *India-Stepmother* (1929). Three Civilians have related their experiences in Madras, viz., Mr. Alan Butterworth in *The Southlands of Siva* (1923), Mr. J. Chartres Molony in *A Book of South India* (1926) and Mr. W. O. Horne in *Work and Sport in the old I.C.S.* (1928). Memoirs of the greatest interest have been published in recent years by two Punjab Civilians—*India as I Knew It* (1925), by Sir Michael O'Dwyer, and *The India We Served* (1928), by Sir Walter Lawrence; and Burma, that province so unlike the rest of India, which seems destined to have its administrative connexion with it severed, has been made familiar to the English reading public by Sir Herbert Thirkell White's *A Civil Servant in Burma* (1913) and *Burma* (1923) and by Mr. R. Grant Brown's *Burma as I Saw It* (1926). Some general studies of Indian life and the problems of its government have also been published by Civilians after retirement, such as Sir Henry Cotton's *New India* (1907), Sir John Rees's *The Real India* (1908), Sir Bampfylde Fuller's *Studies in Indian Life and Sentiment* (1910), Mr. J. T. Gwynn's *Indian Politics* (1924) and Sir Reginald Craddock's *The Dilemma in India* (1929), the last of which must be recognized to be a shrewd and up-to-date commentary on the work of modern administration, whatever may be the view taken of its suggestions for the future government of India.

One fact which emerges pretty clearly from this sketch of literary activities is that the subjects dealt with by Civilian writers are almost exclusively Indian. Their lot has been cast in India, and India has been their absorbing interest. Recently, however, our knowledge of the outside world has been enlarged by books on countries hitherto but little known which have been produced by Civilian authors. The years which Mr. C. P. Skrine, of the United Provinces, spent as Consul-General in Chinese Turkestan, combined with his powers of observation and exposition, have borne refreshing fruit in his *Chinese Central Asia* (1928). Sir Charles Bell, of Bengal, who spent the greater part of his service as Political Officer in Sikkim, and who was for nearly a year in Lhasa on a mission to the Dalai Lama, has written *Tibet, Past and Present*

(1924) and *The People of Tibet* (1928). He was the first white man for two centuries to live so long in the " forbidden city " and is the greatest living authority on what used to be known as a closed land. Mr. H. St. J. Philby, whose travels in Arabia are mentioned in the last chapter, has produced a trilogy on Arabia, viz., *The Heart of Arabia* (1922), *Arabia of the Wahhabis* (1928) and *Arabia* (1930), of which the first was described by the late Dr. D. G. Hogarth as " packed with information about the heart of Arabia more comprehensive and exact than any Briton has collected except Doughty " and as being one of the half-dozen best accounts of it ever written.

A few Civilians have made researches in fields other than those of the East. Sir Warrand Carlyle, of Bengal, is the author, jointly with his brother, Dr. A. J. Carlyle, of Oxford, of *A History of Mediaeval Political Theory in the West*, of which the fifth volume appeared in 1928. Mr. H. T. S. Forrest, of Bihar and Orissa, has explored a literary mystery in *The Five Authors of Shakespeare's Sonnets* (1924), and Mr. David Alec Wilson, whose service was spent in Burma, has made a study for over thirty years of the life of Thomas Carlyle, which he has dealt with in *Mr. Froude and Carlyle* (1898), *The Truth about Carlyle* (1913), *Carlyle till Marriage* (1923), and *Carlyle to Threescore-and-Ten* (1929). The taste for the classics which many men in India retain has also found expression in *Hector and Achilles* (1909), by Mr. R. Sheepshanks, of Bihar and Orissa, in the translations of the Odes of Horace in verse (1912), of Catullus (19124), and of Homer's Odyssey (1925) by Sir William Marris, in the translation of the *Argonautica* (Book I) of Valerius

Flaccus (1916) by Mr. H. G. Blomfield, of Bengal, and, as regards Indian classics, in the translations from the *Ramayana* and *Mahabharata* by Mr. R. C. Dutt, of Bengal. Scholarship of another kind, somewhat rare among laymen, is evinced by *The Fourth Gospel and Its Sources* (1931) by Mr. E. S. Hoernle, of Bihar and Orissa.

Another salient feature of the literary work of Civilians is that its bent is generally grave and serious. Whatever the cause, whether, for instance, official work in India is not favourable to imaginative faculties, it is indisputable that few have produced works of imagination ; much learning is displayed, but it does not err on the side of lightness. The number of writers of fiction among members of the Civil Service may almost be counted on the fingers of one hand. In pre-Mutiny days William Browne Hockley, of Bombay, wrote *Pandurang Hari* (1826), which purported to be the memoirs of a Maratha adventurer, and John Walter Sherer, of the North-Western Provinces, *A Princess of Islam*. They have had few successors. In the case of Sir Mortimer Durand, *Helen Treveryan* (1892) was his sole effort of fiction. Mr. F. B. Bradley-Birt, of Bengal, has written, under the pseudonym of Shelland Bradley, novels descriptive of European social and official life in India, such as *The Adventures of an A.D.C.* (1920). Mr. C. C. Lowis, of Burma, is the author of *Green Sandals* (1926) and other novels in which the *mise-en-scène* is in that country. Mr. John S. Eyton, of the United Provinces, has written some delightful tales of Indian life in Northern India, of which *Kullu of the Carts* (1926) and its sequel *Bulbulla* (1928) have a Kiplingesque flavour. Mr. Hilton Brown, of Madras, whose contributions of light verse to *Punch* are well known, has to his credit, among other novels, *Dismiss* (1923), which describes the life of a Civilian in South India.

There have also been but few writers of light verse. Mr. Thomas F. Bignold, a Bengal Judge, composed much verse of this kind and wrote translations into and from both the classics and the vernacular, which after his death were published in Calcutta in 1888 under the title *Leviora.* Mr. Roland G. Gordon, of Bombay, wrote *R. G. G., his Verses*; Mr. Dudley G. Davies, of Bengal, is the author of a volume entitled *Poems*, and Mr. W. B. Cotton, of the United Provinces, of another entitled *Verses*. Mr. Alexander Rogers, of Bombay, wrote, under the pseudonym Aliph Rae, the *New Lays of Ind*, and Dr. Edward Bennett, of the United Provinces, *Idylls of the East and other Poems*.

INDEX